What People Are Saying about K

"What a shocking ordeal Karin Volo and her _____ _____ through 1,332 Days is a remarkable memoir that illustrates how it's possible to overcome even the darkest of situations and prevail once you've made the choice to be happy and optimistic. Prepare to be inspired by this extraordinary story of resilience!"

~ **Marci Shimoff**, *NY Times* **Bestselling Author,**
Love for No Reason & Happy for No Reason

"The work that Karin was doing, and that she gave us a chance to have a peek preview of and take a look at was very much in concert with the messages that *Conversations With God* would love to share with children everywhere. And so **we were inspired, I would say deeply inspired by her work**, and that's when our office at the School of the New Spirituality made a move to get a hold of Karin to see if we could find a way to integrate our two worlds such that we would both move our messages forward."

~ **Neale Donald Walsch**, *NY Times* **Bestselling Author,**
Conversations With God **series, www.NealeDonaldWalsch.com**

"Karin found herself unjustly jailed for almost four years, away from her family, with no idea what to do. However, Karin made a powerful decision that SHE WAS GOING HOME, and the journey of self-discovery that got her there is one you need to read…but there's more than just her story. After going through what she went through, Karin became PASSIONATE about helping people bounce back from desperate situations, just like she did. Very inspiring!"

~ **Bob Doyle, CEO of Boundless Living, Inc.,**
#1 Bestselling author, *Follow Your Passion - Find Your Power*

"Remarkable, captivating, gripping, spell-binding, and if there is any other synonym for these words, I'd use it! Karin Volo's memoir is an extraordinary story of faith and unconditional love. I highly recommend it."

~ **Peggy McColl, Bestselling Author of** *Your Destiny Switch*

"Karin and Sergio Volo are two incredible people who have faced the worst of times and came through the other side stronger and more courageous than any other couple I've ever met. Now they are turning those challenges into a wonderful, heart centered business where they are helping thousands of people go beyond surviving and learning to thrive through any tough time. If you need any inspiration in your life, read this book because not only will you be moved, your whole outlook on life will change. They set an example and show how love really does conquer all."

~ Lisa Sasevich,
The Queen of Sales Conversion and Creator of the Invisible Close

"When businesswoman and mother Karin Volo suddenly found herself in a frightening landscape on her life's journey, she could have panicked. Instead, she made a conscious choice to be present and calm in her harrowing situation. Jailed thousands of miles away from her home and family, she discovered she could live with courage and faith as long as she focused on what's important- family, love, joy. Anyone who has ever felt imprisoned by life can learn from her story how to make peace with difficult circumstances while working to change them."

~ Colette Baron-Reid, Bestselling Author of *The Map*

"Karin Volo and her family have survived an extraordinary ordeal that would many would find overwhelming. Her story is one of creativity, resilience, and the power to choose our attitude even when we can't choose our circumstances. She is truly inspirational!"

~ Dr. Carmen Harra,
Bestselling Author of *Wholiness* and *The Eleven Eternal Principles*

"Imagine being unjustly incarcerated for 1,352 days in a country 5,574 miles from home. How would you feel? What would you do? How would this affect your family, friends, loved ones? This inspiring book tells how an innocent young mother transformed setbacks into comebacks and breakdowns into breakthroughs by maintaining her faith in God and choosing to FIND solutions regardless of prevailing circumstances! Indeed, Karin Volo is living proof of living truth of the power of faith, love, and determination."

~ Jacquelyn Aldana, Author of *The 15-Minute Miracle Revealed*

"Karin Volo tells an amazing story! An incredible journey both inward and outward."

~ Cindy Powers Prosor CPCC,
The Intuitive Heart Mentor, www.OpeningDoorsWithin.com

"Prepare to be totally inspired by how Karin turned true life tragedy into a cornerstone for living a truly grand life! Quite frankly, she transformed lead into gold. Rather than allowing herself to become angry or embittered, she seized the opportunity to uplift herself, expand her consciousness...and in this book she shows you how all that is possible for you, too!"

~ Kit Furey, JD, CHt, CEHP,
Belief and Energy Transformation Expert. Specialist in Peak Performance and Creativity for Business Leaders Everywhere

"I was truly inspired by the story—I mean, who wouldn't be? Karin has achieved what few people could—take an experience like this and turn it into something that not only results in your growth, but adds significant value to the world through her inspired efforts."

~ **Bob Uslander MD, www.DoctorsOnPurpose.com**

"Unjustly denied the fundamental freedom and comforts of life, Karin turned inward to uncover the profound richness of her spirit and connection to a far greater freedom. Her courage, discipline and commitment to a higher road is a daily source of inspiration and compassion. She openly and authentically shares her life, joy and enthusiasm with all that she does."

~ **Susan Hayward, Business Intuitive Strategist,
www.LivingtheLeadingEdge.com**

"Karin's story is one that has always amazed me. When I first heard about it, I was shocked and inspired. You think that these things only happen in the movies! She had such a positive and deep perspective on problem solving life. Her story can›t help but give fresh insight into our own story."

~ **Cyndi Fine, Creative Instigator, www.cyndifine.com**

"Karin is being used by a higher power in such a profound way. I'm so thankful for all of the reminders and inspiration she's given in her book. She is indeed a messenger of joy and empowerment!"

~ Terri Britt, Award-winning Author of *The Enlightened Mom*,
Inspirational Speaker and former Miss USA 1982, www.TerriBritt.com

1,352 Days

An Inspirational Journey
From Jail to Joy

Karin Volo

Published by A Life With A Fabulous View Inc. in collaboration with Verbii. The views expressed or implied in this book are the views of the author. The events are portrayed to the best of the author's memory. The conversations come from her recollections though they are not written to represent word-for-word transcripts. Rather, the stories have been retold in a way that evokes the feeling and meaning of what was said and in all instances, the essence of the dialogue is accurate. While all the stories in this book are true, some names and identifying details have been changed to protect the privacy of the people involved. The intent of the author is only to offer information of a general nature to help you in your quest for personal well-being.

1ˢᵗ Edition: March 2015

ISBN: 978-0-9837960-5-3

Contents

Foreword

I remember getting the phone call that sent a shock through my entire body like a Taser. I had just finished several long days of teaching a group of business owners the keys to growing their business and living the life of their dreams and I was tired and drained. We discussed the importance of having the right unrelenting mindset, the right skills and the faith that one must have in order to succeed no matter how hard it gets.

We discussed that there is always a way over it, under it, around it or through any of our life or business challenges. Little did I know that one of my students would have other methodologies for dealing with life's unpredictable curve balls and challenges.

It was 2006 when that call came in and Karin's life partner Sergio told me that Karin was in jail here in San Diego. "Jail?" I said. "What the hell are you talking about? You just left the seminar!"

I thought that maybe they went out to celebrate and she had a few too many margaritas or something, but I was way off the mark in my quick assumption.

The day she left my seminar and went to the airport to go back to Sweden surely wasn't a normal day for her, as you will come to find in this amazing book.

Although I didn't really know Karin well at the time, I knew that she had amazing potential and applied to her business and life what I was teaching. What I didn't know is how much she would end up teaching me from jail.

They kept Karin for almost four years—1,352 days to be exact! Keep in mind that this was not a prison. This was a small jail they hold people accused of federal crimes that are in transition.

Over the next few years, Karin and I kept in touch and she kept me abreast with the case whenever I went to visit her or via her letters. The highs and lows, the trials and tribulations that went on month after month, would be enough for most people to just want to roll over and die.

Not Karin, however. Somehow, she found the courage, wisdom, and inner faith to keep strong and to trust her inner guidance and divine power. I was always amazed when she told me how many books she read and how she was teaching yoga and meditation to the other inmates. Her attitude was something to behold.

Having a positive attitude is one thing. Knowing in your heart of hearts that you are here for some higher purpose or reason even when faced with being extradited to a Mexican prison for many years is another. Karin had a faith I have never seen before.

She somehow was able to see past her circumstances and continue on her journey. The love and faith that Sergio had in Karin was remarkable. Their story is amazing and shows that love really is the most powerful force in the world.

Like many of you, I have faced many challenges in my life, but I don't know if I would have had the courage to do what Karin did. From the first day she was in prison to now, all I saw and see is a woman with dignity, calmness, and unrelenting faith in her connection to a higher power.

This book will take you on a soul searching mission to find your own core, your own inner strength and your true spirit that will guide you through whatever journey and challenges you face today or may face sometime in your life.

Karin is an amazing teacher and has so many wonderful stories, lessons and incredible insights that will touch your heart and stir your spirit and soul.

She moved my heart and soul and now through her book, she will move yours.

—John Assaraf

Chapter One

•••

A Tap on the Shoulder

I am not what happened to me. I am what I choose to become.
—Carl Jung

You never forget those days that irrevocably change your life. It was 6:30 A.M. on March 29, 2006, and I was standing in line at San Diego Lindbergh International Airport with my business and life partner, Sergio, waiting to board our homebound flight to Stockholm, Sweden. It was good to be going home after a week of intense business mentoring with inspirational speaker John Assaraf and Murray Smith of One Coach. Sergio and I were excited about the future of our business and where our new skills would take us. The Law of Attraction was indeed "the secret" to our burgeoning success. We had seen this extraordinary new film, *The Secret,* twice during the conference, and I was certain it would be a huge hit. There was no doubt in my mind that we attract into our lives exactly what we need, yet the mystery of how and why we draw in the unexpected continued to engage me. "Dumb" luck and coincidences, along with an inner passion to make the most of my life, had led me here to where I needed to be right now. A bad marriage was long behind me. I had a new lover who was not only devastatingly handsome but who happened to be the perfect business partner for me as well. The right books seemed to come into my hands just when I needed their guidance. Our office phone rang again and again as potential clients called to ask about our services, and they often told us that they had heard about our executive search firm in the most serendipitous

1

way. The universe seemed to be conspiring to support my dreams.

Even so, I was a bit unsettled today. When Sergio paid the cab driver and we gathered our bags, I tried to release the nervousness that had been shooting through my body. Life was good. We just needed to get to the gate and back to Sweden where we would implement all that we'd learned in our weeklong conference.

It had been a strange day ever since the moment I opened my eyes in the morning. For some reason, we didn't get the hotel wake-up call we'd ordered, and although we awakened in time, both of us were feeling harried. We had to be at the airport by 5:30 A.M. to ensure that we'd have time to grab a bite for breakfast before the long flight and switch our tickets for two seats next to each other. The taxi we had ordered was due at 4:30 A.M and when it didn't arrive, we phoned and discovered they had no record of our call. They promised to send a car immediately and we stood outside the hotel checking our watches every couple of minutes.

Finally, we were on our way with a driver who took all the short cuts so that we got to the airport on time, although just barely. Walking quickly, Sergio and I made our way to the check-in desk and discovered that my ticket was coded *"secondary security pass."* Sergio's had no such notation.

"What does this mean?" I asked the clerk as I pointed to the unfamiliar words.

"They'll tell you when you go through security," she said, and with a perfunctory gesture, directed us to the security checkpoint.

Sergio and I stepped up our pace because we were concerned this new development would slow us down further. Aside from the flight out to L.A., I hadn't been on an airplane since 9/11, and I assumed there was some sort of system for giving extra attention to random passengers. *Just my luck.*

"Wow, they've really got tight security," I said to Sergio.

"Well, maybe it won't take too long," he said as we maneuvered through the crowd. Nothing strange happened and we went through the normal checks.

Sergio's prediction was right, but after we pulled our carry-on baggage off the X-ray scanner's conveyer belt, it was clear that we wouldn't have time to sit down and eat breakfast. I knew I'd feel better when we got to the gate, so we stopped just long enough to pick up a snack before boarding: a banana and espresso for Sergio, a lemon poppy seed muffin and cup of Earl

Grey tea for me. I juggled the tea carefully, its cardboard sleeve barely thick enough to keep my hand from becoming uncomfortably hot.

With a little speed walking, we soon arrived at the gate. A quick glance at the sign departures board told me our flight was on time. I asked the flight attendant at the podium if she could seat us together after all, and she reassured us it was no problem. In a few minutes, she handed us new boarding passes and said, "You're good to go."

Sergio and I walked to the back of the line and I began to unwrap my muffin and bit into it carefully to avoid getting crumbs on my cashmere sweater. Sergio gingerly peeled back the plastic tab on the Earl Grey tea I'd purchased and handed it to me. After a few sips, I happened to glance up again at the departure sign.

Delayed.

Now that was odd. But then, given the crazy morning we'd just had, it seemed to be just another wrinkle in our day. I hoped we wouldn't land too late. The plan was to take a taxi straight to the office. We could catch up on some work, pick up the girls at 3:00, and go home to sleep off the jet lag a bit before starting dinner.

I folded up the muffin wrapper and stuffed it in the paper bag, and then made a quick call to our office, since it was afternoon there. Our assistant told me we had a new client waiting to give us some new business. Excellent!

And then, a tap on my shoulder.

I turned. I didn't recognize him. The man looked like an ordinary traveler but he swiftly stepped between Sergio and me as two men in dark blue windbreakers and jeans standing behind me each took one of my arms. One of them asked me, "Are you Karin Volo?"

"Yes."

I noticed some papers rolled up in his hand. He gave me his name and said, "I have a warrant for your arrest….. . " Just seven words. My mind froze.

He was still talking, but the only other words I heard were *Mexico* and *Leo*, the name of my first husband. I blanched in shock. Then I looked over at Sergio. In his amber eyes, I saw confusion and helplessness.

One of the men took my carry-on bag and black Esprit leather backpack from me and said, "If you go with us quietly, we won't put handcuffs on you."

"Can I just kiss—"

3

"No!" said the man who had my right arm. He tugged at me, and quickly pulled me away. "No physical contact."

My mind raced for words but drew a blank. I turned to see Sergio's face. It reflected back to me my own fear.

"It'll be okay," he called out, as much to convince himself as to convince me.

The men hurriedly escorted me away from my freedom, each holding one of my elbows as I looked straightforward. Where were we going? It seemed crazy! Why the grip on my arms? I was no criminal!

"Who are you?" I managed to ask.

"U.S. Federal Marshals." No more explanation was offered and as I passed curious onlookers, I was too stunned to formulate any other questions. The marshals led me into a room that appeared to be a kitchenette and conference room, furnished with the bare necessities. They seated me at the table and I looked out the window into the open sky and focused on the sight of a jet as it silently rose into the air.

I was still speechless and sinking deeper into shock. It was as if a deep freeze had settled in and thoughts were barely able to move through the rapidly solidifying ice that had become my mind. My eyes looked around and I took in details both familiar and unfamiliar—the marshal's badge, a coffee ring on the table, the flickering of a fluorescent light under one of the cabinets. Papers were placed in front of me. They appeared to be legal documents. The men were saying something but none of it made sense. My mind struggled to push through the frozen sludge.

I saw my name and my ex-husband's name and then the bold words that would be seared into my memory for the rest of my life: *Warrant for Arrest*.

"We need to handcuff you now and take you into custody."

I moved with dreamlike slowness. Between themselves, the men talked about my luggage and wanting to retrieve it from the plane. They discussed whether they should continue to delay the flight and decided against it. The marshals, still talking to each other, said Sergio's name wasn't anywhere in the arrest document—they weren't interested in him. I felt a momentary sense of relief. He would go home and take care of my girls until all this was cleared up and they let me go. Sergio was a family man, with kids of his own. My daughters adored him. They would be safe. Everything would be okay just as soon as this madness ended and I was on a plane going home.

One of the marshals asked me to come with him, and I began to follow him awkwardly, my shoulders stretched back to relieve the discomfort of my hands straining against the handcuffs. As he and another marshal each held one of my elbows, I walked with them through the airport again. I knew the plane I was supposed to be on would depart any second, taking my beloved Sergio home to Alexa and Megan without me. When would I see him again? How would he explain to the girls why I wasn't with him? What would happen? I couldn't think about that. At that moment, home felt much, much farther away than the 5,400 miles between San Diego and Stockholm.

As I walked between the marshals, I felt confused and completely mortified. I passed men and women in business attire, and thought, "What if someone I met at the conference sees me?" We walked outside to a car and one of the marshals settled me into the back seat. Then the other marshal got behind the wheel and put my bags in the front. Just as we were getting ready to pull away from the curb to wherever they were taking me, another marshal ran up to the car. He explained, "The man she's traveling with doesn't have his tickets. He says they're in her handbag. He needs his ticket."

That jolted my mind back into action and I began to beg. "You *have* to get the ticket to him! He *needs* to go home and take care of my daughters!" They searched my handbag and found our tickets. As the third marshal took them and began to jog back to the terminal, I wondered how Sergio was coping. I prayed that he would have the strength to do whatever needed to be done to handle things at home and keep our business going. God only knows what he would say to my girls.

"Where are you taking her?" Sergio asked.

"She's being arrested," said the third marshal, "You should take your flight and get out of the country."

"Please," he said as the marshal began walking away, "ask Karin whether I need to stay or go home and take care of the children."

The man nodded.

Sergio lingered helplessly, unable to take in what had just happened. The flight attendant began checking boarding passes as the line of passengers began to enter the walkway to the aircraft. Leaving was unthinkable, yet an eight-year-old and a six-year-old in Sweden needed him home that night. In a daze, he waited, and then the marshal returned with the tickets—Sergio had completely forgotten about them—and said, "She'd like you to get on the flight."

It was the hardest decision Sergio had ever made, but he knew he had to put the girls' needs first and leave Karin behind. He had no idea where they were taking her or what sort of danger she'd encounter. Loyalty and guilt intermixed, but he pushed aside his emotions to do what made sense.

The first leg of the journey home would last six hours. As he settled into the long flight to Chicago's O'Hare Airport, Sergio realized he hadn't asked the security official for his card or even his name. All he knew was that as soon he could, he had to start making some phone calls to track down where Karin was. His mind began to race. Who were these people? Were they the police? The F.B.I. or C.I.A.? He was irritated with himself for not getting more information, but it had all happened so quickly. For a fleeting moment, he thought maybe Karin had been kidnapped. Then he brushed the idea aside. The men had certainly looked and acted official.

He wondered when he would be allowed to speak to Karin again. Where would they take her? When would they allow her to make a phone call? Would they let her call his cell phone with its unfamiliar area code? Would he have touched down by then?

Chatter from the many passengers became an undistinguishable murmur. With no answers, no information that might help him understand what had just happened, Sergio found himself experiencing a vacuum of sound as he withdrew into his thoughts. A survival instinct kicked in and he grasped at the security of logic. He pulled out his notepad and pen and began to list the calls he needed to make. Strategy was key.

He had to create security for the children somehow. Although he and Karin were only committed partners, with no plans of marriage, and they had lived together only part of the time, he was the only father Alexa and Megan had ever known and he loved them dearly. He would tell Karin's two daughters that their mother hadn't been sick; there had been no accident; that it wasn't their fault she hadn't come home; and, most importantly, that she hadn't abandoned them. He'd say she'd been detained on business and he wasn't quite sure when she would come home.

How long would this nightmare last? A few days? Weeks? He decided he would call his ex-wife and tell her that he wouldn't be able to spend as much time taking care of his own two children from his previous marriage, at least until Karin *was home. He hoped she would agree to take their children more often although they shared custody.*

There were dozens of practical matters to address. He would have to work with Karin's mother to coordinate taking the children to and from school and their various activities. He'd have to take care of expenses both at home and in the business, look at all the contracts that needed to be completed; figure out how he might cover living expenses temporarily if Karin couldn't return quickly and get back to generating income. Was he getting ahead of himself? Maybe, but he felt the need to plan as much as possible. It was the only thing he could do right now.

One thing at a time. Locating and working with the attorneys—he made notes of who might help him with that. His first call would be to John Assaraf. Surely he would know a lawyer in San Diego. Sergio checked his watch again. It would be hours before he landed in Chicago.

The more he thought about the situation and the possibility that it might not end quickly, the more the fear that was churning at the base of his spine began to spread through his body. His skills in project management took over as he wrote his lists. Sergio had only three years' experience in his and Karin's executive search business, and an uncomfortable thought arose in his mind: Could he handle the workload all on his own? It was Karin who drove the sales and marketing and hired and managed personnel. How would he fit that in while she was gone?

And how long would she be gone?

"Slow down," he told himself. "Think. Just think. Who else do I need to call?"

Sergio knew the situation was serious but had no idea just how serious it was.

A bitter metallic taste rose in his mouth but he chose to ignore it. Focus—that was what he needed to do. Focus and plan.

The bitter taste would remain with him for almost four years.

It wasn't a long drive from the airport to the courthouse where I was formally placed under arrest. I sat in the back seat of the car with the U.S. Marshal, waiting to be told what would happen next. I looked out the window and though "how ironic"—I was finally seeing some of San Diego after spending an entire week in hotel rooms in Del Mar, where I'd eagerly soaked in all the information and inspiration John and his team offered at the seminar.

I tried to remember what the marshals had said to me as I sat at the table in that little room at the airport, but everything was surreal. It's as if I forgot how to read, or to process spoken language. I had no idea what had gone so horribly wrong. I was sure there must be some type of mistake. The frozen sludge in my mind was of no help to me, and I made no attempt to think through what was happening. A primitive part of myself told me to stay alert and observe, like a wary animal being stalked.

When we arrived at the courthouse, they escorted me into the building through a back entrance. It was dirty, dark, and hideous. Ancient grease stains and scuff marks dotted the shiny, sickly yellow walls. The smell of sweat and fear permeated the stale air. I sensed complete desperation emanating not only from me but from the cages that held so many people. I looked straight ahead and allowed my peripheral vision to blur the images. I didn't want to look into anyone's eyes. It reminded me of visiting the humane society and seeing all the anguish and despair, only this was a hundred times worse. Who were these people? What crimes had they committed? I couldn't bear to imagine the possibilities.

A clanking sound told me the bars behind me had been locked. The sound of metal on metal reverberated and faded away as I heard shouting begin far down the hall. Around me was a quiet buzz of conversation, mostly in Spanish. More metal clanked as doors opened and inmates were escorted back and forth to the hidden courtrooms. The blueish-white fluorescent lights illuminated the empty holding room they'd locked me in, and I sat down on a metal bench that was ice-cold from the air-conditioning. My eyes hurt from the harsh lighting so I put my head on my knees and hugged them. Then, I tried to calm myself by closing my eyes, focusing on my breathing, and pretending I was anywhere else but here.

I'd arrived just before 7:00 a.m. and sat there for hours, rarely raising my head or listening to what was happening around me. For long stretches, I simply waited and wondered when I would wake up from this horrible nightmare. They were required to itemize my belongings so they lead me into another room to fingerprint me, take my photograph, and empty my small leather backpack so they could make a list of the contents. To my surprise, they didn't open my carry-on, but asked me to tell them what was in it. They confiscated all my jewelry and the scarf I'd been wearing, and explained that they had to remove anything I might be able to use to strangle myself.

I had enough presence of mind to surreptitiously remove two photographs of my girls from my wallet and sneak them into my pocket.

I wasn't sure I would be allowed to keep them, but I needed my girls to be near me, if only in the form of wallet-sized school photos.

The guards moved me to a different room and frisked me. Somehow, they missed the photos. I was so relieved, but I didn't dare take out the pictures to look at them the whole time because I was afraid they might take them away. Then I was returned to the ice-cold holding room, where I sat for what seemed like an eternity. My stomach was in knots. My back hurt terribly. I just sat there with my eyes closed, rocking myself back and forth, pretending this wasn't happening and feeling so afraid of what was coming. I didn't want to see that filthy, disgusting room, which had by now filled up with other women. Unlike me, most of these women were in standard jail attire, which reminded me of hospital scrubs.

I remember asking some man in a suit who stood outside the cell for a minute, "What's going to happen?" The blunt answer came back: "You're going to be arraigned." I had no idea what that meant.

It seemed an eternity that I sat there. Finally, someone came and took me to the courtroom. Once again, I was handcuffed while they walked me through long corridors that snaked under the building. I picked up on the strong scent of body odor mixed with urine and blew air through my nostrils to clear them, but the close smell simply filled them again.

It was a very dark journey in every way. Maybe it was because I was dressed nicely in slacks and a sweater rather than a uniform, but when I walked by cells full of men it was as if someone had turned on a switch and all of them began shouting catcalls. "Mamacita, looking good!", "Ooo, pretty lady!", and exaggerated kissing sounds that accomplished exactly what they intended; by the time that long walk was over, I felt violated and naked. I had no idea how much worse I would soon feel.

A suited male marshal led me to a service elevator where I joined some other prisoners and we rode up to the main floor to the courtroom. There, I was placed in another smaller holding cell to wait. When it was my turn, the marshal escorted me through a set of doors, into a plain vestibule with lush carpeting and one lonely wooden chair that seemed out of place. The next set of doors we went through brought us into the courtroom. The cherry wood walls and railings and the majestic judge's bench provided a jarring contrast to the space I'd just left. I looked over at the American flag placed near the front of the courtroom and, for a brief moment, felt a glimpse of hope. This was a hall of justice, in the United States of America. Although I'd been born in Mexico to American parents, and currently lived in Sweden, the homeland of my mother, I'd grown up in Arizona and Connecticut. I had recited the pledge of allegiance as a child. *With liberty and justice for all.*

The arraignment lasted about two minutes. I finally learned why I was there: Mexico wanted me and I was being extradited. That was all I knew. Somehow, I had the clarity and courage to announce, "I need an attorney." A representative from the Federal Defender's Office gave me a business card and promised that someone from their office would be assigned to my case and would come to visit me. Someone did come for a few minutes, asked basic questions, and wrote down my information. I still didn't understand why I had been arrested or what crime I had been accused of committing. I thought I would have a chance to defend myself or make a plea, or something. Nothing could have been further from the truth as I was moved around from room to cell to hallway as if I were on a conveyor belt, with no one showing any more interest in me than they did the other inmates despite the fact that I was dressed in street clothes. We were simply bodies to be escorted from here to there in some bizarre ritual.

At noon, a guard came into the holding room and handed me a sack lunch consisting of two dry slices of bread with an unidentifiable slab of meat between, a piece of crumbling cake, and a slightly mealy apple. I managed to eat the apple. Time lingered in the air like a plume of smoke as I watched the hand on the industrial wall clock slowly move. I spent the entire day there as women wearing prison garb were led in and out although I was too scared to ask anyone what had brought them to the cell. I had no idea if they'd been tried and were awaiting sentencing, for what crime they'd been arrested, or from what institution they had come. All I could see was that there were three different uniform colors: evergreen, light brown, and khaki, but I didn't know exactly what the different colors meant.

Not knowing what to expect, unsure of whom these women are, whether any were violent or might want to intimidate me, I remained silent. I tried to keep my head down and not look scared. I spent a lot of time examining my hands, as if there were something fascinating to be learned from them. It kept me from taking in the unsettling sights all around me.

When I did look up, I could see that nearly all the women were of Mexican descent and ranged from young to middle aged, thin to heavy, and

10

pretty to plain. None seemed to be all that interested in me after I softly replied in response to their questions, "I don't know what's going on. I don't know what I'm being charged with." They sat around, most of them talking, half in Spanish and half in English. They asked each other, "What did they get you on?" Some had a swagger in their voice as they told the others about their lives and the trouble they'd seen. At last, a pleasant girl in green asked me, what was going on? I told her I didn't know, that I'd only arrived a few hours before. "Maybe you'll end up at GEO," she said.

I had no idea what GEO was but didn't dare ask, although it seemed to be a place she was familiar with. She seemed nice and stayed close by me, but we didn't speak much. Between my shock and fear, I couldn't bring myself to ask her to answer my questions.

At one point in the late afternoon, the guards brought in a woman in a micro miniskirt, garish purple rouge and lipstick, and a low-cut tank top. She cursed loudly in English and peppered her angry rant with Spanish. I saw her go behind the short wall that barely obscured the toilet and heard odd noises I tried to block out mentally. "Hey, get this bitch out of here! She's crazy!" shouted one of the women to no one in particular as she strained to look through the bars and down the hall. Some of the other women snickered and gossiped in low voices as the loud woman in the bathroom grumbled to herself. Never having seen anyone who was high on street drugs before, I had no idea what she was doing. I only knew that as soon as a guard did appear, she brusquely escorted the woman out and into another cell.

Toward the end of that eternal and grueling day, I came to the realization that I would be wearing one of those uniforms. That was okay, I decided, because until I was out of this place, I wanted to blend in. The nice girl in green had left, and now I didn't want anyone to notice me or try to talk to me. After what had happened today, I'd had enough of that to last a lifetime. I gazed at my hands again. They were shaking. I folded them underneath my armpits so no one would see.

I looked up and a male marshal with a thick mustache walked by. I remembered another man in an unfamiliar uniform, many years ago in Mexico. He had insisted that he would need to search my house. Alexa had squirmed as I balanced her on my hip, a task made more difficult by my ever-growing belly. Pregnant at the time, feeling vulnerable, I'd been unsure what was happening and was too scared to ask. Faces suddenly appeared in the dark windows of the first floor. My friend showed up at the door in response to my frantic phone call and told me not to panic.

That was all so long ago. I squeezed my eyes shut to block out the memory. *Sergio will get a hold of a lawyer and all this will end.* I pictured the girls running to hug me at the airport and Sergio walking toward me, a huge smile on his face. *Make it real,* I told myself. I held on to my vision, drawing comfort from it.

Around 5:00 P.M., they moved me by van to a different holding cell—at GEO, which I would later learn was the nickname for the jail, a company called GEO that was under contract with the Office of Federal Detention and the U.S. Marshal's Service. GEO provided high security for adult male and female detainees. I was being taken to the Western Region Detention Facility in San Diego, which housed 784 temporary inmates.

I moved clumsily because of my handcuffs and shackles with a short chain between my ankles. Then I entered the van and took a seat. It had very dark windows with reinforced steel grills, so while the seats were normal, I felt as if I were in a moving prison. A grille between the driver and guard and the detainees' section reminded me that some of my fellow travelers might be violent, and I felt my muscles tense at the thought. The only other passengers were a couple of male detainees who were seated behind me. Like me, they were handcuffed.

My mind was a blank and I can't remember how long it was before I arrived at GEO and was escorted through several metal doors to another holding cell. It was dinnertime, so I was handed a tray with a meal that consisted of some inedible food. It had an unsettling plastic sheen to it. I tried to eat a bit, but I had no appetite for the congealed and rubbery mess. A female guard in a beige GEO uniform that showed every roll and bulge took away my nearly full dinner tray without a comment and said something about starting the intake process.

She led me to an empty room and told me to remove all my clothes. I removed my shoes and trouser socks and tried not to make eye contact as I got down to my bra and panties and then removed those as well.

It was mortifying to stand completely naked in front of a total stranger. "Bend over and spread your buttocks with your hands, then cough." She spoke with no emotion, as if she were simply relating the instructions to locate the nearest exits on the aircraft.

I bent over and tried to distract my mind with the patterns on the stone floor as she checked for anything hidden in my body's orifices. Apparently, that's a good place to smuggle in makeup or drugs, so the strip search is a standard part of jail life.

My feelings of degradation and violation began to overtake me, and I felt every muscle fiber in my body tighten further. My throat was tense and my skin seemed to grasp my forehead in a painful grip, and my head began to throb.

The guard suddenly told me to stand up. She pulled some clothing from a nearby cart as I tried to compose myself. Then I quickly put on what I would later realize was the standard green scrubs uniform of GEO: a sports bra and granny panties, a white t-shirt and white tube socks, dull green pants and top (they looked like hospital scrubs), and cheap navy sneakers. As foreign as the clothes felt, at least my humiliation began to fade and I was feeling slightly less dehumanized. The guard led me over to another guard who was standing at a table, getting ready to fingerprint me.

As the guard prepared the form and the ink pad, I looked closely at her. Unlike most of the women I had seen today, she was rather pretty: Long eyelashes, beautiful high cheekbones, skin the color of a smooth river pebble, her sleek black hair thick with shiny curls and pinned up in a bun. Her lipstick was slightly glossy and perfectly applied. She was young, maybe 25. I couldn't understand it: Why was she working in a prison? She looked more like a receptionist in a modern office building, the type of woman who can handle four incoming calls and a visitor without missing a beat. Why would she want a job like this? None of it made any sense. The sludge in my mind had barely budged.

I could see she was having a little trouble positioning my pinky finger above the form and moved my wrist slightly to accommodate her.

"DON'T MOVE!" she barked. I nearly jumped and felt a rush of tears fill my eyes as my throat tightened. Her grasp on my wrist tightened and I meekly submitted to her maneuverings. Any semblance of normalcy had been erased. Like everyone here, she was all business. Who I was, what I was thinking—none of it mattered here. I could tell my guilt or innocence was irrelevant to everyone here. I was an inmate to be processed, nothing more.

The shock of this woman's rudeness was still reverberating when I was again directed to walk with other guards to yet another unfamiliar room, this one in the medical unit. I sat silently, alone, for perhaps fifteen minutes, in what looked to be a small infirmary with six metal beds fastened to the floor. Then, they brought in a woman who wore the same cheap, ugly clothes I had just donned. The guard left, and the woman turned to me and introduced herself as Ellen. She was very jittery, and kept getting up and pacing, sitting down again, then popping up to repeat the ritual. She was very tall and stout, with wild wiry hair reaching out in all directions, but despite her manic appearance, she didn't seem intimidating or threatening in any way. Maybe it was because she was so obviously fearful herself. "I can't believe this. I have to get a hold of my boyfriend. He's got no idea what happened," she kept saying.

Ellen looked disheveled and in need of a shower, and I suspected she had been shuttled from holding room to holding room for a few days. She said something about how hurt and disappointed her children were going to be. "I tested dirty. And I'm on probation. This is bad," she told me. I murmured a sympathetic sound, but it didn't seem to have any effect on her nervousness.

Only much later would I realize that her anxious pacing and darting eyes were the result of being high on crystal meth. Like so many women in the jails and prisons in the U.S., Ellen had a long-standing drug problem and certainly needed to be in treatment but, the system being what it was, she was locked up and shunted about instead. Whatever petty dealing she had done to support her habit, whatever she had done to cover her drug use, she had not been sufficiently discreet and now she was scared and remorseful. All I knew at this point is that she, like me, was more concerned with her children than anything else. "I don't know what I'm going to tell them," she said.

It was my dilemma, too. What would I tell my mother and my girls? I felt certain that Sergio wasn't going to stick around. My predicament was crazy. Why would he put up with it? Ellen listened sympathetically as I told her my girls were thousands of miles away, surely confused about why I hadn't returned.

Soon, a guard walked in to tell us that since all the medical staff had gone home for the evening, there was no way to do the required physical examination and we would have to stay there overnight before being moved elsewhere. With nothing else to distract us, Ellen and I simply talked for a few hours. Our conversation turned to the everyday details of what our kids were up to, how many siblings we had, and where we had lived. Ellen's face brightened when I told her I had been born in Mexico and lived there for a few years as a child and later, as an adult. That made me a sister of sorts because she'd lived there too, even if the thread of our connection was as thin as the blankets they'd issued us. It gave each of us some comfort to reveal a little about who we were and to find that we had something in common.

At some point, a guard handed us a small toiletries kit and Ellen laughed as I stared at the toothbrush I'd just received, clearly puzzled by it. "Bet you never saw a toothbrush that short," she said.

I looked at her in amused confusion. "No, I can't say that I have!"

"They make it stubby so you don't carve it into a knife." She grabbed hers by the tiny, fat handle and brushed her teeth with an exaggerated scrubbing motion. "Oh, can't kill anyone today, I guess I'd better just brush my teeth instead."

I laughed. It was all so absurd. Ellen told me, "They always give you toothpaste, even if you still have some. Some of the ladies wash their clothes with it. It makes a pretty good laundry whitener. You'd be surprised."

"They have to wash their own clothes?" I asked.

"Well, only because they want to. There's a laundry but no one uses it. The clothes here are pretty nasty even when they're clean. But soooo pretty, aren't they?"

I shook my head and smiled. I hoped I wouldn't be here long enough to discover what she meant exactly. For now, I was just going to concentrate on not letting myself panic. Talking helped.

Time ticked away as we carried on, tentatively establishing a bond of sorts between us. Then, sometime around midnight, they dimmed the lights. Ellen quickly fell into a quiet slumber but sleep refused to overtake me. I lay down on the bed and ignored the distant metal doors clanging shut. I began to direct a movie in my mind: I wrapped my arms around my girls and hugged them. Next scene: sitting down to dinner with Megan, Alexa, and Sergio. Then another scene: lying next to Sergio in bed, his toned chest and strong arms wrapped around me. I willed myself to pretend he was there with me. I knew that I was not only calming my agitated body and soothing my frayed nerves, but training my mind to trust that these wonderful scenes I was creating in my mind would become real. I couldn't think about "when" or "how." There was so little information to help me understand my predicament and at this moment, I didn't want to understand, or think. I simply wanted to escape the horror.

Then I closed my eyes and simply waited for my mind to immerse itself in the river of a dreamless sleep.

Chapter Two

· ·

The Middle Way

Life is either a daring adventure or nothing. –Helen Keller

D addy's long fingers turned the pages of an oversized book that was rich with photographs of European buildings and landscapes at sunrise. I sat in his lap drinking in the swooping arches, intricate details, and exotic images as he explained that soon I would see these grand structures up close, because he was going to take my mother, my older brother and sister, and I on a magical trip overseas to Sweden, France, and Italy.

I soaked up his stories and wriggled past my older siblings each night for months to ensure that I had the best view of Daddy's books as he performed this ritual of preparing us for our European adventure. By the time we arrived in Florence, I knew the titles of paintings and sculptures by Michelangelo and could light up my father's face with pride as his four year old daughter pointed out the dome of the Cathedral of Santa Maria del Fiore and Giottos' bell tower. My parents, my older brother and sister, Tom and Sue, and I all squeezed into a small RV we'd rented and traveled from city to town, the vineyards of France giving way to cobblestone streets and buildings with ancient oak doors that I was sure opened to Cinderella's hearth. I opened my eyes to the wonders of architecture and museums and my ears to the sound of foreign languages mingling with the flapping of pigeon's wings as I gleefully chased birds in a plaza.

I lived in a comfortable space nestled between security and adventure, and I'm still happiest when I have equal measures of both. Fortunately, mine was a solidly middle class American family that treasured the excitement of exploration and learning. My mom, Birgitta, had been a Swedish exchange student at Willamette University in Oregon when she noticed the charms of the good-looking captain of the basketball team and student body president named Neil. Well-mannered and handsome, he came from very humble roots and could only afford to take my mom out for coffee, never a meal, but she didn't seem to mind. She simply smiled quietly when her sorority sisters would coo that she had captured a prize bachelor who was sure to be a good provider. After all, these were the days when even the most educated women were likely to set aside their ambitions after marriage and devote themselves to mothering and homemaking.

A few months after they first met, my parents became engaged, my dad graduated and began to earn his master's degree in Mechanical Engineering at Stanford University, and my mom followed and finished her undergraduate degree there. They had a beautiful wedding in Sweden that my grandfather, a famous photographer, documented in one of my favorite books that he self-published, *Those Happy Years*. My parents' lives were unfolding smoothly before them, and whenever I would hear the story of their courtship, I didn't give a second thought to how easily they came together and began creating a secure relationship. It seemed to me that's just how it worked when you fall in love.

My father earned his Masters from Stanford, his M.B.A. from Harvard, and then Union Carbide sent him to a job in their Mexico offices. My parents uprooted themselves without hesitation although neither knew any Spanish beyond perhaps counting to ten and saying "hello" and "good-bye." Nevertheless, both picked up the language quickly—enough so that my mom earned a master's degree in Psychology at a university in Mexico. It was a degree that would serve her well given the troubles she would encounter in her life. At the time, she had no hint of rough patches ahead.

In 1968, seven years after my parents left the United States, I entered the world as baby sister to Tom, who was six, and Suzanne, who was four. With American parents and a Mexican birth certificate, both countries would claim me, although I never did think of myself as Mexican. I definitely didn't imagine that some day that heritage would make any difference one way or another. Mexico was simply the place I spent my preschool years. When I got older, I found it held no special appeal for me, although it seemed like a nice place to take a vacation someday.

I was close to my mom, but to my youthful self, my tall, handsome Daddy was pure royalty. He was my prince and my king: brilliant, kind, gentle yet powerful, my grand protector. He would duck through doorways gracefully despite his lanky, 6' 7" frame, then look over at me with his brown eyes, the dimples on his cheeks deepening as he smiled broadly. Some of my favorite memories of being with him were in the courtyard of our large, three-centuries-old Spanish-style home. Daddy would sit by the fountain, thick black Ray Ban sunglasses shielding his eyes from the bright rays as he read books on engineering and architecture. After my bath, I would dash out to the courtyard in my birthday suit to dry off in the warm rays before my mother corralled me into using a towel and putting on some clothes. Later, I might take a trip to the bustling market across the street with my mother. I was mortified and resentful that she put me on a leash—"like a puppy!" I thought bitterly—so that I couldn't run off and get lost in the crowd of buyers and sellers. Of course, now I can see that a leather harness on a toddler might be a sensible choice when you've got two hands, several packages, and three children to manage, but at the time it felt like a humiliating assault on my budding freedom and independence. My lower lip would jut out in protest.

After our European trip, my father learned that he had developed skin cancer, probably from exposing his fair complexion to the hot sun near the equator each day when we were living south of the border. Cancer therapy was very crude at the time but everyone held out hope that such a young and vibrant man would be able to beat it. He asked for and was granted a transfer to New York City, which had far better medical care than the Mexican city where we lived, and my parents bought a house in the suburbs in Connecticut. Whatever fears they had, my mother and father had hopes for their family's future together.

It was the early Seventies and time moved slowly in our neighborhood, where mothers scurried from kitchen to car to playground with a line of little ones behind them, while fathers disappeared to offices each morning and came home to a gin and tonic at 5:30. My dad let me take a sip of his evening cocktail a few times and was amused that I actually liked it, so he let me make plain tonic water a regular beverage—as long as I drank my milk at suppertime as well. My parents drank socially like the other couples they knew. A cocktail or two, a vinyl record on the hi-fi stereo, some chips and dip, and your family den became party central. The up-and-coming businessmen daringly donned the new leisure suits that promised a freedom from the old grey-flannel-suit conformity while their wives showed off new, fashionable, polyester pantsuits with collars that jutted out like the wings of birds about to take flight.

Despite his disease, my father continued to work for three years, although he sometimes took a few days off after surgery or chemotherapy to recover at home. On the surface, nothing changed for us kids, but secretly, I felt my father had morphed into an unfamiliar and frightening figure as his cancer spread to his brain. His big brown eyes were now partly obscured by eerie sci fi glasses with multiple horizontal lines running through them, which I was told helped him to see double rather than quadruple images. When he wanted to use the bathroom, he had to lean against the wall or my mother to balance himself as he walked tentatively down the hall. His thick brown hair had been replaced by a wig that often slipped into a cockeyed position. None of us discussed this hairpiece, or saw him without it. My father was probably embarrassed by what seemed like a loss of virility. And being so young, I found this new figure in my household scary. I was ashamed to feel this way, because I knew he was still my dad, but I would silently slink away when he entered the room.

My parents tried to be as positive about the outcome of my father's treatment as possible, and never talked to me about what was happening, or what might occur if he didn't regain his health. My mother was doing her best to take care of him and us kids, and didn't realize that I now saw my father as a disturbing imitation of the prince who had charmed me when he scooped me up and put me on his shoulders, or who had mesmerized me as a swarthy pirate singing a lead role in the community theater's production of *Pirates of Penzance*. My guilt was so great that I didn't dream of telling her, much less him. I hid the painful emotions swirling inside me.

One day, my brother got into trouble for tackling my sister—and knowing what a little monster I was around those two, it's probably safe to say I'd started the entire scene by picking a fight with Sue, which always brought Tom rushing to my defense. My father came running from across the house. He had never used corporal punishment because the mere threat of a walloping was enough to keep us in line, and now he began to unbuckle his belt as he took off after Tom. "You come back here!" he demanded as my teen brother dashed up the stairs toward his bedroom. My dad ran a few steps after him but suddenly stopped to grip the handrail. He looked dizzy and weak. My mother hurried to his side, and Tom wordlessly retreated to his room. I looked away, an uncomfortable witness to my father's frailty.

After that, Tom's rebellions became more pronounced. He knew my parents didn't have the time and energy to devote to discipline, and he probably was as frightened and confused as I was by the secret in our house. My father was slipping away and taking normalcy with him and we had no idea what to make of this. Sue responded to the uncertainty by becoming ultra serious about school and insisted that she couldn't be bothered with a social life given her ambition to become a doctor. She was the classic bookworm, and being a full head taller than all the boys in her class, she felt awkward socially around the more petite girls who obsessed about boys and high school dances. Novels, nonfiction books, and the library became Sue's sanctuaries.

I spent more and more time at my friend Kathy's house, building igloos outside in the winter and forts inside, which we created from blankets, chairs, and ropes. Inside our little hideaways, we'd play board games. One of my favorites was Life, and I carefully counted my money as I drove my little plastic car around the track, picking up pink pegs for baby girls and blue ones for baby boys and hoping I would amass enough of a fortune to win the game when I reached the last square.

At home, I tiptoed around my father. He was never an affectionate man by nature, so when I stopped running into his arms, he didn't reach out for me. I did notice that he had begun to hold my mother's hand, which he never used to do. But I wasn't certain I wanted him to hold mine, so I shied away. When I wanted my mother's attention and the two of them were in their bedroom next to mine, I'd walk into my closet and tap on the wall to let my mom know I needed to talk to her. She never questioned this odd behavior, and I don't know if she understood how uncomfortable I was with this strange man who now inhabited my father's deteriorating body.

The cancer didn't respond as the doctors hoped, and my mom told us we would have to prepare ourselves to lose Daddy. Hospitals, waiting, the monitors going quiet, an urn lowered into the ground and a gathering at our house afterward, with too many neighbors offering us too much food—it's a blur to me now. I had no idea what to say when they offered sympathy or asked how I was doing. I tried to scurry away whenever someone started to approach me and longed for an escape from this unfamiliar and awkward ritual. My brother had the same notion, I guess, because he literally disappeared with our car. The cops brought him back but the next day he ran off again, without the car, and we wondered how far a fifteen-year-old could get on foot.

As it turns out, the answer was "as far as Florida." Tom spent three days hitchhiking and for years later bragged about how with seven cents, a crucifix necklace, and a gift for gab, he'd finagled rides from a group of Christians who didn't question what a kid his age was doing on the road and, in fact, treated him to a hearty steak dinner along the way. After that, Tom began running with the local crowd of pot-smoking teens. He'd grown his bushy brown hair long, like John Lennon and the hippies, and would skip school and generally create enormous stress for my mother.

Months later, we all escaped the frigid and dreary Connecticut February with a family vacation to Arizona. As we jumped into the swimming pool at our relatives' home and basked in the sun, we all knew it was time for a change. My mother got the idea that by moving to Tucson, near my dad's relatives, we could start anew and she would get some much needed support. My Uncle John (my father's brother) could serve as a male role model to Tom, or so she reasoned.

My mother sent Tom ahead of us and our furniture to spend a few days guarding our new home until the rest of us arrived. Uncle John was supposed to supervise him, and maybe even have a heart-to-heart talk about starting over with a new attitude in a new place. But when he caught sight of my long-haired brother's collection of marijuana plants under purplish grow-lights spread out among the empty rooms, my uncle responded with a loud voice and a tight grip on a baseball bat he began to wave around menacingly. "I don't need this crap!" my brother shouted, and my uncle was forced to step aside as Tom stomped out the door. Tom went missing for a few days and, after this fiasco, my mom adjusted her expectations of him downward. She accepted that at sixteen, he was a high school dropout who mostly spent his time avoiding all of us but never getting into trouble that was too serious. Tom was a big guy, bearish even in his teens with his bushy brown beard and mustache and his wide shoulders, but despite his biker appearance and his Harley, he wasn't cruel or mean. We didn't know much about his friends and didn't necessarily want to either, and Tom didn't try to bring us into his world. He'd found his place among the biker crowd and that's where he felt at home.

I was an avoider as well although I found a much better way to escape my family and the unpredictability that each day held. I loved them, but they'd taken on an unrecognizable form. Divorce was becoming more common, but I didn't know anyone whose family looked like mine. I spent as much time as possible at my friends' houses. In their bedrooms, I'd practice the latest dance moves with them as the Bee Gees sang about their night fever. I just wanted to recapture the stable, suburban, nuclear family life I'd lost.

Sue and I seemed to be coping, so my mother wasn't worried about us girls. In fact, the only time she considered therapy for anyone was after I had an attack of appendicitis shortly before we moved to Arizona. In retrospect, maybe my grief and unspoken fear had taken its toll on my body. Maybe my mother felt that I was holding in my feelings too much, or the doctors might have said something to her about how I seemed a little too well adjusted to my father's death. Whatever her reasoning, my mom brought me to see a child psychologist who used play therapy. The counselor seemed nice enough but right away she wanted me to play with a dollhouse with a miniature family. "How does the mother act when the daughter is alone in her room? Does she come to her and ask her what's wrong? Where is the sister?" she would prompt me. I thought it was artificial and ridiculous, and I had no interest in playing with a bunch of chewed up dolls when I had much nicer ones in my own dollhouse. After a few completely unproductive sessions, my mother decided that maybe this wasn't such a great idea after all. I was doing okay in school, after all, and seemed to have plenty of friends.

In those years after Dad's death, when we lived in Arizona, my mother worked hard to provide us with stability. With uneven income and piles of bills plaguing her, my mom had to move us more times than I could remember. When she worked as a realtor, she was always struggling to sell this house or that one it seemed. After a short and disastrous marriage, she told me that now that the divorce had gone through she would buy a condo for us. "And you'll still be able to go to the same school," she told me. I give her credit for doing her best—and succeeding—and keeping me in that school district, with my friends, despite the many changes in our address.

While I was in high school and Sue was attending Stanford, we learned that Sue had Hodgkin's disease. Our aunt had suffered from it as well but had been in remission for years, so Tom and I never felt Sue was in any real danger, and I think my mother felt the same way—and fortunately, Sue did come through the radiation and chemotherapy treatments and continued her studies. It was Tom who seemed destined to die young given his fast lifestyle. "Let's face it," he'd say, "The way I live, I'll never make it to 30." In fact, he almost died in a serious motorcycle accident when he was 19. He came home to recover and afterward lived on disability checks and money from odd jobs—and, I would guess, petty dope dealing here and there. I didn't ask.

Tom wasn't the only one with financial problems. The life insurance money from my father's death had long since run out and I could see that with each move, my mom and I were slipping further down the socioeconomic ladder. There were medical bills, too. One afternoon, I came home from school to find her king-sized bed covered in bills she had spread out to try to make sense of it all. We began to take in boarders, including a mentally unstable woman who was on the brink of a post-divorce breakdown. I wished her drama didn't have to fill our home. Frustrated by what was going on in my house, I spent more and more time at my friends' places.

I'd had a small scrap involving a friend's parent's car where I got in trouble for doing something dumb and decided that the reckless road was not for me. I saw how unstable my brother's life was and I didn't want that life. But when I looked at my sister, so studious and unable to cut loose and have a little fun now and again, I knew I needed to find balance between rebellion and conformity. The middle road would be the one for me. After that, my rebellions were limited to occasionally ditching school, buying a few boxes of donuts, and driving up to the mountains with my friends to hang out. We would talk about how much we hated our geometry tests, hypocritical teachers, and whether we might get our own color television sets for Christmas if we worked on our parents enough.

As for ambitions, I was of the first generation of women to assume they could do anything if they had a college degree, and I knew that I was smart and had a lot of options. My family highly valued education, and I knew that was my ticket to success. I'd come to be close with my grandfather, or Morfar as we affectionately called him (the Swedish word for mother's father), who would become my biggest mentor. Morfar had moved to Phoenix in a luxurious home in the suburbs with his new wife, a woman who was much younger than him, the scandal of his leaving my grandmother for her now faded in the family's memory. Morfar taught me to see my potential. Always

24

elegantly dressed, even when he was simply reading a book on the patio, he seemed the epitome of success. Morfar was a brilliant photographer who had begun his career as a war photographer (there was a family tale of him helping to smuggle Jews to the U.S. through Sweden at the time, which only made him more heroic in my eyes). After the war, he began photographing industry leaders and celebrities, won many awards, and eventually published over 100 books of his works. "Whenever a book sells," he explained, "They send me royalties. That means I make money in my sleep. I don't have to do anything but cash the checks!"

That's what I wanted for myself, but I knew from talking to him that I would have to work hard to get to that point where I could enjoy passive income and the kind of success that would allow me to have a home like his.

Morfar gave inspiration to my dreams as we walked up Camelback Mountain by his home when I'd come to visit. Whenever I would walk around his house, I would pretend it was mine, earned through hard work and determination. It was the beginning of my belief that you can attract to yourself whatever you desire if you truly believe you can have it, and you make that future real in your mind. I would have a home like this someday. I was sure of it.

He encouraged me to try out for Miss U.S.A. or Miss America. "You're as pretty as any of those girls, and you can earn scholarship money, get a good education on their dime."

"I don't know," I'd say. "I can't see myself in a pageant. I can't imagine strolling across a stage in a bathing suit. It just seems kind of weird."

"No matter," he'd say with a friendly shrug as his long legs propelled him up the mountain. I tried to match his stride as he continued. "You can do anything with that mind of yours. Women today have so many opportunities."

I believed him thoroughly. After all, my mother's education had netted her some decent jobs—which she'd ended up losing only because her life kept being disrupted by caretaking for one ill family member after another. Besides, it was the 1980s and women in floppy little silk ties were flooding the workplace, enrolling in law school, earning MBAs, and driving nice cars they'd bought for themselves. That's what I wanted. Morfar and I stopped to look down at his home from the road above, and I caught the reflection of the early morning sun in the swimming pool. I was determined to start earning some money and getting some work experience so I could one day have a life like his.

Through my school, I'd gotten a job working as a bank teller at a local bank in the afternoons after classes ended. The pay was good, much better than when I made minimum wage selling concessions at a flea market snack bar on the weekends as a junior. By the time I was a senior, I was bringing home as much money as my mother, who had moved out of social service work and into selling real estate. I would have saved my earnings for college tuition, but I knew she needed help financially so I paid bills and bought groceries. I didn't resent helping to support the two of us, mind you. I could see my mother was trying her best to provide me with a good life despite all our challenges. If I had it harder than some of the girls at school, there was no point in wishing my circumstances were different. I could only do what I could do, and keep my dream of wealth and security alive as I plugged away at my job and learned all that I could so I could make the most of the opportunity.

When it came time to leave for college, I chose a place far away, yet familiar in a sense: Willamette, the place where my parents went. I qualified for student loans and decided I'd take the heaviest load of classes possible so I could graduate in three years and begin working full-time.

Leaving Arizona was easier than I thought it might be, because by the time I was a senior I'd broken up with my high school boyfriend. David was very sweet, affable to all, and affectionate to me, but as we entered our late teens, he started drinking heavily and ended up in A.A. I was glad he'd straightened out his life. He had a good heart and deserved happiness, but I saw that he could never match my ambitions. What kind of future could we have together? Besides staying sober for another day, he really didn't have any goals.

I, on the other hand, was going places.

At Willamette University, I had some of my happiest times in my life. I would meet another very stable, nice guy from a good family, who ended up dating me during those college years. Doug and I got along great and had lots of fun, even with the stress of studying. Looking back, it was probably my most healthy relationship. But life seemed to have other plans for me.

Everything was going well with my classes and my life when my sister called at the beginning of my last semester in college to tell me she was worried about Tom because she hadn't been able to get a hold of him for days. Had I heard from him?

"No," I said. "I wouldn't worry, though. You know Tom. He always turns up."

We'd last seen him just a few weeks before, at Christmas time. The family had all gathered at home in Tucson. It had been a wonderful holiday. At one point my sister, mom, and I were in the kitchen with Tom, snacking while we chopped vegetables for dinner, and Tom was saying to my mom, "You know, I'm really very happy. I know my life isn't exactly what you'd expect it to be, but you should respect my choices. It's my life."

"I do, Tom," she said. "I try not to worry about you. Although you've always given me good reason to worry!"

"What, because I'd take off with seven cents in my pocket?"

We all laughed.

"Seven cents and a slick story," my mother reminded him with a smile.

"Come on, admit it. I've always taken care of myself just fine. So I don't have a traditional job or lots of money. Big deal. I get along."

His words reassured all of us at the time—but things weren't going so well after all.

"Karin," Sue told me over the phone one day in early January, "I had a really scary call from him three days ago." By this time, Sue was back in Tucson, attending her first year of medical school. "He told me, 'you shouldn't go home—go stay with a friend until I call you back. It's dangerous for you to go home.' I said, 'What are you talking about?' but he wouldn't explain. He just said, 'you should not go home.' I figured it was just some sort of paranoia, maybe the pot talking, because he wouldn't explain why I'd be in danger."

Sue decided to wait a few days until my mother returned from her trip to Sweden, where she was visiting relatives, before bringing up her concerns, but unfortunately, our mom hadn't heard from Tom either. We called everyone we could think of, and finally, Sue and my mom placed a call to the police.

"Can you give us a description of the missing person?" asked the officer on the other end.

My mother started to describe my brother, beginning with his being 6' 8" with a huge beard—not exactly your typical fellow on the street. And to her horror, the officer said, "Ma'am, I think you should come down here. We've got a John Doe in the morgue that fits that description."

It was Tom.

What had happened? We were in shock. All we could piece together was that something had frightened him enough for him to take his own life. He'd left a disjointed note that didn't really make sense. My mother thought for sure it was murder. After all, Tom's circle included some very shady characters. But the investigators insisted there was no evidence of foul play.

After the funeral, I went back to school feeling devastated. I knew Tom had predicted he would die young, but this was beyond imaginable to me.

I kept thinking back to a play I had written for a class the previous semester. The assignment was to take two characters that don't know each other and put them together in one place, and write a dialogue. I created a character who was a busy-haired, bearded man who stood 6' 8" tall. As the play begins, he's sitting on a park bench holding a brown paper bag with a gun in it, contemplating suicide. The other character, a professor who is sitting next to him on a park bench, is talking him out of it. The play ends with the two of them going for coffee. I got an A on the assignment, and showed my script to my brother, who couldn't have missed the obvious similarity between the suicidal man and him.

"It's really good," Tom told me. But he didn't say anything about how perfectly he fit the suicidal man's physical description, and I didn't bring it up or put much thought to why I'd chosen to model the suicidal man after my own brother.

Now I wondered, was it a premonition of sorts? Did I somehow know he would end his life? Was the professor me, trying to reason with him and talk him out of a violent end—a conversation I wasn't able to have with Tom?

I'd never had an experience like this before, seeming to have picked up on a terrible event before it happened. I began thinking more and more about the games I'd play at my friend Sarah's house when we were in high school. Her grandmother was a little "out there"—friendly and warm, but strange, because she claimed to be psychic and a healer. She would heal Sarah's twisted ankle simply by holding her hands over it, which fascinated me. She would talk us into sitting around a card table with our palms resting on it and trying to get the table to levitate. It actually worked, several times, and I never knew why. It would tip in a certain direction to answer our yes/

no questions, and Sarah's grandma explained that we were communicating with a spirit. Once, she asked the "spirit" who was talking to us if it was my father. The table tipped twice—*yes.*

Very cool, I thought. I didn't actually believe it was him, but what if it was? Wouldn't that be something? Maybe I could actually ask him a question.

"Are you okay?" I asked "the spirit."

Two more dips of the table.

"He loves you," Sarah's grandmother said. "He's communicating that to me. He loves you very much and wants you to know he's okay. He's not suffering anymore."

I liked that thought, and couldn't think of anything else to ask. What do you say to the ghost of your father, if that's what it was? I figured this was all some clever trick that the old woman had figured out in order to reassure people that their loved ones were better off in the next world. And it did make me feel better, so I didn't want to look at the experience too closely.

A few years later, I had the most unsettling, powerful, fantastic dream I've ever had. I was 17, and my father appeared to me wearing a trench coat and standing in a mist. His face clear and I could see he was handsome and healthy again, and he said to me, "I know you were scared of me when you were little and I looked so different, but it's okay. Don't ever feel ashamed of that. You didn't hurt me. There's no need to feel guilty. I understood. I love you so much, and I'll always be there for you."

When I woke up, the room was so cold I shivered, despite the fact that I'd been perfectly warm when I fell asleep (it was the springtime in Arizona—definitely not cold!). I couldn't shake the feeling that this wasn't just a dream. I had to ask Sarah about it now that her grandmother had died.

"What did you think? It's weird, right?"

"Amazing. You know, my grandma swore that spirits come to us in dreams and if they actually talk to you, it's really them."

"Do you really think so?" I wanted to believe her.

"Yep. When a dead person talks to you, you know that they are really there."

She sounded completely certain about it. Although I still thought the table tipping was some sort of parlor trick designed to comfort me, I decided I believed her about the dream. Maybe if it had simply been a normal dream that you remember the next morning I'd have been more skeptical, but this was too real. And how else could I explain the chill in my room, except for that somehow my father's energy was affecting it so that I would know it was him?

I felt lighter knowing that he was there for me and that I was forgiven. I hadn't realized just how much the weight of my guilt had burdened me for years. Although I was now old enough to understand that children react to situations in immature ways, I hadn't been able to shake off my shame. Understanding is not the same as believing; I now believed I hadn't hurt my father as I feared. I was not guilty and released the heavy shame I'd carried unnecessarily.

And now that Tom was dead, I pondered what would become of my brother's spirit? There were so many unanswerable questions. Was Tom's death before the age of 30 something that couldn't be avoided? We'd joked about it so many times, Tom and I. Did he know? Did I know, somehow? Could I have prevented it? Could anyone have guided him to a different road that didn't lead to such an ugly end?

My boyfriend, Doug, tried to console me in my confusion after Tom's funeral, but I could see he was unable to fathom what I was going through. He'd led a charmed life, upper middle class and sheltered, and had never experienced any losses other than maybe a childhood pet. Much as I cared about Doug, I felt he couldn't understand why I was so unfocused, depressed, and lost. I was floating around in a daze miles away from him, and from all that he was concerned about, whether it was work or where our friends were going to get together Friday night. Being a year older than me, he had already taken a job in a city three hours away. The commuting was taking its toll on our relationship. My emotions were all over the place, and I don't really know what he was thinking of me. All I know is that I really hurt him when I broke up. I couldn't tell him about the play I'd written, Tom's unsettling predictions of death before 30, or any of these odd events that I couldn't stop thinking about. I thought he couldn't possibly understand. I felt like an old soul next to him, and yet I didn't know what to say that might help him understand why this great chasm had opened up between us.

For weeks, I walked in a state of agitation and confusion, pulled this way and that by my roiling emotions and troubled thoughts. In my fragile state, I was looking for someone, anyone, to be a strong, male figure to rely upon. I was working part-time as a secretary for a private investigation firm at the time, and my boss, Aaron, immediately provided me with the sympathy I was craving. He never questioned why I would become teary or space out and forget what it was I was supposed to do, but would say, "It's hard, I know" as he held my gaze. His kindness went straight to my heart. Aaron even decided to investigate Tom's death. He told me all the details he'd uncovered. Apparently, Tom had gotten in too deep to a drug ring. "He probably didn't see any way out," Aaron said.

I thought back to the mysterious note Tom had left, and his warning to Sue about going home. The pieces came together and I felt myself tearing up. Any doubt I'd had that Tom had taken his own life was erased.

"Thank you," I said quietly. "I just can't believe you would do this for me."

"Listen, it's the least I can do. It's my job. I know how to find out anything. Anything. You don't have to wonder anymore."

I was deeply moved by his thoughtfulness and generosity. My feelings toward Aaron grew stronger.

He was sixteen years older than I was and married. I was young, about to graduate college, and at an exceptionally vulnerable time in my life. I wanted to believe him when he said he and his wife led separate lives and would someday divorce. Our relationship grew physical, and suddenly I was living in an apartment he was paying for, and he would leave my bed to return to his wife with some mumbled excuse to me that I willed myself to accept. I was too needy to acknowledge the clues that something was very wrong.

The signs of mental illness can be very subtle. My mother helped me to understand this later; because of course she had studied about personality disorders those many years ago in graduate school in Mexico. I had no idea what I was dealing with—Aaron's behavior was disturbing, but I didn't know what to make of it. He was extremely jealous and controlling. He had a license to carry a concealed weapon and in one of his tirades, he threatened to kill me and then shoot himself.

I didn't share any of what was going on with my mother or sister, or my friends. I was too embarrassed, I guess, and definitely too afraid. All I knew was that life was getting weirder and weirder. I'd insist to him that there were no other men in my life, that there was nobody to be jealous of, but Aaron would go on manic, angry rants and rummage through my purse looking for evidence that I was cheating.

"I'll find him!" he'd shout. "So help me God, you will *not* make a fool of me."

He'd storm out, then call a few hours later to apologize profusely, and then take me out to dinner at a fine restaurant—and repeat the scene all over again a few days later. He even punched a tree in front of my apartment, bloodying his knuckles in a rage because he thought I was with another man when I was fifteen minutes late coming home. One night, he took me to see the movie *Sleeping with the Enemy* with Julia Roberts, which we had heard was a good thriller. As I watched her being stalked by her insanely possessive husband, I found myself leaning further and further away from Aaron. I knew in my gut that I was in serious trouble because this movie was too close to my reality. But how could I get out? Aaron could always tell me where I'd been and what I'd done. I had to be accountable for every action to him so I was pretty sure I was being monitored on all levels by him— otherwise, how could he know things I was doing when I wasn't with him?

"I think we should cool our relationship," I told him one day, my simple speech well rehearsed.

His eyes grew dark.

"It's not you, and you know I'm not seeing anyone. I just think things have gotten a little intense, and I . . . I need to sort through my feelings. It's been a very difficult ever since my brother died."

What I said was perfectly logical, and a stable and mature man would have agreed quietly to a few weeks apart from each other. That was not Aaron's reaction.

I could see the muscles in his neck and face tighten and he stared at me with eyes full of hatred. "I will find you. I will hunt you down. Wherever you go, you can't escape me, you bitch. And I'll kill any man you are with." The words were frozen yet red hot with rage.

Somehow, I ended this terrifying scene. My friend Sharon came to stay with me overnight like we'd planned, and soon after she arrived, she asked how it was going with Aaron.

"Can't talk here," I scribbled on a piece of paper, too afraid to say anything in my own apartment.

She scrunched up her face in confusion.

I motioned to the door and made a walking motion with my two fingers. She looked at me sideways, puzzled, then shrugged and grabbed her coat as I opened the door.

After we'd turned the corner, I finally answered her entreaties.

"I know this sounds nuts but I swear my apartment is bugged. He can do that, you know. He's ex-CIA. He knows everything about me, Sharon. Stupid stuff no one could possibly care about. He knows when I went to the grocery store and who I waved to on my way down the street. I'm scared to death of him."

"Why didn't you tell me something before?" she said, her eyes wide.

Embarrassed, I felt tears escaping down my cheeks. I couldn't help it. I hadn't told anyone how bad his spying and controlling behavior had gotten and now it came pouring out of me.

"I was scared and I thought I could figure out what to do, I guess. For all I know he's watching me now. He's a lunatic!"

"It's going to be okay," she said, wrapping an arm around my waist as I choked back a sob.

"I tell you what. We'll check into the Intercontinental in Portland. I'll put it on my card. We can talk there, as long as we need to. We can figure this out, I promise."

We returned to my apartment where I pulled clothes out of my closet, a few toiletries, my purse and passport, and who knows what else my eyes, wild with fear, caught sight of before I tore out of there with Sharon right next to me. We drove downtown in her car, taking side streets in case I was being followed. I was shaking with fear and sure he was going to show up any minute.

As we sat together on one of the prim queen-sized beds, she grasped my hand.

"I'm an idiot. I should've seen this coming," I said.

"Don't blame yourself, Karin. This crept upon you. You can't think about all that now. We have to get you away."

I scoffed. "Where? Where can I go?"

"To Sweden. He'll never find you there."

"How am I going to get to Sweden? He's a private investigator. He said he'd find me! He'd hunt me down!"

"No," she said firmly. "Look, we're only a few hours away from Vancouver in Canada. You can fly out of there." I started to see that this might work, I could escape.

My hysteria had subsided in the face of Sharon's determination and faith that we could come up with a plan of escape. We were up most of the night and caught a few hours sleep before putting the plan into action. Sharon would drive me from Portland to Vancouver, Canada, where I could catch an international flight that she would pay for on her credit card so that Aaron couldn't trace the purchase. We would stop at the mall to buy some warm clothes because I would certainly need them in the Swedish winter weather. Then, Sharon would return to Portland and post my letters to Sue, Morfar, and a few close friends which basically said that I needed to get away for a while to clear my head and I'd be fine, so they shouldn't worry—and I would get in touch soon, but couldn't tell them where I was going.

The careful plan worked out perfectly and I arrived on the doorstep of my very surprised mother. My mother heeded my pleas not to reveal that I was with her when my friends, Morfar, and my sister started to call her. In my panic, it didn't occur to me that when Sue read my words she might think that like Tom, I had become suicidal. Terrified, Sue called Mom, who reassured her that yes, she knew exactly where I was and I was safe and there was no need to worry. But after a week, I felt so bad about making everyone so worried; I decided to tell them all exactly where I was.

About twenty-four hours later, Aaron called me.

In my hurry to leave my apartment, I'd left my address book that had my mother's phone number in Sweden. It scared me that he just "happened" to call 24 hours after I placed calls to my sister and Morfar in Arizona telling them where I was. I knew Aaron had the capacity to bug people's phones, and much as I'd feel better telling myself that the timing was a coincidence, I couldn't help believing that he had illegally placed wiretaps on their lines.

When Aaron called, my mother denied I was staying with her. Then I received a gushing letter from him, filled with apologetic words and empty promises to make it all up to me. Wisely, my mother brought me to a female minister who had some experience with domestic abuse situations and stalkers. The minister had simple advice: "Write him an unemotional letter saying you need to focus on your own needs right now and do not want him to contact you further. Two sentences, at the most. Don't acknowledge anything he said or express any emotions. Keep it as short as possible."

Fortunately, her idea worked—I'm not sure why but was grateful that it did. I never heard from him again.

Now what? I wasn't ready to go back to the States. I needed time to heal, and to breathe. What had happened was so unsettling that I had to process it all.

Sweden became a haven for me, a place to take my time calming my nervous system and learning to take baby steps into the unknown. I cleaned apartments and did a little office work for family friends while learning the language. I ventured out and got a job for a summer as a nanny in France, which was fun because I didn't speak French and I liked the family. I even backpacked through Europe. It was like a pilgrimage for me when I returned to Florence, 18 years after my first visit, and climbed the hundreds of ancient stairs of the Duomo. I felt my father's footsteps behind me.

Somehow, this international travel really boosted my damaged self-confidence. I realized that I could manage and take care of myself—even in foreign countries where I didn't speak the language. I felt safe, enough so to begin thinking about my life and what I'd been doing.

I discovered books American self-help books that spoke to what I was going through, and the situations I'd unwittingly created for myself. For the first time, I thought about my subconscious thoughts and feelings and how they were affecting me. Now that I knew myself better, I felt ready to start over and return to my original plan of becoming successful through hard work and determination.

The job market in Sweden wasn't great, and neither was my grasp on the language despite all the classes and tapes I'd purchased, so I decided to return to Arizona. I got a job selling perfume door to door and I found people were willing to talk to a friendly and persistent young woman with a professional manner and a case full of samples. I traveled all over the western United States by myself and a team of three others, consulting road maps from Rand McNally and discovering new towns. I wasn't afraid of cold calls and almost always made the sale. With the energy of youth driving me, I worked 80 to 100 hours a week and quickly was able to open my own office, then trained 20 sales associates who worked under my supervision. I made a lot of money quickly, but I also couldn't keep up that pace and within 18 months burned out. I didn't have any life outside of work and was tired of constantly recruiting and training people, and of course, I was ready to leave all that road travel behind. I decided to sell my interest in the business to a partner and find a position that was less demanding but still challenging.

Morfar said to me, "You're so good at selling. Why not sell something that offers a higher commission for the same amount of work?" That made a lot of sense, and soon I started working for a conservative family executive search business that matched employers and employees. I found I had a knack for putting people into the right jobs, and for selling the position to the potential employee and the potential employee to the company.

I started a new healthcare division for the company and soon had people working under me whom I had trained. We were a strong team and I paid off all my student loans and my car. Mine was an enviable position. I had no debt, excellent income, and a gorgeous, light, airy three-bedroom house with a professionally landscaped backyard and a Pebble Tec swimming pool featuring its own waterfall. But as I walked through its rooms, I felt it wasn't quite enough. I wanted to get married and have a family.

I was independent and successful, and I'd left uncertainty and insecurities long behind me. I was clear on what I wanted, and I felt I deserved the good life. My friends laughed at my very specific list of rules for potential romantic partners: After my disastrous relationship with Aaron I'd decided I would never date any man who was more than ten years older than me or who had been married or had children. He had to love jazz, skiing, hiking, and dancing, and be successful in business, and have a great sense of humor and strong family values. After I found this man, I imagined, I'd quit my job, have a few children and be a stay-at-home mom while they were little. He and I would create the stable family life that I'd always longed for. I truly believed that if I envisioned exactly what I wanted and held on to faith that I could attract or create it in my life, it would be mine. I knew what I needed, and what I wouldn't settle for ever again.

What I didn't know is that I had not yet learned how important it was to trust my instincts and resist the pull of security when red flags are waving. My yearning for a solid family life was so strong that it blinded me to a dangerous path I was about to take with a man named Leo, who would one day bring me to Mexico.

Chapter Three

· ·

Spellbound

Stay away from him.

Now why would my instincts tell me that? I hardly knew the man standing across the room. We were both members of a singles social activity club and attending a meeting for an upcoming ski trip to Taos, New Mexico. I didn't know him—so why the instinctive resistance? He seemed friendly enough, but I certainly wasn't attracted to him, with his silk shirt buttoned down an extra button so that his three gold chains glimmered through his chest hairs.

I took little notice of Leo as he flirted with the other women. He wasn't my type—too old, for one thing. Seventeen years was a huge gap, and I wasn't looking for a father figure. I'd read enough self-help books to know that losing my dad at an early age had been a factor in drawing me into that terrible relationship with Aaron years earlier. I was in a better place now and clear on what I wanted. When we got on the bus for the single group's ski trip a few days later, I was the last person to board. There were only two seats left: one beside Leo and one beside a quiet man who was an engineer. I sat by the engineer.

But then Leo and I kept bumping into each other at so many events. He was always full of generous compliments and oodles of charming comments that impressed my friends. Whether the club went skiing, dancing, or hiking, or to brunch or a jazz concert, or shopping in the quaint stores on our ski trips, he was always there. I couldn't be rude and ignore him. Besides, we had a lot in common. I didn't see the harm in talking to him, and he often had girlfriends with him anyway. I told myself I wasn't going to fall for him as I could tell he was a player. But our friendship grew as we had more and more chances to talk about our shared interests. We got to know each other better over the following months.

One night, about six months after we met, we met up at a bar for happy hour and his eyes seemed to glow with warmth as he said, "You're exactly the type of woman I want to be with. I'd love to date you."

I felt a rush of blood and my heart beating faster. And I remembered my list. Leo did not meet my carefully selected criteria. I found myself saying, "You'd have to be exclusive with me."

It's okay, as long as he promises to be faithful and break it off with any other women he's seeing, I told myself.

I wish I'd realized what was happening. I thought that my fear was ungrounded, or at least overblown. It's only in looking back that I can recall how quickly I dismissed the strong sense that I was making a mistake by moving forward with him. There was a sense of adventure and recklessness as the inner voice that was connected with my first impression of him faded into the background. I wanted to be loved and cherished. I wanted romance. Was I being too rigid? I wondered. I was feeling very lonely and was ripe to be swept off my feet.

For the briefest of moments, he pondered the boundary I'd just set, sipped his cocktail, and said, "Deal. Let me make some calls in the morning." We hugged and agreed to talk the next day.

The next morning, a huge bouquet of stargazer lilies and roses arrived at my door. Shortly after, he called me to tell me he'd spoken to every woman he'd been seeing casually and told them he had found his special someone and was breaking it off with them. "I want to take you out to dinner tonight," he said, and I didn't resist.

I can look back at my journals and see how thick the self-deception was as I went back and forth between honest observations about what I wanted in my life and too-cheery descriptions of the time I was spending with Leo. I was 28 and longed to settle down and start a family soon, with someone who was financially stable—and that he certainly was. Leo courted me royally and I believed he really did love me. I told myself that maybe those rules I'd set up were meant to be broken. The man for me had to be loving and affectionate and want to start a family soon. Check and check. Besides,

I usually was more comfortable with people older than me. I decided to forget about my list of criteria. My friends had already told me I was overly rigid with my list and needed to allow the right person to come into my life.

Leo seemed to be committed to making a marriage work, which was important. He had been married twice before but said his first ex-wife wasn't emotionally stable. With sadness in his eyes, he told me he'd left the relationship with great reluctance after she became abusive and he caught her in bed with another man. He had two teenage sons with her. It pained him that he couldn't see his sons, and he cried when he told me how he had sent airline tickets for them because they lived hundreds of miles away, but his ex-wife refused to let them come. He also had a six-year-old daughter with his second ex-wife, who was living in California—at least he got to see that child occasionally. Having his children spread so far apart, unable to get together with them, he missed having a family. *Poor guy,* I thought. Leo hadn't proposed yet, but we had several discussions probing each other's thoughts about our future together.

I didn't want to go back to trusting in an older man with a great smile and an armful of promises, but I told myself I'd misjudged him. I felt bad that he was estranged from his parents and had an unhappy childhood— troubled people, very dysfunctional, he explained in a quiet voice. I could understand why he was so eager to create a new, healthy family and romantic partnership with me.

Within two weeks after we started dating each other exclusively, he surprised me with a diamond ring placed in a crystal goblet, which the waiter brought to us as we were about to order dinner at a fine Italian restaurant in Phoenix. My eyes welled up with tears as I said yes, and he immediately ordered the most expensive champagne for us to celebrate. Because I had just gotten braces on my teeth, I told him we had to wait until the braces were removed before we got married. I thought a long engagement would be good since everything was happening on warp speed. Besides, how can a bride have braces for her wedding pictures?

Leo played right into my fantasies by portraying himself as a very successful businessman. He brought me to the house he had recently purchased, saying he was waiting to find the right woman to share it with him. It was a beautiful, new home on a manmade lake, and he told me he'd paid $350,000 cash for it. Although I had a home of my own, this one was so majestic that even though living there meant a long commute to the office for me, it seemed like the perfect place to begin our lives together. We decided I'd rent mine out and we'd live in this new one.

One Sunday afternoon, we were walking in the nearby mall after I'd checked in at the office to prepare for the coming week. We stopped into a furniture store that I had walked by hundreds of times. I'd often admired the display of the elegant living room furniture in the window, and it was clear that Leo, too, was drawn by it. We meant only to look, but Leo proceeded to purchase the entire collection—well over $50,000 worth of furniture and accessories—all in one swoop. I was surprised, but he did have a lot of money, enough to be very generous with our friends, buying them gifts and fine bottles of wine. Leo even told me that the ring cost more than a lot of people's yearly salary. It was so big I sometimes felt embarrassed to wear it. Sometimes, I felt as if I were his trophy wife, dressed up to reflect how successful he was.

I enjoyed my job, but I wanted to be a stay-at-home mom, and neither Leo nor I wanted to wait a single minute to have kids after we got married. "You should quit your job now," he said after we became engaged. "You'll get pregnant soon!" I thought about doing it but felt a little uneasy. I decided to get off the birth control a month before our wedding.

We knew what we wanted, but it was as if there was a low-grade infection in our relationship. I wasn't always aware of it, but sometimes, I felt uncomfortable. I started to see that Leo readily made cracks about my successes at work and my awards I'd earned—he'd minimize them, and then quickly say, "I'm just joking." Maybe it was just his way and I needed to work on being less sensitive? He was tremendously subtle in undercutting me, and it was making me feel more dependent on him and less certain of who I was in the relationship. These observations rarely made it into my journal, where I was talking myself into a story about a magical romance.

After several months, he kept encouraging me to quit my job. He said he'd take care of me and that we didn't need my income. As the wedding approached, I lost my passion and focus for work and only wanted to start my new life and start making our little family with this wonderful man.

The first few months of our courtship were delightful in many ways. We were madly in love. We did a lot of traveling together. I was on top of the world. In my mind, we were already married because the commitment had been made, so I felt no unease moving into our new house with him. I'd had only a couple of glimpses of how Leo could be Dr. Jekyll one minute and

Mr. Hyde the next. I made excuses for him. I'd noticed he was under stress or drunk at the time each his darker side emerged. I figured things would get better as we settled into a life together. Even my family thought Leo was terrific, and their opinions mattered to me. He charmed us all.

It was Leo's idea that we get married in Sweden. I was surprised but took to that idea quickly, as I missed my mom and my Swedish family. I looked forward to hosting the dream wedding in a country manor house by a Swedish lake, with dozens of guests watching me walk down the aisle. My mother had carefully packed away her Christian Dior wedding dress, the one I'd envisioned myself getting married in ever since I saw it in one of Morfar's books. When I was a little girl and my mother let me take it out of storage to stroke its intricate lace with my fingertips, I felt I was enjoying a special treat. Now I had the exquisite pleasure of wearing this exquisite gown of hers on my own wedding day. Unintentionally, we even chose the same wedding date my parents had—June 28.

The wedding was the stuff of fairytales. I trusted Leo completely and didn't even hesitate when he told me, "I'm a little short until my next deal goes through, so you'll have to cash out your retirement fund to put the money up for the wedding. Don't worry. I'll reimburse you later when my money comes in." So I paid for the wedding of my dreams myself, but I didn't mind.

One thing did really bother me: When Leo said his wedding vows to me, he closed his eyes and didn't look into mine even once. Afterward, when I asked him about it, he said he didn't want to cry in front of me or get emotional. I wanted to believe him. He always had a good explanation ready for anything I questioned.

There were other signs that day that things were not quite right, but I didn't want to acknowledge them. For example my grandmother's string of pearls broke minutes before the wedding ceremony. At the dinner, my veil caught on fire from a candle. I laughed off these little accidents—at least, that's how I thought of them. Now, I believe the universe was trying to tell me something.

For our honeymoon, we traveled throughout Europe. He paid for the trip, and we had a marvelous time. When we returned home, we learned I was pregnant. We were both thrilled and I prepared for my new life as both wife and mother. Everything was perfect. We didn't need my income because of course, Leo had the money to provide for the two of us—and for the children I was sure we would have.

But when I asked Leo to pay me back for the wedding expenses, he told me in a businesslike way, "What's mine is yours and what's yours is mine." I was shocked and didn't know what to say. "Besides," he continued, "I bought our new house and the furniture, and paid for the honeymoon." I got the feeling he thought my request was out of line, even selfish, and that I needed to think differently now that I was married. I should have protested because what was really important wasn't the money but the broken promise. Still, I said nothing.

I was starting to see that Leo had a curious way of making me feel that whenever there was a disagreement, I was in the wrong, even if logic indicated otherwise. It's hard to explain, but I've since learned that this ability to turn matters around to make you question yourself is a special skill of abusive men.

On our honeymoon, Leo had talked a lot about moving to Mexico, which he said would be a great place for him to do business. With my ability to instantly receive Mexican citizenship and renew my childhood passport just by sending in my birth certificate, it would be easy for him to set up a business there, he explained. By the end of 1997, he and I made plans to move to a house he'd found on a short trip he made to Mexico while I was struggling with morning sickness and fatigue. I agreed to move but wasn't entirely on board with the decision. Something about the plan bothered me.

It was easier to brush aside my discomfort about certain things Leo said or did than to face the reality that my new marriage might not be what I thought it was. That was not a thought I was ready to entertain given that I was pregnant and legally married to this man now. He wasn't physically abusive to me, just extremely irritable and secretive. It was a subtle change since our courtship, and I kept waiting for him to return to his old, loving self. He'd say ugly things and apologize later. "It'll be less stressful once we're out of this transition," he promised.

I was left alone to do all the packing and moving. As I was nearing the last few weeks of the pregnancy, I was uncomfortable physically, but I managed somehow to finish up. I placed our two cats in the car and put all of our furniture in storage, and then got into the Infinity SUV by myself for a two-day drive to Central Mexico that really wore me out.

Leo met me outside of a larger city and drove with me to the house he'd rented for us. My face fell several inches when I saw it for the first time: It was tiny and dirty, and as it turned out, the electricity and water worked only sporadically. But I felt I had to make the best of it.

Just a day after we arrived, Leo became angry when he couldn't find his garlic press in the kitchen gadgets box. "I'm sorry, honey," I said. "I put that in storage. I figured we had to pack lightly because you said the house was small."

Leo blew up at me and called me all sorts of names, telling me I was incompetent and stupid. I was stunned and felt myself shaking ever so slightly as he scowled and went off on me. I rubbed my hand over my extended belly, looking for comfort from within, feeling I had the weight of the world on me because I was bringing a child into this volatile marriage.

Then, I found my voice but did my best to keep it even and calm. "You're mad over a garlic press? Do you have any idea what it took for me to pull off this move when I'm eight-and-a-half months pregnant?"

He quieted down a bit and said he was sorry, that this had been the only house available on such short notice. He promised to find a better one. But this was just one of many incidents of verbal abuse. In the coming months, his belittling increased.

So here I was in a foreign country without family nearby, trying to be optimistic about the challenges in my marriage while setting up a new household and dealing with the discomfort and fatigue of being pregnant. I was scared to let my thoughts wander to the question, "Did I make a big mistake by marrying him?" I decided I was probably being too hard on him—after all, he *was* under a lot of stress. He'd told me he'd fought in Vietnam—and had been honorably discharged with a purple heart. I wondered if his experience in the war had made him more vulnerable to anxiety.

I was always a hopeless romantic while I was growing up. I dreamed of finding *The One*, the man who would fulfill my romantic fantasy of what a husband and marriage should be. As a little girl, I always loved *Cinderella* and how her prince whisked her away to live happily ever after. When I met Leo, he seemed like my prince. Now, I was carrying his child. Despite the signs that something was very wrong, I chose to trust him implicitly. He was my husband after all, and I'd given a vow to death do us part. Given how

43

vulnerable I was in the situation, I can understand why I did that—but it still hurts to even think about it.

A few weeks after moving into our little house, and after over forty-two hours of labor, I gave birth to my first child on my thirtieth birthday. Alexa was the best birthday present I ever received! Leo was wonderful through the entire process. Having three children of his own from his previous marriages had prepared him well, and he simply took charge and made decisions I was too distracted and inexperienced to make at the time. In retrospect, this was the only time during our entire relationship when I felt he was really there for me.

However, with the sweetness came bitterness. My mother called from Sweden to break the news that Morfar, who had been in ill health, had died. I knew I couldn't fly back for the funeral. I had to say good-bye to him without my family around me—that is, my mom and sister and grandmother. I had a new family now. I tried to focus on Alexa.

It wasn't long before several incidents and Leo's unexpected behavior caused our marriage to take a major turn for the worse. I began to see that his drinking was getting out of control, which frightened me. He'd hit the bars and I'd fall asleep in the baby's room so I wouldn't have to have him crawl into bed with me smelling like tequila. I said nothing about this new, scary habit of his. We moved to a new house, my mom came for a visit, and Leo cut down on the drinking. My world seemed to be looking up a little: new house, new baby, wonderful husband who was returning to his old self.

His business seemed to be doing well—I overheard him tell his son over the phone, "You don't need to go to college. I'll teach you to be a millionaire!" and offer to send him money. He always seemed to have plenty and to be generous with his kids. Then again, I wasn't sure he was giving his son good advice. Leo's son was very different from him, from what I could tell. It seemed as if Leo was projecting onto him the ambitions he'd had when he was younger—to be a millionaire—and not tuning into what his son actually needed. The boy was more introverted than his father. Why couldn't Leo see that? Now, I realize it was his narcissism, but then, it just registered as not quite right.

Leo was turning back into the old, charming man I'd dated who was focused on making big money. That was fine for him, and it gave me some hope for our marriage, but a niggling feeling that I couldn't quite name colored our relationship.

One day, he asked me to help him out by signing some papers that his Mexican attorney had drawn up. "It's just a formality," he explained. "A Mexican citizen has to sign them." I didn't speak Spanish and even so, I probably wouldn't have understood the legalese, but I trusted my husband. "It'll be much easier to get the monies to flow through the bank system this way," he quickly explained. "No big deal."

Looking back on my time with Leo, I realized when he had access to money, he was a happy man. When he was struggling financially, he didn't want to be around anyone. His identity was wrapped up in dollars and business deals. I fully believed he would change back to how he was in the beginning of our relationship and the new Leo would disappear as his business starting gaining momentum.

Although Leo didn't work a lot those first few months we lived in Mexico, he frequently assured me he would always be able to take care of me. He'd read books all day long, and then get up to cook—and he was excellent at that. But then he'd open up the wine, and when the bottle was empty, he'd drink tequila, and then move on to whiskey. And as the liquor got harder, so did his personality.

I wanted to make a trip to Sweden to introduce Alexa to my side of the family. I had just sold my house to the renters and decided to use the proceeds toward the trip so Leo wouldn't get upset about my spending any of his money. But he became upset anyway—not about the money, but about my taking our daughter away from him for three weeks. "I told you about it," I said, but he didn't remember. Now I know that people who drink heavily often have memory lapses. At the time, I felt guilty and bad about miscommunicating, or not communicating clearly enough.

The ticket had been paid for so I went anyway and had a wonderful time, and returned to find that Leo's financial company was now involved in several projects, including the construction of a hotel. I was glad the tiff had blown over. We were a family, and we needed unity. I helped him out here and there with secretarial work, but mostly took care of Alexa and depended on Leo to run his business and make money. He was really quite busy. Back on track with his career, he reverted to being happy and motivated. I felt relieved.

I also felt alone. All affection had disappeared from our marriage. We rarely made love, which was difficult for me. We now had a great group of friends and, to the outside world, my life looked wonderful. Leo rarely became angry anymore, so I pushed my own needs and fears aside and told myself to enjoy what I had with him.

In the fall, we were able to move to a very nice three-story house with a pool, situated on a hill overlooking a lake. It was a very comfortable house with exquisite views—we loved it! We began traveling a bit and spent a night at a lovely hotel in Puerto Vallarta, where we made love for the first time in many months, but when we came home, Leo's trips to the liquor cabinet and the bars began again.

Whenever he was drunk, he'd tell me how stupid I was, and how I ought to listen to him because he was brilliant. I learned to avoid him, and his verbal assaults, by going to sleep early.

I was still breastfeeding Alexa when I began to suspect I was pregnant again because I was constantly hungry. Sure enough, that rare night out of town had culminated in me conceiving. I was happy—I always wanted children, plural—but when I told Leo, he turned very pale and seemed very nervous. We toasted—him with wine, me with water.

About six weeks into my pregnancy, we were hosting a birthday party for his best friend at our house. There were twenty of us about to enjoy the cake, including my sister and mom, who had come in from Sweden for a visit. I placed candles and lit them, and everyone started singing "Happy Birthday," Leo's friend blew them out, and the next thing I knew Leo walked into the room and began yelling at me.

"How dare you sing 'Happy Birthday' to *my* best friend when I wasn't even in the room?"

"But—I had no idea you—"

"I'm the reason you have food on the table! How could you *not* know I wasn't here?" He was livid with everyone, but I was the main target of his wrath. Some of our friends tried to make a joke of it and it blew over, but later, he brought it up again when he, my mother, and I were sitting in the living room together "I have immense power," he bragged. "I can get anyone killed with a snap of my finger."

I could tell my mother was scared to death. She tried to calm him down and get him to stop talking that way, but he sneered at her and said, "It doesn't take anything to get anybody killed in this country. I have all the right connections."

I didn't hear all of it—I went to sleep, hoping he would apologize in the morning.

As I began to prepare breakfast the next day, he walked in and said in a low, even voice, "You will never disrespect me like that again. I can take care of you very easily if you don't respect me and treat me the way you should."

I tried to apologize and explain, but I was quaking with terror. I'd always thought it was the liquor that made him so mean to me, but this time he was completely sober and had ice-cold eyes and razor sharp hatred.

Leo refused to talk to me directly for a couple of weeks. My mother went home and in phone calls, she urged me to leave him and move to Sweden. I thought about it, but I was deeply committed to my marriage. I really wanted to make it work. "I don't believe in divorce. Once you marry, divorce is not an option." I told my mother. "Maybe he's scared of supporting another baby and that's why his mean streak is showing."

Excuses—he had plenty and when he ran out, I made excuses for him. He stopped interacting with me and gave me the silent treatment, only rarely saying something and even then, it was always an insult or a complaint. When we traveled, or if we were around other people, he became a nice, happy person. Then when we'd get back home, he'd be aloof and drink a lot. Christmas was strained that year.

On the spur of the moment, Leo decided we should go to Cabo San Lucas in Mexico for our New Year's holiday. We would really have to scramble to find a place to stay, but I thought it would be a good idea to reconnect in a romantic spot. The two of us made up and he promised to cut down on drinking, but when we got home, it was the same story as it had been ever since we moved to Mexico.

In March of 1999, Leo came back from one of his business trips only to learn that his work permit in Mexico had been revoked. He didn't know why. His attorney and business partner, Eduardo, had supposedly had taken care of it for him. A policeman came to our house saying he had to take Leo's work permit temporarily. I woke the next morning with a premonition that something important was going to happen. Good or bad, I didn't know. I didn't tell Leo, who left for work. Then, around 4:00 p.m., I received a call from Eduardo.

"They've taken Leo," he said.

"What do you mean?"

"I don't know. They've just *taken* him. The cops."

I shrieked, "No! How can they do that? Who took him? Where is he?"

Eduardo promised to call back as soon as he got some answers. I sat down, my hands shaking, for I don't know how long. Then, the phone rang again.

"They're taking him to the airport," he said. "Back to the U.S. They won't say why."

I decided that I might be able to intercept him at the small airport in Guadalajara, as I knew there were not very many flights going out. I'd better get some answers for myself.

I asked our maid to watch Alexa, jumped in the car, and sped to the airport to try to find him—no luck. Eduardo called at 7:00 p.m. while I was still there and told me the FBI had Leo and had taken him back to the U.S.

I drove home completely confused and dazed. I put Alexa to bed and sat down in the kitchen. I hadn't eaten but wasn't hungry for anything but news of Leo. The only thing I could think of was to call my mother, who told me to come to Sweden as soon as possible. In the meantime, she would fly to Mexico. She was at my door in 24 hours. That's my mom, my rescuer.

I heard from Leo a few days later when he called me collect from a jail in Houston, Texas. He told me that he was swept away by the FBI and taken back to the U.S., even though there was no extradition order—a legal document demanding that the Mexican authorities return him to the U.S. for trial. He said that he was wrongly accused and that it was just a matter of time to get things straightened out. "My attorney's working on it and says it's just a matter of paperwork. It's a bitch, but it'll all clear up," he promised.

Day after day, Leo called me from jail collect for about twenty minutes and swore up and down he'd been falsely accused and that his business partner and attorney, Eduardo, would fix everything. I wanted to believe him. But I kept hearing from friends that there was a group out to *get* Leo, who were extremely happy that he had been arrested and extradited. I heard rumors that our car was going to be repossessed. How could that be? It was paid for! A week later, it was repossessed—they showed me the documents, and as the truck hauled it away, I looked up to the sky and said, "Okay. What *else?*"

A few days later, at our three-story house overlooking the lake, there was a banging on the metal door at the ground level around 10:00 p.m. Someone was yelling, "Let us in! Let us in!" I peered out through the darkness and saw a group of men. One man was climbing up the hill to look into my bedroom and bathroom windows. Alexa's crib was in my bedroom, and the noise from below woke her up. She was crying, so I held her against my big pregnant belly.

Someone yelled, "Open up! It's the police!"

Boldly, I yelled back, "Police don't act like this!"

My voice may not have betrayed it, but I was scared. I called a friend who knew a lot of people in the area and asked him to send the police. He came over, too, and arrived just as the police did. I let them in. Then, some more police showed up at our door. The police inside the house were looking at the police outside of the house—it was surreal! The police who were with me said to the police who were outside, "What are you guys doing here?"

One of the other cops said, "We've had complaints of screaming in this neighborhood. We need to check inside the house to make sure everyone is okay. We have to come in and walk through the place."

I let them in and they looked around without actually searching anything, and left a few minutes later. The other cops left, as did my friend, so the drama came to an end, leaving me bewildered. I certainly didn't feel safe, so I closed all the doors and locked everything.

The baby had calmed down a bit, but I lay in my bed, rocking and wondering what else was going to happen. "This is bad, Karin," my mother told me, stroking my arm. "I really think you should consider coming to Sweden." I started thinking, "What type of people was my husband doing business with and who is out to get us?"

"I can't. Not until this is resolved."

The next day, my mother pushed food in front of me and insisted I eat. "You're pregnant—you can't skip meals!" she scolded me. I was living in a nightmare and was totally overwhelmed with everything that seemed to be going wrong. I was so nervous about how my stress might be affecting my unborn baby.

About ten days before my due date, the doctor told me, "She's not growing. If you don't go into labor on your due date, we'll have to induce." When the day approached, I was admitted into the hospital. For eight hours, the induced labor carried on, but something seemed wrong. The baby's heart rate wasn't regular. "You need an emergency C-section," the doctor said. I was prepped for the procedure and when Megan came out, she cried and cried—but as soon as she heard my voice, she stopped. Nothing was wrong with her—in fact, she was perfect! I drew her into my arms, grateful for this little gift of joy.

When I got home, a few friends came over. I explained to my older daughter that this was the baby that had been inside me. Alexa had kissed my belly goodnight every night while I was pregnant. She didn't quite understand at first, but then her face lit up and she pointed to her sister in my arms and said, "Baby!" It was one of her first words, and I laughed and said, "That's right" as she pointed to my now deflated tummy—very sharp for a 16-month old! Regardless of all the darkness and uncertainty surrounding me, my daughters were the light in my life.

Even so, I had severe postpartum depression and felt pressure from every angle. My new baby was the reason I got out of bed every morning. Alexa amused herself—she was developing some independence. And Leo would get angry with me over the phone, telling me I had to be strong. I could tell he was relying on me, and I still had faith we were going to be a family again. I really loved this man, in spite of everything. I truly believed he was a good person and I had to stand by him no matter what. He was just a victim, I thought.

My mother, my girls, and I went to a nearby seaside town to spend the holidays. On New Year's Eve 1999, I woke up my daughters to take them to see the fireworks from the beach. I remembered wondering years before when I was eighteen, "Where am I going to be when the century turns to 2000?" I had a vision of myself standing on the beach holding the hand of a small child and holding a baby on my hip. Back then, I'd been puzzled about why no husband had appeared in that spontaneous vision. As Alexa and I stood on the sand under the stars, with Megan in my arms, I realized my vision was fulfilled. I knew now why there had been no husband in the picture in my mind those many years ago.

It was because Leo wasn't meant to be there.

I decided I had to get out of the town where we had been living and move to a vacation condo we were renting. Life was just too difficult there after all that had happened. Then, Eduardo died of cancer. Over the next few months, I discovered through a friend of Leo's that Eduardo was a complete fraud who had swindled an elderly woman he knew in a phony land deal that ate up her life savings. Eduardo wasn't even a licensed attorney! I began to feel really scared. Leo had done so much with him for the business and now everything began unraveling.

By summer, Leo had signed a plea bargain and was scheduled for sentencing in August. The girls and I were at the vacation condo. I had some savings, but our money was dwindling. My mother helped me as much as she could, but my finances were so tight I felt the air escaping my lungs. I just wanted to breathe deeply again.

For Leo's sentencing, I drove with the girls up to Phoenix, Arizona, where he was incarcerated. Alexa, who was now two-and-a-half, visited with him for 20 minutes. Megan, who was one, just cried and I had to take her out right away. That was the only time our younger daughter ever saw her father. Neither of the girls remembers him.

A vision became clear in my mind. I would move with my girls to Sweden, where I could figure out my next move and rely on the support of my family. My mom would be happy to have the girls nearby again. I didn't leave my mother's home address with Leo, just a post office box number. I needed distance from him because now I was doubting my own safety and judgment. The thought of him calling me, like Aaron had so many years before, scared me. After Leo's sentencing, he was transferred and he couldn't call me anymore. I never spoke to him again, but the echoes of our relationship would reverberate far longer than I could have imagined.

To raise money for the airfare to Sweden, I sold a lot of jewelry and stereo equipment. I also sold the diamond in my wedding ring set and replaced it with a cubic zirconia. I wasn't ready to part with my ring or my marriage, but on some level, I may have realized that switching out the stone was a small step toward reclaiming my values and my power.

The flight was incredibly long, but my girls were remarkably well behaved on the entire trip. I felt blessed and rejuvenated by spending these hours with them and seeing how resilient and sweet they were. I felt hope for our future together.

When we arrived, autumn had already set in. It was the end of a chapter of my life, and now it was time to reflect on what had happened to me.

I was soothed by the fact that my mother took us in despite cramped quarters. She lived in a complex for the elderly in the middle of Stockholm and had only two rooms. We stayed a week, but decided to temporarily move to her old country house she had inherited from her mother. A few rooms had been turned into a livable space, but the rest of the space was laid out in a hodgepodge manner fitting the building's former life as a storage space. It was named *Tulebo* after the lake that was a five-minute walk away, but it was hardly an estate worth of a name. I'd say it was the original money pit, because my mother had been pouring money into it for years. Still, it was in a serene area, and that was very good for me at this point.

Always the worst month in Sweden, the entire month of November was dark, rainy and dismal, but that was okay. Free from my nightmare, I had a new resolve. I cleaned like mad and made improvements, painting one room at a time. Scrubbing away the old dirt felt good. "It's my restoration therapy," I said to my mother with a smile. The girls had room to run around inside, and two neighbors had children they could play with. It was a very cathartic month for all of us as we began to heal. I spackled, painted, and spent a lot of time cooking. And I began analyzing my life.

Leo had been sentenced to three-and-a-half years in prison for fraud. I tried to take it in. At this point, I hadn't heard from Leo for over a month. During that time, I felt something lift off me and I saw my life clearly for the first time. I had been so desperate to keep my dream of a happy marriage and family alive that I became blind to how our marriage really was, and how taking care of myself and the girls was up to me. I came quickly to a clear decision within those weeks: I needed to file for divorce. But I also decided to wait until after Christmas to send a letter to Leo with the news.

I had been so afraid of being a single mom. But I already *was* a single mom, and already *had* been for a long time. With that thought in mind, I affirmed that I could handle this—that I had the power and wisdom to move forward into a new life and that my girls and I would flourish. I could make my own money again. The house Leo and I had owned was confiscated by the government, but I had some cash from selling my diamond—and I had faith in my ability to find employment again.

When I looked back over my time with Leo, and read my journals, I was surprised to see how unhappy and afraid I had been for so long! For two years, I'd hated my life—even though I tend to be a pretty positive person. I had been waiting and waiting for Leo to turn back into Prince Charming, not seeing that it was actually getting worse and worse. He had succeeded in crushing my self-confidence and self-esteem, and nervousness and fear had become part of the fabric of my daily life.

Denial and justification are two defense mechanisms of protection in an abusive relationship. You find excuses and keep thinking it'll get better. I found out later in studying psychology, when someone makes a decision, or a commitment, it's hard to back away. For me, it was my marriage vows—till death do we part—that made me want to stay, and made me unable to see things as they really were. The reality is that you have to be totally honest with yourself to find your way out of the situation and reclaim yourself, your power, and your voice. It took a month for me to face the truth about my circumstances and reclaim the truth about myself, but it took me *years* to heal from the scars of my marriage.

More and more, I began to question who was Leo…really. What truths had he hidden from me? And did this have something to do with post-traumatic stress disorder from Vietnam?

But it turned out he hadn't fought in Vietnam. That was one of the first bombshells that I'd discovered as I began to investigate his story, calling his relatives. His ex-wife wasn't mentally unstable—he'd been the one to physical abuse her and cheat on her! Leo's criminal attorney, called me to say, "My advice is don't spend any more money on this case. He's not the man you think he is. You're too nice to be taken by him." As horrible as this situation was, I was grateful for his blunt honesty.

When I spoke with Leo's parents, they were wonderful and so happy to hear from me! There was an outpouring of love and support and caring for the girls and me. We talked for two-and-a-half hours. I went through everything Leo had told me about himself. Everything from day one had all been based on lies but Leo was so talented as a liar that he was able to weave in untruths and remember what he said to whom. I guess a pathological liar believes the reality he portrays.

I felt dizzy as my world turned upside down. I had believed in him and stood by him through so much and it was all a scam. *My entire marriage was a scam.* I couldn't understand how I could have fallen for someone like that.

Betrayed, hurt, shattered, and even humiliated—the emotions were overwhelming. How could I have been so blind, so stupid, to fall for him? Why was I so weak? Why hadn't I seen him for who he was? The last three years played like a movie on the screen in my mind. I met Leo, quit my great job, had a wonderful wedding, gave birth to his children, stood by him believing in him and telling people he was a good man—and now I learned it had been one lie after another.

I had been conned, and felt ashamed and embarrassed. It had affected my family as well. I beat myself up for being so gullible and naïve.

Anguished thoughts filled my journals. *How could I have been so stupid?* And yet, how could I have known he was involved in something so shady? My mind began to clear when I received a 35-page long handwritten letter from Leo. It was a rage-filled, twisted diatribe that blamed me for all his problems and went on about how he'd been a victim of women like me all his life. It was so irrational and venomous, so revealing of his personality, that something inside me told me to hang on to it. I felt no one would ever believe just how far out of touch this man was with reality. I read the letter one time—really just skimming it before putting it away. I'd now had two committed relationships to older, charming men who turned out to be hiding their true nature. Both took advantage of me and became aggressive and even threatened violence—that pattern was going to end right here.

As I rebuilt my life, I continued investigating his past and learned the extent of his pathological lies. Painful as it was to admit, I'd married a psychopath. I turned to books like *Codependent No More* and *Women Who Love Too Much* to try to get some insight into what had just happened, and I started to build up my confidence again.

Years before, I'd read *How to Stop Worrying and Start Living* by Dale Carnegie and I reread it, this time taking the ideas to heart. I had to put this experience with Leo behind me and not let it color my perceptions of myself. I didn't want to believe that I was destined to attract men who had deep-rooted problems. At the same time, I would be very cautious in the future, keeping my eyes open and remaining alert to any signs that a man was not what he seemed to be.

Leo had no interest in a relationship with my daughters, who didn't remember him, and that was fine with me. A four-year chapter in my life ended. I was moving on and would never again have to deal with Leo and his madness. I was safe once again.

In Sweden, Alexa, Megan, and I all blossomed and really started to live. The physical distance from the place where we had been caught up in the mad web of my ex husband helped tremendously, as well as being surrounded by people who loved us. I could think clearly. In time, I made new friends, and some of them became like a second family to me. I began to think that maybe I could be happy again. How great it was to be surrounded by people who cared about me! The girls loved both the house and Sweden. We went back to my mom's tiny apartment in Stockholm at Christmas and enjoyed the holidays with her.

I was trying to reestablish my work permit and had also started the divorce process when in mid-January 2001, I registered the girls in daycare in Stockholm. Two children in full-time daycare cost me $40 a month, since

I was unemployed at the time. Knowing I had low-cost daycare relieved some of my stress.

My mother was my rock and indescribably supportive, and never criticized me for missing the signs that Leo was bad news. She has a great relationship with the girls. Sometimes, I'd reflect on the challenges she went through and say a prayer of gratitude that I come from a very strong line of women.

I was able to sublet a small apartment in the same complex where mother lived, so we had our own two-room apartment for three months. It was so nice to have our own space. I started taking intensive Swedish classes so I could look for a job.

It was time to build something for myself and a good life for the girls. So with a major effort, I put it all behind me and focused on the future.

Eventually, I realized there were undoubtedly a lot of women who had fallen into the same Cinderella-Prince abyss that I had found myself. I was sure I would never be able to entrust my heart to a man again. I was determined to be a great mom and provide for my daughters without a husband in the picture, and as the weeks and months passed, my faith in myself was slowly rekindled.

Chapter Four

∙ ∙

Far From Home

Sergio had no idea where I'd been taken—and between touchdown and takeoff on his connecting flight to Stockholm, he had a grand total of 50 minutes to make calls and check in at the ticket counter. He called our mentor and friend, John Assaraf, to ask for assistance and direction. After all, Sergio knew nothing about the American legal system, or to what facility I might have been taken. John diligently did research while Sergio finished up his 16-hour flight to Stockholm. As soon as the plane landed, Sergio checked in, but John said he'd had no luck finding me. It was time to start contacting the jails in the San Diego area. Sergio did—but got no answers. He also called our business partner and dear friend, Steffani, who lived in the U.S. to fill her in and ask her to help as well.

It was several harrowing hours before he got through to someone at GEO who said a woman who fit my description had come in but had collapsed and was taken to the hospital. This miscommunication seemed to stem from my routine medical exam in jail, but Sergio wouldn't learn that until much later. He was sick with fear, shock, and uncertainty, not knowing if I was alive or dead for several days. And he ended up going without sleep—in part, because he was dealing with a nine-hour time difference and had to be awake when working people in San Diego were. But also because he was also terrified about what he was going to say to the girls. He worked hard to maintain a strong presence of normality for them.

Meanwhile, I was awakened at 7:30 a.m. that second day when ten new women came into the medical unit. Ellen and I scrambled to move our personal things because the beds were the only places to sit in the room. I was disoriented by this sudden invasion. The women all found space to sit on the beds and started talking loudly to each other, wanting to know what they had been arrested for and whether they had been to GEO before. The lack of privacy and invasion of personal space was something totally new to me, and it made me very nervous and scared. It felt like an alien world and I wanted to observe it and understand it from a distance, but I had no control over who was in my space.

Fortunately, by this time I felt pretty comfortable with Ellen. She kept asking when she and I would be taken to our tank—the common term for cell block at GEO. The same Corrections Officer, or CO, who had processed me when I arrived came to fetch Ellen and me and escort us to our new quarters on the third floor.

Ellen smiled and acted friendly to the CO, and then asked her, "You think we could get in C tank? Together?"

I looked at Ellen, puzzled by her request, as the CO thought for a moment. "Sure, why not? Not too full right now," she said with a shrug. It seemed odd that Ellen's request was granted easily. Here it felt I had no power—what did she know that I didn't?

There was an east side and a west side to this women's wing, and as we followed the CO, she led us to one of the six tanks that consisted of four to seven cells. I peered down the long hallway as we passed one set of tanks, then another, and looked out the long line of barred windows on the opposite side. The view was of a bleak rooftop and a grey, windowless building directly across from GEO. Layers upon layers of security just made me feel more invisible, locked away from anyone who knew or cared about me. When would they find me and contact me? What was happening to Sergio? And to my girls?

Some of the women inmates in the cells recognized Ellen from when she had been there before and called out greetings to her. For Ellen, it was *welcome back*; for me, it was like *The Twilight Zone*. I kept waiting to wake up. I did feel safer coming in with her, however, and it made it somewhat easier for me—almost as if she were my guardian.

The CO who processed us finally directed us to our cell and pointed to our assigned bunks. Ellen's had a mattress but mine didn't. "I'll get you one. I just have to call up for it," promised the CO. I began to put my few possessions in a large storage box under my bunk, as instructed, and then

I heard her keys jingle as she walked away. I tried not to react, and kept unpacking, but then I sat down on the cold metal bunk and took in the harsh reality of that cell and its simple furnishings. The stainless steel stool and desk. The toilet without a toilet seat, out in the open for all to see. The tiny ceramic sink with a tiny hole for the drain. The bare, dingy white cement walls that, along with the bars, carved out our 10 feet by 12 feet space. The bars on the cell weren't closed, but I could hear the solid steel doors clanking as the CO opened and shut them at the end of the hall when she exited the tank.

"It's a good thing she knows me," Ellen said, plopping down on her bunk and breaking the silence after the CO had left and was out of earshot. "We got a good one. If you're new, they assign you by what you're charged with. C is probation violation—that's me. You might've ended up in D. That's for really serious stuff."

I managed a smile. "Thank you for looking out for me. That's really nice of you."

Ellen shrugged. "No problem. You're cool. So now we're bunkies."

I don't know why they granted her request, but they did and I was glad to be assigned to bunk with her. *Bunkies.* The term rolled around in my head. There was so much that was unfamiliar. *Bunkies. I can live with that.* I didn't want to think of us as "cell mates." I felt just a tiny glimmer of hope that I would be safe.

After sitting on the cold steel bunk for a couple of hours, I asked a CO as she walked by what was going on with the mattress for me.

"I don't know about your damn mattress. This isn't the Hilton. It's not my problem. You keep your mouth shut or you won't be getting a mattress, ya hear?"

I tried to be discreet as I gulped for air and fought back tears.

Silenced and scared, I sat for another three hours waiting before I got a mattress, my mind wandering but now numb to my emotions. I just couldn't bring myself to let my fear rise in me. What if I were to start crying? I thought about my girls and tried to imagine what they had done after school, what Sergio had cooked for them, and how peaceful they must look right now as they lay sleeping safely in their beds with Sergio there to watch out for them. Then, I realized he might have gone home and asked my mother to watch the girls. What was happening?

Although we weren't married, Sergio felt Alexa and Megan were as much his children as mine, but he had a son and daughter with his former wife, too. Later, I would learn he had called her after he found out that I "had collapsed", letting her know that he wasn't going to be able to take his own children at that time. She was very understanding and agreed that Sergio simply wouldn't be able to spend much time caring for his own two children for a while until everything was resolved and I was back home.

Unbeknownst to me, Sergio *had* stuck around and was with the girls when they weren't at school. He was operating in crisis mode—taking care of the kids, handling the business and delivering what we had promised to our clients, talking with my mother and sister, and trying to track me down and find an attorney in the U.S. too. He was not going to rest until he found me. But I knew none of this at the time. Keeping my fears from overwhelming me was very difficult.

At dinner time, Ellen and I walked down the tank's hall to a big dayroom that had one shower, two metal tables with attached round stools, an open toilet and a urinal, a big sink, three phones, and a television enclosed in a metal box with a plastic cover that was placed high up on the wall. We sat down together and she introduced me to a few other women she knew. She explained that there was only one floor for women but several devoted to men. I began to understand why so many of the women knew each other. It was, after all, a very small space.

Everyone was polite to me, and after I'd gently rebuffed their requests to know what I'd been arrested for, they left me alone and out of the conversation. I ate little—just enough of the tasteless, colorless food to keep my strength up. The women were allowed to watch the television and turned on a Spanish-language soap opera, but I didn't want to join them. Until I felt safe, I just couldn't bring myself to socialize with anyone—except Ellen. Even then, I was far more close-mouthed than normal. I felt I understood what it was like to be a monkey in a zoo, wary of being watched, unable to move freely.

That night, I tried to sleep, but the bright lights shining overhead and in the hallway brought on a migraine. It didn't help that there was a constant amount of noise, including the unsettling sound of metal bars being slammed opened and shut. I knew I had over-the-counter migraine medicine in my purse but of course, it was not accessible. I called for the guard when she walked by and she told me I could get some Motrin or

Advil when the medical cart came by that evening. I knew those medications probably wouldn't do anything, being so much weaker than my Excedrin Migraine pills, but what choice did I have?

By now, we had four women in the cell, and one of them was nice enough to offer me her extra sheet so I could put it over my head and block out the florescent light. I thanked her, but even with that and the painkillers that I took later, the stabbing, cold ache in my head continued.

As I lay there, I tried to remember what it was like to sleep in my own bed and snuggle with my two daughters. And I thought to myself, "How long will Sergio stick around?" He was responsible and loved my daughters as if they were his own, but why should he put up with this situation? It was my problem. My mind raced with doubts and uncertainty. I had family. *No matter what, I'll always have them. I'll always have my girls.* I repeated it over and over to console myself. It didn't make me feel better, because my heart had shut down. But it kept my mind from racing with thoughts that would agitate my fears. And then, I thought, *Tomorrow, I'll go home. I'll be home with my girls the day after that.*

This is what happens to mothers who go into jail: Your heart hurts so much for your children that something protective comes up and numbs you to the pain. You cannot deal with it because your mind and heart know it will overwhelm you. I didn't realize I would become accustomed to being numb and not feeling the pain of separation. There would come times when I would break down and cry all day. And soon, I would let myself cry myself to sleep at night. At this early point, even in the midst of my deepest pain, I wept quietly, always quietly. I didn't want to show my tears in a place like this. I needed to appear strong. And for my girls, I needed to be strong.

I had no idea Sergio was exhausting himself trying to find out what had happened to me. GEO's phone system wouldn't let me call collect to Sweden, so I felt helpless. I couldn't even phone anyone I knew in the U.S. and ask, "Would you mind making a call to Sweden for me? Sergio will pay you back." All their numbers were stored in my mobile phone and try though I might, I couldn't remember any of them.

I spent a lot of time just thinking, and I still didn't understand exactly why I was there. I had heard the words *extradition, Mexico* and *charges of fraud*. And I had heard all the names of the investors in Leo's business. I had the big picture but no details were given to me. That nightmare had somehow returned, and I couldn't bear to let it into my head—not until I had some answers, and a lawyer.

The Swedish consul showed up and left that third day. He was a very nice and sympathetic man, but there was nothing he could to do help. Even though I had recently become a Swedish citizen, I was still a U.S. citizen. I had entered the U.S. with my U.S. passport as required by law. Therefore, Sweden could do very little to help me since I wasn't considered a Swede in my circumstances. All they could do was monitor the situation closely. I thanked him but didn't feel reassured. The situation was so complicated because of the various countries involved that I wondered if he could do anything at all for me.

The next visit I had was from the public defender assigned to my case. Mike looked to be in his early 30s, with a shaved head and serious brown eyes. He looked a bit haggard, as if his caseload was very challenging. But I could tell he was intelligent and I felt he was genuinely concerned about me as he asked me how I was doing and listened to my not-so-convincing reassurance that I was okay. Then, he got down to business.

"So the reason they're holding you is that Mexico has filed papers to extradite you so that they can try you on charges of fraud. Do you know anything about those charges?"

I took a deep breath. "Not really, but I think I know where they stem from. I was married to . . . a con man."

Mike didn't blink at the hesitation in my voice. It felt odd to be speaking the truth about Leo at last, to someone I had just met.

"He had used me. It turned out our entire marriage was based on lies and that I was his 'cover' that made him look like a respectable family and businessman. He asked me to sign some papers." I explained about what had happened, or at least as much as I could remember. Mike nodded and took notes.

"I have to be honest, Karin. Your situation is pretty bleak. I'm not sure on what grounds I can get the extradition orders dismissed. We can fight this, but it's very likely they'll still send you to Mexico. I'm happy to take the case and do my best. There aren't a lot of extradition cases, but I'm the most experienced person in my office. Do you want to fight this?"

"Yes!" said. There was no doubt in my mind. "If you're willing to take me on."

"You'll have a hearing," he said, and I didn't ask when. "Have you talked to your partner back home yet? What's his name?"

"Sergio. And no, I haven't talked to him. I asked the consul to get me the phone number of my cousin Rhonda in Connecticut. I'm sure she'll place a call to Stockholm for me. But couldn't I get out of here on bond or something?"

"Unfortunately, because you're a resident of Sweden and you've got a Swedish passport along with your U.S. passport, they'll consider you a flight risk. I'll ask, but I can't guarantee anything." He looked into my eyes and quickly added, "But I'll try."

In his wake lingered promises so vague that holding on to them would have been like hanging my hopes on a wisp of mist. But what choice did I have?

"Your best bet at the moment is to get the extradition charges dismissed by the U.S. because they didn't follow proper procedures. I don't know if that's the case, but I'll look at everything carefully and see if there's anything that we can use to convince the judge," he said. "You need to know that under the treaty law, you have fewer rights than the Mexicans crossing the border illegally. It's a tough spot to be in, but I'll do my best with this case. That I can promise."

Seven days after being arrested, I placed a collect call to John Assaraf on a GEO phone in the day room. He had sent a letter urging me to do this, and his secretary patched me through to John's cell phone.

"Karin!"

My eyes welled up at the sound of a friendly, familiar voice calling my name.

"How are you holding up?"

"Okay, I guess."

"Listen, I'm really sorry. When I heard you were arrested at the airport, I just couldn't believe you were arrested. I've put money into your account so you can make calls and get what you need. I don't know what they have there, but I wanted to be sure you had some credit in your account."

I was extremely grateful and overwhelmed by his thoughtfulness and kindness. It had been days since anyone had been kind to me and it was almost more than I could handle. Later, I would find out he came from a pretty rough background, which might explain why he knew to help me in this way. It made me reflect on how, like him, I could be mistaken for someone who always led a solid and stable life, free of any sort of difficulty—or troubles with the law.

John's secretary thought to call Sergio and connected us. What an incredible relief! I hadn't heard his voice in a week. When he answered the phone, I tried hard not to cry.

"I'm taking care of everything. The girls are fine." He rattled off a list of reassurances as fast as he could, and I told him about John's call and the money he gave me.

"What a great guy he is," Sergio said.

I told him what little I understood about the extradition. He knew about Leo, although I had never gone into detail. I didn't want to revisit that part of my life.

"Do you want to talk to the girls?"

"No," I said. "I know it's been a week but I don't know what to say. Tell them—tell them I could only call you while they were at school. Next time, we'll figure it out." I needed to discuss strategy and dozens of details with Sergio, so I knew that when I finally did talk to Alexa and Megan, it would have to be a super short conversation. At $1.27 per minute, I didn't have enough to call Sweden directly for more than a few minutes here and there until John's money was credited. Fortunately, we'd discovered a way to talk through conference calls. All I had in my account was $64.27, the cash in my purse that they had credited to me.

When we hung up, I felt much better. I thought about my girls, and how even though Sergio had only known them for four years, he was very close to them—the only father they had never known. The next time I called, I talked to them. I was evasive when they asked where I was, when I was coming home, and why my business trip was taking so long, but they didn't press me for details. Being just six and eight, they had their attention on their daily lives, and it was easy to divert the conversation to what had happened that day, what they were planning to do that night, and how school was going.

I began to rapidly deplete the balance in my account because I had to spend time on the phone talking to and strategizing with Sergio. I told him he could find my journal from those Mexican days somewhere in the storage area of our apartment, along with the 35-page letter from my ex that showed how crazy Leo was and that might reveal some clues to his illegal shenanigans. As he read the journal and letter, Sergio learned for the first time just how hellish those years had been for me, how Leo had threated my life multiple times, and my reluctance to get married again made a lot more sense to him. After all, I had only offered him a commitment ring, and we'd never made plans to walk down the aisle together. I used to always joke that I was allergic to marriage, but Sergio understood that I was dead serious. He'd known few details about my past relationships and simply accepted that I was "not the marrying type," and that I was quite happy with an indefinite engagement. If people wanted to say we were engaged, we didn't correct them, but we also didn't discuss getting married.

After leaving Leo, my focus had been on emotional and financial survival. I did realize, however, that I needed friends and a social life. I knew I owed it to myself and to my children. I was quite sure I was not ready to date—I felt too fragile, and my divorce wasn't final. Until it was, I just couldn't imagine seeing someone. And anyway, I didn't trust my judgment where relationships with men were concerned. I would take very slowly to the idea of a relationship with any man if one showed up in my life.

I'd met Sergio one February day after I'd begun working at an executive search firm. When I was told about the job, I found myself thinking, *You know, I could do that again.* It was such a clear message to me—I could feel it was the right move to get back into the executive search field. Besides, I'd received an e-mail from a dear friend, Margaret, an intuitive psychic and a *feng shui* consultant, who said I should get back into headhunting and that I could end up working for a company I had worked with before. All of this gave me the direction I needed, but little did I know it would also send me in the direction of a man who would change my life forever in the best way possible.

The first time I met Sergio, he seemed very nice and gentlemanly—and very handsome. He was originally from Spain, had been married nearly twenty years, and now was divorced with two children. He was the Country Manager (similar to a Sales Director), responsible for Nordic sales for a company in a related field. I could tell he was smart and reliable. After my disastrous marriage to Leo, I had reverted to my earlier rule about not getting involved with men more than ten years older than I was. No more older men for me! Sergio was only seven years my senior, so there went *that* excuse to not see him again! It had been three years since Leo's arrest, and I was ready to start living a normal life. I wasn't looking for a relationship. I just wanted to have a social life with friends and fun activities.

Two days after our first date, Sergio and I went for a walk, talking Swedish together so I could improve my fluency. As we strolled, we passed a neighborhood where I had often dreamed of living. "Funny," he said, "I always dreamed of having an apartment there." It soon became apparent to both of us that we had a lot of similar interests and similar goals.

I was very comfortable with him and as we became better acquainted, he let me set the pace for our relationship. He knew some of what I had been through and was very patient and non-demanding. We had several dates before we even kissed. A relationship was a big step for me *and* for him. If we were going to be seeing each other, six hearts would be involved.

Sergio says he was attracted to my personality because I'm lighthearted and positive. But he also says that underneath my outgoing manner and behind my smile, he detected a deep sadness. I was definitely more reserved than I had been in the past. My heart had been wounded badly. Sergio wanted to show me that not all men treated women badly. Plus, we were both unafraid to take risks or start over, so we could see ourselves becoming very close friends and even working together as business partners. He was sensitive to how vulnerable I was, despite my strength, and let me take the lead.

After we had been seeing each other for a few weeks, the two of us had lunch together one day and then we went for a walk through a large park in central Stockholm. Spring was coming and the sun was beaming down on us. I finally leaned over and kissed him. It was our first kiss and he was a little surprised. "Wow! He has such kissable lips!" I thought. "I want more!"

We got together after that, but we still hadn't met each other's children. He often came over to my apartment after I'd put the girls to bed, and we'd have some time alone. It was so refreshing to find someone with whom I had so much in common, and we found we could talk about anything with each other. Sergio is a very serious person but I have a knack for making him laugh, which I think he appreciated.

We finally decided to "accidentally" bump into each other in the park while we each had our children with us. All of us went to a café and had hot chocolate. Gradually, we began doing more things together. Sometimes, it was just the two of us, and sometimes, all the kids came along. All of them were under ten years old and played really well together.

That summer, Sergio had planned to take his children to Spain for a month to spend time with his family there. The girls and I went to *Tulebo* again in July. My sister finally came to live in Sweden from Arizona. We had a great time, but I missed Sergio while we were apart, even though we talked regularly on the phone. I knew in my heart of hearts that I really wanted to be with this man. By the time we both came back from our separate vacations, the level of commitment for both of us was much, much deeper.

After several months, my position at the executive search firm changed to straight commission instead of a fixed salary. The market was slow as the technology bubble was bursting in Sweden and some months I had income while some months I didn't. Not being able to predict my income flow was a stressor—and so was the fact that the girls and I would soon have to move out of our six-month sublet. My home has always been a very important place for me. When I can't relax at home, it affects other aspects of my life as well. Home to me is where my heart is and where I feel safest. The insecurity was difficult.

During the Christmas holidays, I went apartment hunting and found a better and larger place, since my sister was living with us as well by this time. I made plans to move in, and wondered whether the bursting of the technology bubble would make it difficult for us to make ends meet. I tried my best to remain positive.

Sergio's position at his company was eliminated shortly after that. Meanwhile, I was getting burned out by working strictly on commission at my company. I was especially tired of being the only one bringing in new clients.

One night while he and I were walking, Sergio suggested we start our own executive search company together. The idea both surprised and intrigued me. I called my friend Steffani, with whom I had worked previously. She had left and started her own company a couple of years before. I asked if she wanted to open an executive search office in Sweden with Sergio and me and she said yes, so he and I opened a branch office for her. We were all taking a risk at a scary time, but everything fell into place. By the end of March 2003, the business was up and running. We were pleased and amazed that it was such an easy transition. The excitement rose as we imagined our little business growing more and more successful.

One principle I learned from this experience is that when you are on the right track, the universe makes things happen easily and smoothly. It was a leap of faith for both me and Sergio to start this business together, and Sergio put up money for the venture. Fortunately, we worked together beautifully—we really complimented each other. First, we clarified our roles: I'd be the face of the business and Sergio would run things behind the scenes. He saw huge potential in me, he says, and that motivated him more than getting the glory and attention. "What drives me," he said, "is to see you becoming all you want to be. They say behind every successful man is a strong woman. But I see us as the opposite. I'm the strong man behind the successful woman." It was a partnership of the heart as well as the head.

When our first client hired us, it was such a relief because I knew we were going to make it. Then things started happening quickly. I taught Sergio the business and he ran with it. Within a couple of months, we were doing international placements working from Sweden and placing people in several European countries. All our interviews were by phone, and we delivered to our clients just what they needed: reliable, dynamic employees who were an excellent fit for their companies.

That summer, I was in *Tulebo* again with the girls, who were now five and four. Sergio and I took his children to Spain for a week and then they stayed longer. With my relationship with Sergio even more solid, I knew I had to talk to my daughters about the changes in our family. I sat down with Alexa and Megan in their bedroom, and began, "I need to tell you a story. I'm going to tell you where your father is and what's going on with him. He's sitting in prison right now because he's stolen from people and lied. You go to prison when you do things like that. I never want you to lie to me or steal. Those are two things we do not tolerate in this family."

They both were a bit relieved to know the truth about why their father was not involved in our lives. It seemed they accepted it and took it well. I told them no one knew about this, and I was ashamed that I had married a man who was now in prison, ashamed that I didn't know who he was when I was with him. They understood why there was to be only absolute honesty in our home.

By this time, I was divorced from Leo and was just waiting to hear about whether I would get full custody of the girls. The Swedish judge granted it to me temporarily, but I had to file for permanent status. I kept tabs on Leo over the internet while he was in the Arizona prison system and when he was released, that first summer I was with Sergio, I lost track of him and didn't try to find him. The courts couldn't find him either. It took 18 months to get full custody of the children under Swedish law, and only then did I feel that my girls were truly safe. What a relief! My mother and I celebrated with a glass of wine. I intentionally kept the same mailing address for years in case Leo wanted to communicate with the girls—but he never did.

Sergio's apartment in Stockholm was installing new plumbing and he had to live in another place for four months, so we decided on a trial run of living together: He moved in with me and the girls. We all got along, but Sergio had hesitations about living together on a permanent basis because he knew he would probably spend more time with *my* children than with his own and that really bothered him. He struggled with guilt and really wanting to have his kids with him more often. One of the things that really impressed me about Sergio was what he did when he divorced his first wife and moved into an apartment in Stockholm. He continued to drive to their home an hour away every morning to be there when his children woke up. Pappa was there to make their breakfast and take them to school and daycare just as he always had. He did this for the first year after they had divorced. I could tell this was a man who really loved his kids and would do anything for them. The contrast in commitment between him and Leo was huge.

Soon, Sergio purchased a very small, old house with a nice lot, close to his children's home. His plan was to tear down the old house and build a new one, but he ended up with a prefab house that was constructed in a day while we watched. Very quickly, we were able to nest together as a family on the weekends—the girls and I still lived in the apartment during the week. All four children chose their rooms' furniture and colors. It really felt like a place where we all belonged.

By 2005, it was pretty obvious to everyone that Sergio and I were committed to each other. I had told him I didn't ever want to get married again, but I loved him and wanted to be with him. We were now living together about three quarters of the time between his home and ours, and the arrangement was good for both of us. It gave me time to be alone with the girls, and him to be alone with his children—plus, we had time together. It was a good balance. We were each able to do our own thing and still enjoy each other even though we were together many hours each day.

Once or twice a year, the two of us would enjoy a weekend trip together without the children—usually in England, Scotland, or Spain. Many of my best memories are those weekends. Sometimes, we just looked at a map and picked a city and went there. I loved to take the big red tourist buses that gave guided tours of whatever city we visited. At first Sergio thought it was embarrassing to be such obvious tourists, but then he realized it was a great way to get to see the city and no one knew us there anyway. We were so happy together!

Even though Sergio and I were very committed to each other, I was flat out against marriage. We had discussed it, though. He never wore a wedding ring with his first wife. "But if we do get married someday," he said, "I'd wear a ring."

After that, I started thinking about taking another risk. What if we each had a ring to show our commitment to each other? So for his birthday, I let go of my fears and decided to buy rings for us. I fell in love with the style of a now-famous jewelry designer, went to see him, and commissioned him to make us two rings in time for Sergio's birthday.

I had given Sergio several presents throughout the day, saving the rings for last. When the time came to give Sergio his birthday present, I was incredibly nervous! The kids had gone to bed and my palms were sweating. I came downstairs in my pajamas and robe and sat beside him with the ring box in my robe pocket.

I told him, "I'm committed to you, and I want to be with you. You had said you would wear a ring to symbolize our commitment to each other. Well . . ." Then my sweating hands gave him the box. It took him totally by surprise. He realized what a big step this was for me and how much trust it took. I added, "I got one for myself too." I opened a matching box for me, and together, we put our rings on.

This simple exchange both strengthened and deepened our relationship. That was a major turning point for Sergio. He had been thinking I was the right person for him, but maybe *he* wasn't the right person for *me*. My willingness to take that step forward showed him that I really was committed to him. It was as close to an engagement as I was comfortable with—an indefinite engagement without a wedding in sight.

Most children feel more secure when they have two parents and the girls actually wanted us to get married. I always answered, "NO! Absolutely not!" Sergio was understanding. For both of us, the rings and our commitment of the heart was enough.

"When you gave me the engagement ring," Sergio explained later, "it meant that you'd chosen me, and appreciated me just as I was. And the whole thing was so bold, so brave of you."

In GEO, I couldn't wear my commitment ring. I looked down at my fingers and my rapidly deteriorating manicure, and the faint light ring of skin where the ring, now tucked away in a locker with my other belongings, used to be.

I continued to call Sergio in Sweden by calling John Assaraf's office and having them set up a conference call. "You phone him as often as you like—don't worry about the money," John insisted. "I've put more in your account for you." The freedom to buy snacks and toiletries, luxuries by jail standards, would turn out to be major factors in my ability to keep my spirits up. John's generosity continued to overwhelm me with gratitude. I did get a counselor to track down the number for my cousin Rhonda in Connecticut, and was able to talk to her. She offered to relay messages to Sergio for me, and even set up some conference calls as John had. What a gift she was for us!

GEO was not meant to hold inmates for long, so there was a continual rotation of bunkmates in Ellen's and my cell. I realized how lucky I was that Ellen had brought me in with her, because the women who showed up at all hours to share this tiny space with us were simply probation violators. I shuddered to think about what crimes the other women—the ones I sat next to in the dayroom or saw during the recreation time—had committed. I kept quiet and avoided conversations, but you can't give people one- and two-word answers to their questions forever, so soon I got to talking more with the women around me. They treated me as one of them because I'd been born in Mexico, which I thought was curious, but if that made me more likeable and worthy of their respect or friendliness, I wasn't about to argue. I started to realize that most of my fellow inmates were drug dealers, addicts, and women who had participated in smuggling Mexicans across the border illegally. None of them were hardened criminals.

For me, the countdown to my hearing had begun. It would be only three more weeks. I knew I could stay positive if I worked at it, especially since the worst of my fears about the other women were finally beginning to fade.

But then my hearing was pushed back eight weeks to June 28! I felt the wind had been knocked out of me. That seemed like a lifetime away!

I cried quietly in my bed, and Ellen either didn't notice or decided to let me be. Each day, I told myself *As soon I have my hearing, it'll all be okay.* I didn't understand exactly what would transpire and I hadn't asked too many questions of my lawyer. I needed to believe that everything would get cleared up and I could get out of this place quickly.

I don't believe in coincidences—I believe in synchronicities—so I wondered, what could be the significance of June 28? It had been my wedding day, and my parents' wedding day. Did it have some sort of karmic meaning? I decided that it didn't signify the beginning of something terrible happening to me, but the beginning of a lesson about my relationship with Leo. I was open and willing to learn it—but really, I didn't need to be in jail to learn it, did I? I willed myself to believe that my nightmare would end on June 28, that I'd figure it all out, and having learned what I needed to, move on with my life, free of legal woes.

In May, Sergio had some good news for me.

"I found two Mexican lawyers!" he told me in one of our daily phone calls. "They think they can get the extradition charges dropped on their end. And get this—Mike and one of the Mexican attorneys studied at the same university! What are the odds?"

"That must be a sign! Mike said he might find something in the papers that could get the charges dropped. But it's complicated because he doesn't know Mexican law. If they can all work together—"

"Exactly. Between all three of them, they're sure to find some sort of procedural error. That's the strategy for now."

I took a breath. "That's good."

"Very good."

"Yes, I've told them everything about your marriage and what happened. No matter how small, just in case it helps the case."

He told me that the attorneys had advised us to stay confidential about the entire situation. There were strong indications that my life and our family's security were at risk, given the uncertainty of who had been involved with my first husband and his threats against me. But mostly importantly were the girls…they were far too young to understand the legal complexities we were facing.

Sergio said, "I'm not going to rest, you know. I don't care what it takes. We're getting you back here as soon as we can. Don't lose faith."

I promised I wouldn't. And I set my heart on June 28, and imagined the judge dismissing the charges and pounding the gavel. And then, I would go home.

71

Chapter Five

· ·

"Today Is the Day I Go Home"

"Martinez! Roll out!"

The harsh voice woke me from a light sleep. I heard a groggy woman mumble after the CO loudly instructed her to get dressed. For the next couple of hours, I was half awake, willing myself to relax and let a deep sleep come over me. As Ellen and I ate breakfast the next day, I asked what had happened that caused someone to be taken out of the tank in the middle of the night.

"The call you around three in the morning if you've got a hearing," she said, digging into some watery oatmeal with her orange plastic spork. She glanced over at my tray. "Huh. Breakfast. The one meal where they don't give you cake! You should get a diet tray, like mine. Less bread, more fruit. And overcooked vegetables. It's still fresher. You just have to request it."

"Really? Thanks. I'll have to do that. I sure don't need cake twice a day, and I could use some healthier, less fattening foods. Although I have to say, this bread isn't bad." The facility baked its own bread, but I didn't want to live on it, either.

"You get apples mostly and sometimes, bananas," Ellen continued. "Or an orange. And for lunch and dinner, some carrots or green beans. You look at some of these women and they've put on twenty pounds in a month!"

Ellen wasn't exaggerating. I'd seen women start to blow up from stress eating—and from lousy food. The meals I'd had so far were highly processed, with lots of carbohydrates and little appeal. Because there were so many

72

Mexican women in GEO, we did get rice and beans. The Mexican food was better than the rubbery chicken or dry hamburger on buns so lacking in fiber they crushed flat as soon as you picked up the burger with your fingers.

"Why would they take someone out of GEO so early in the morning?"

"Well, it's a long day," she said. "With the whole transportation routine, strip searches, shackles—it all takes time. You eat breakfast and dinner downstairs. And you get a crappy lunch bag at court. All so you can show up in front of the judge for about three minutes."

Would my hearing be like that? In and out? And "out" might mean out of GEO. Mike had cautioned me not to get my hopes up, but I chose to be optimistic.

It might sound crazy that it would take an entire day for a hearing, but if there's one thing I'd already learned, it was that moving inmates, or "court bodies" as the COs referred to us, took time. For instance, when we were going to recreation, or "rec," fifteen minutes would pass before the hundred or so women on the floor could be brought out of their cells into a holding area, then to the elevator and the eighth floor, where the recreation room, chapel, library, and the outside rooftop were. The return trip took just as long, so while we had recreation for an hour, it was often cut short to only 45 minutes.

"I guess with hearings, it's like that long day when I was first booked. Lots of waiting around. You were pretty tired out from it, as I recall."

Ellen nodded and chewed, and then confessed, "It wasn't the long day that did me in. I was on meth when they arrested me. You get really hyper. I was probably talking your ear off. And then, when the meth wears off, you totally crash and sleep for a long time."

I felt a little foolish. In fact, Ellen had slept for three days. I'd had no idea that she was on drugs, or recovering from being high. I'd never known anyone who used meth. I was certainly getting an education!

Many of the women at GEO, like Ellen, originally got in trouble with the law because of using crack, crystal meth, or other drugs. They often had been caught buying or selling narcotics or marijuana, or transporting the drugs for someone else—a dealer, a boyfriend, or maybe a boyfriend who was a dealer. I got the impression that plenty of the women had been through rehab at least once. Ellen had told me she was an addict, but I hadn't considered the possibility that she was high the first time we met. She had just seemed nervous and extroverted to me.

73

Rollouts were common. They were disruptive, but I liked to think that when a woman was called, she was going before a judge to be sent home—so naïve!

Unsettling as they were, rollouts were nothing compared to shakedowns. A shakedown involved the whole tank rather than just one woman, and a dozen or so COs suddenly shouting at us to get dressed and patting us down quickly—too quickly to notice or care if they touched our breasts too closely. Everyone jumped to comply with their orders.

The first time it happened, I'd been reading, and I felt my heart race as the loud voices from all around the floor and the sounds of women hurrying to line up in the hall began. It felt like chaos, but I followed the other women's lead and kept silent as I watched as some of the COs begin to enter our cells and roughly go through our possessions to look for contraband. They even ran a stick with a mirror on the end under the beds to see if we'd hidden anything there. Meanwhile, other COs herded us like cattle toward the day room, where they locked us in. Ellen explained to me that the COs would go through everything we had, stripping beds, turning over mattresses, and tossing items into the hallway.

"If you've got extra food, they'll throw that out. Extra pads or tampons, they'll take those away, 'cause you're not supposed to have them except when you have your period," one of the younger women explained, overhearing Ellen talk about the routine. I hadn't thought to keep sanitary supplies, since it was easy enough to get them simply by asking. But given how little control we had, many of the women took advantage of any chance to stock up on something useful, including extra clothes and sheets.

After twenty minutes or so, the shakedown ended and let us out of the day room. We crowded into the hall, where the COs were wheeling away several big white canvas bins filled with extra clothing, razor blades removed from pencil sharpeners to serve as makeshift scissors, and extra food. When Ellen and I got to the cell, it looked like a tornado had hit it. I began putting everything back together. I had very few items in the storage box under my bunk—some clothes, a stack of white notepads, some toiletries, and that sort of thing. Cleaning up didn't take long, but I felt rattled. It was clear some of the COs had enjoyed the sudden disruption and the chaos they left behind. A couple of them taunted us, while the others just went about their job as if they were simply sorting through garbage, not people's possessions. We weren't people here. We were more like animals in cages.

74

Later, I learned that if they found containers of "pruno" (a homemade alcoholic beverage) or medicines that the women hadn't gotten with permission from the medical chart, they pulled the woman aside and would give her a write-up, which was a report about the incident. Then, the woman would be targeted: The COs would keep coming back to do cell searches in addition to the shakedowns involving the entire tank. I had heard that these things could be used against you when it came to getting sentenced. Apparently, the attitude was, "A troublemaker is always a troublemaker." But the way I saw it, women were just trying to have a little bit of control over their lives at a time when their fate was in the hands of the justice system.

The cell, or room, searches were less scary and intense than the shakedowns, fortunately. How invasive they were depended on the CO. If you were lucky, they just poked through your possessions and you didn't even know they were there. One CO always came in early in the morning, opened the boxes, counted the clothes, and left without waking anyone up. If you did wake up and rolled over, her face would be right there in yours!

In that first shakedown, they missed my extra shirt, which I was glad to see. I'd already come to realize that if you held on to an extra shirt or pair of pants, you wouldn't have to have your laundry done as often. You were only supposed to have three outfits, and while laundry service was provided, it was a good idea to hand wash your clothes—I'd learned that from Chata.

Chata was the matriarch of a family drug ring who was swearing she wasn't involved in "the business" anymore. She was like a big kid and as down to earth as it gets—passing wind loudly and laughing about how she couldn't help herself. She had explained very shortly after I arrived that they throw all the clothing bags together, mixing white T-shirts and underwear with dark green uniforms, which is why the whites would always look so dingy. Worse, they overstuffed the machines and if they did use laundry detergent, the lack of agitation left clothes and sheets dirty. We slept on black sheets—black to hide the stains, I imagine—so I tended to believe Chata. "I'll do your laundry if you pay me," she said. "I love hand washing. It's relaxing. And I use toothpaste to get the whites really white."

I made a deal to have her clean my clothes for the price of two foil packets of tuna a week, purchased from the commissary through my account—which Sergio was now supplementing. Sitting in the conference room at the Del Mar Hilton Hotel hearing him speak about our power to attract what we want and deserve felt like it happened in a different lifetime. On the phone, Sergio and I would discuss issues with finances—our own and our business's—but here, I was negotiating the price of scrubbing my underwear with toothpaste. It felt surreal.

Could the Law of Attraction workshop Sergio and I had attended been just a month ago?

I couldn't help thinking that the lessons we'd learned that week applied here too. I felt that I had attracted this experience. I didn't feel it was some sort of punishment from a God who blamed me for what Leo did, or for not catching on to his crimes earlier and blowing a whistle. But I also didn't believe that some random piece of terrible luck had brought me here. I was here for my soul's growth—that was clear to me. I knew I had to start thinking about the spiritual work that I'd been neglecting.

It was time for me to start letting go of old emotions like grief, anger, and fear, and forgive Leo—and myself, for not catching on to what he was doing. I'd moved forward with my life after Leo, and read a lot of self-help books and done journaling to acknowledge anything uncomfortable that I had pushed out of my mind. Yet I knew I was still holding on to anger and shame. Of course, I was upset about where my choices had taken me—and what his actions had brought about. I needed to reflect on that and start the process of forgiveness.

But how could I be reflective in GEO, when it seemed that at any moment, my focus would be broken by a shouting CO or a sudden outburst from one of dozens of women who shared the small, echoey space in the tank? I affirmed over and over, "Today is the day I go home" and imagined the scenes of the judge dismissing my case on June 28 and me getting on a plane, flying home, and hugging my girls outside the gate. But the days here were long, and the stress was high. I knew I had to start developing my skills for changing what I was attracting—and managing my stress. There was no time like the present to begin.

I was starting to learn the GEO routines and creating my own, like the walking and the yoga on the roof, to give myself a sense of control. Sergio was doing the same nine time zones away from me. On top of trying to manage our business and my case, he had all the pressures and obligations of being a single parent—as well as a divorced dad with shared custody. Sergio and the girls and I wrote letters every day and they posted them every week to me by Federal Express. They also created affirming and positive prayers and visualizations and said them together at 8:00 p.m. before bed. The prayer went, "Thank you, Father. We are so happy and grateful for having our Mommy with us now." Then, they would visualize Mommy coming home and pray to the angels to make this wish come true. This helped them feel secure even though their mother was not physically there with them. Sergio made sure they followed this routine almost every day because he knew it would help them feel secure if he maintained a stable home environment. He kept them involved in activities so they could have their friends around them as usual and to keep them busy so they couldn't think about why their mother wasn't coming home.

Sergio was fighting a war on two continents and all fronts. When people were reachable by office phone in the U.S. or Mexico, Sergio was making calls, and staying awake by drinking plenty of water and green tea. He knew they would help his system flush out toxins and support his immune system, but also, coffee and wine tasted bitter to him. Maybe his body simply knew that he needed the water and green tea to keep going at his breakneck pace, sleeping only two or three hours a night. He lost about twenty pounds from the stress.

I talked to the girls, and to Sergio, almost daily. But with Sergio, there simply wasn't time to get into detail with each other about anything except business and my case for the twenty minutes we were on the phone together. My letters to him were like journal entries about my day. I wrote about my feelings, but I didn't tell him I was afraid he'd leave me. Every day that I talked to him, it seemed like a miracle that he was still there.

Sergio told me the girls weren't asking too many questions, and when they did ask, he was telling them that I couldn't come home until some paperwork is done.

I'd written him about reading *You Can Heal Your Life*, and we'd discussed in letters how it fit in with what we had learned about the Law of Attraction. I'd always meant to read it because I had been intrigued to hear that the author had used the power of her mind to heal herself of cancer. As I understood it, the book was for people with physical problems, which I didn't have—aside from the migraines—so I hadn't gotten around to it until now. One afternoon, Paula came running into my cell with a big smile.

"Karin!" she said excited, "I know how to help you with your migraines."

"What do you mean?" I said as I noticed the book she was holding in her hands—*You Can Heal Your Life*, which I'd heard about and wanted to read. To me, it was a clear sign that the universe was looking out for me, even here.

"I found the cure in this book," Paula said laughing. "You're never going to believe this, but guess what the best thing for getting rid of them is?"

"What?"

"Masturbation." She smiled, and I laughed aloud at her "medical advice."

"It does not say that! Let me see the book."

"I'm serious!" she said. "You gotta take your chances, when no one's around."

I wasn't feeling the need, but I wasn't about to tell her that! It's not that I wasn't yearning for Sergio, or having sexual feelings like any healthy woman would have over the course of several weeks. But even when I tried to imagine myself naked next to my handsome lover back home, I felt nothing in my body.

One of the women, Julie, had told me that they put saltpeter in the food—a filler she said they use in the Navy to keep the men from having sexual feelings and getting into trouble. She insisted it wasn't an urban legend and that she had the same experience when she was enlisted. Julie was young, confident—and an attractive blonde with blue eyes. She was pretty enough to be a Barbie doll, and I tried to imagine her in a military uniform—or doing heroin, which I knew had landed her here. I was coming to realize that appearances can be very deceiving.

At GEO, the food was so highly processed, and our rights were so casually violated, I wouldn't have been surprised if Julie were telling the truth about the saltpeter. Whatever the case, my libido was pretty much nonexistent and it felt very strange. *I guess it's just one more thing they strip from you.*

Being in jail robs you of little things you never think about in ordinary life. Mirrors, for example. I wanted to say my affirmations properly, like *You Can Heal Your Life* prescribed—Paula had given me the book and I was working with its exercises now. I was supposed to look into my reflection as I said my affirmations with strong emotion in order to give them the most impact. Finding a mirror to use was a problem, though. Since mirrors were glass and could be broken into shards that had the potential to be used as weapons, we couldn't have them. The commissary had sold me a nail clipper, and I held that at just the right angle so I could look into the narrow reflection of my hazel eyes as I said, "Today is the day I go home,"

"I am willing to set myself free. All is well in my world," and "I love myself". Hard as it was to muster up positive feelings, I did my best so that the affirmations would send a powerful, clear message to the universe that what I was saying was true. I believed what the book said—that when you infuse your affirmations with genuine emotions of joy, hope, and enthusiasm, the universe responds by changing your circumstances to match your energetic vibration.

In addition to reading *You Can Heal Your Life*, very soon, I was able to read letters from Sergio and the girls that he sent me via Federal Express once a week. The letters were only a few days behind, so between those and my daily calls to Sergio and the girls, I was in contact constantly. I know now that hearing my voice every day gave Alexa and Megan great comfort—and it did the same for me. I continued to keep their photos with me and I looked at them constantly. Then, I would close my eyes and imagine myself running toward them as I came from the airport gate, and the feeling of their hugs as we wrapped ourselves around each other. I smelled their hair as I kissed them, and said, "I love you" over and over in my mind as I played out this scene.

Meanwhile, Sergio and I had no idea when I actually would get on that plane. Mike told me he would keep me posted on my hearing, and I focused on that, imagining myself going before the judge and him saying, "Charges dismissed."

I was going to need physical, emotional, and spiritual strength to get through these days—that much I knew. So, for starters, I needed exercise. I began walking in the hallway of the tank and picked up another woman's habit of using a deck of playing cards to keep track of my laps. I'd hold the deck and place a card on top of an intercom at one end of the hall before heading back in the other direction. Walking back and forth along the whole row of cells for 40 minutes was 26 steps each way, so the deck came in handy. There were 52 steps in one round trip, and I made 52 steps 162 times per day. That worked out to 8,424 steps on an average day. Talk about boredom! I figured out the number of feet per stride and tried to calculate how many miles I'd walked per day, for a total of what was eventually 1352 days—it came out to 11,389,248 steps! You could say I was dedicated to exercising.

I went through a pair of shoes at the end of a first month and had to buy a $26 pair of Keds—the kind we wore back in the 1970s, with little tread on the soles—at the commissary. And when I was walking, I imagined I was walking through the customs at the airport, getting ready to go through the door to see Sergio and the girls waiting on the other side. And that the solid steel door was the sliding door at Stockholm airport that would open up and free me to walk into the arms of my loving family.

I also walked around on the roof, but this got boring quickly. I was like goldfish swimming around and around a small fish tank. The roof was eight stories up, but they weren't taking any chances at GEO. The area was surrounded by fifteen-foot high grey cement walls, from which metal poles held up chain link fencing that enclosed the area like a canopy or cage. I couldn't take much comfort in the clear blue San Diego skies when the view was marred by the steel reminder of my imprisonment.

Just before I'd come to John Assaraf's conference, I had started learning yoga from some videotapes I'd bought. Steffani promised to send me some yoga books after I'd mentioned to Sergio that I was trying to refresh my memory by using *Yoga for Dummies,* which I'd found in the GEO library. I began doing some poses on the roof. A couple of the women asked what I was doing and I told them, demonstrating what little I knew. By the end of a week, a dozen women were joining me in the yoga moves. Often, people get nicknames in jail and I became known as "the yoga teacher", a nickname that stayed throughout the entire time I was incarcerated. Although I was self-taught, I was able to develop a good routine to help with relaxation, improve sleeping, dealing with the stress, breathing, and exercising all the major muscle groups and share it with the other women. A few of the COs even said to me, "I wish I could join your class!" Instead of stretchy pants and tops, we had to make do with our shapeless cotton-and-polyester dark green uniforms, but we managed anyhow. Many women told me about how much it helped them stay calm and feel better. It really made a difference and I was hooked on it myself. In a situation where you have such little control, there was something soothing about being able to control your body by focusing on your muscles and holding different poses. Getting in touch with your body, your individual self—that was important when you were treated like just another body to be moved from point A to point B.

Because I had so much time during the day, I also picked up some mysteries to read from the library. I enjoyed reading the ones by Sue Grafton and a few other authors, but avoided the ones with graphic violence—I didn't need to be putting that in my brain! And I wasn't looking for courtroom scenes either. I just wanted a bit of an escape. There was a chapel that held services during the week, but the only time I could go was during our free hour, and I didn't want to miss out on fresh air and exercise.

Using Ellen's advice to avoid the regular trays and ask for diet trays let me avoid what I was observing all around me: Women managing their stress by eating bread, starches, and cake and ballooning in weight. Some of these women would take extra cake from those not eating it (like me!). As Ellen had pointed out, it seemed some had gained fifteen or even twenty pounds in just four or five weeks. In contrast, I'd lost a dress size and had to ask for smaller sized "greens"—our term for the dark, dull green uniforms. I was stressed and had little appetite, especially for the highly processed foods we were fed daily.

I was feeling less frightened of the other women and having more conversations with them, and that's how I learned that I shouldn't even begin to consider standing trial in Mexico. They would send me straight to a Mexican jail, where I would have no chance of bail. Several women, and Mike, told me that in Mexico, you're considered guilty until proven innocent. One of the women told me she'd been raped in a cell right next to the one where her fiancé was being held, and other women confirmed that rape in Mexican jails was common if not standard. It made my stomach tighten with the fear of what I was facing.

I didn't share this with Sergio. It was too terrifying to consider. But there were things he wasn't telling me, either. The child protective services department in the area where we lived in Sweden had sent over a social worker to check on the situation with Sergio taking care of my daughters— and my odd disappearance. He told them the truth, just as he told my family—but for our clients and extended network, the story was that I'd had a health crisis and had to stay in the U.S. This was true as far as Sergio knew a couple of days into my incarceration, and it seemed best to us to keep that story alive rather than try to explain about my legal situation which was far to complex and uncertain. Obviously, someone had informed social services of our situation—but who? Sergio felt uncomfortable knowing that someone had gone to them instead of to him with their concerns. He dealt with them and they were satisfied with the answers he gave, but later described his experience at the time as being like a man in a sinking boat. He plugged the hole that was the inquiry from social services, and then another would appear. He didn't want to worry me, so he kept his tone positive on the phone and in letters—and he avoided telling me what I didn't need to know.

Sergio was very afraid that the police or government would decide to take the kids away, while I was afraid he'd say, "This is crazy" and call my mom to take in the girls, abandoning them. He says he instinctively knew if the girls were okay, I would be okay, so he became devoted to providing them with a loving, stable environment. So much of his life felt out of control that he was fastidious about the things he could control. He kept the house spotless because he never knew if someone would come to check on him and the girls. Through all of this, he says, he missed me terribly and could only imagine how devastated and lonely I must feel.

By the end of May, Ellen had "rolled out" and been discharged, and the tank was half empty—with around 15 of the 28 bunks filled. I even had the entire cell to myself for two weeks. With more privacy, I could cry in my bunk without being so easily noticed, but then, when I was crying, the other women were discreet enough not to say anything. It was an unwritten rule that you didn't confront anyone who was crying in her bunk—or sleeping during the day. Being under your blanket and sheets was one of the few times when you had privacy. Similarly, no one looked when you announced you needed to use the toilet, which had no walls, only a flimsy light green sheet that we could hang between the metal corners of the bunks to give a little privacy.

Fortunately, there was privacy in the showers to some degree—you could drape your clothes or a towel over the top of the cheap plastic shower curtain, which was transparent on the top third. The sound of the water hitting the mildewed cement floor and walls was loud enough to hide the sound of crying, and I did plenty of that.

A jail is a holding facility, which is very different from a prison. There's no certainty about anything—who shares your space, when your hearing will be, or anything else. And there are only three ways to get out (legally, that is). You can get transferred to another jail or prison if you've been convicted. You can be released on bail. Or, your case is dismissed and you go home—but that's rare. Life in jail was one continuous invasion—of privacy, of personal space, of free will to make choices, and of liberty and justice.

You could always tell how much some of the COs and the sergeants enjoyed doing shakedowns and cell searches. To them, this was the fun part of the job. They would gloat about being able to come into our space, and yell or laugh at us. Other CEOs were professional and matter-of-fact. I didn't resent them. They were just doing their jobs, and they would say so by way of apology sometimes. As for the crueler COs, I imagine they had their own problems if they felt the need to pick on us when we already were being punished—even though many women had committed no crime. I'd always taken for granted that in the United States of America, you are innocent until proven guilty, but isn't how you're treated in a jail like GEO.

The treatment is tough to take. The lack of privacy, control, and respect makes you feel dehumanized. I felt the cell searches, particularly the shakedowns, were less about safety than about keeping everyone feeling scared and powerless. It seemed they wanted the women to feel insecure, depressed, and even worthless. Although I was working hard to stay positive, even I lost my sense of balance and felt completely helpless sometimes. How do you stay confident and hopeful in a situation like I was in?

I needed good news—and soon.

Chapter Six

Faith the Size of a Mustard Seed

"So what do you say we get married?"

I paused for a moment, taking in what Sergio had just proposed. I think I was in shock.

"I know you're allergic to marriage, but it feels right to me."

How could he want to marry me in my situation?

"Yes!"

I'd said it. *That wasn't hard after all!* I laughed in spite of myself. The fact that Sergio was sticking by me made me realize I wanted to be with this man for the long haul.

The details of planning the wedding gave us hope and something to look forward to in those first weeks at GEO. I drew a picture of the dress I wanted. It was not your typical white wedding dress. I'd already done that one. I wanted a white, fitted dress with a flowing skirt, a square neckline, and large flowers on it. I made a sketch of it and sent it home, and Sergio took the girls shopping to try to find what I'd drawn. They got so excited when they found a dress that matched that they couldn't wait to tell me in our next daily phone call. In letters to them, I told my daughters that as soon as I got home, we go shopping together to find the dresses they would wear. I wanted to buy matching dresses for the three girls—my daughters and Sergio's daughter.

In each of our 20-minute daily conversations, Sergio would tell me about some detail or another that would encourage me to focus on the joy that awaited us: We wanted an outdoor wedding and he found the perfect place in a beautiful rose garden with a lovely restaurant that could accommodate us. I wanted to keep the guest list small, with just our closest friends and immediate family. One day, he announced that he'd found an officiator to perform the ceremony, and her last name was Valentine. Now that was auspicious!

After these conversations, when I would look around at the dull grey of my surroundings, I would close my eyes and envision how beautiful our special day would be, and how much fun we would have riding in a horse-drawn carriage past the gardens along Strandvägen, one of the prettiest streets in Stockholm lined with trees and overlooking the water. I imagined us pulling up to the Grand Hotel, which is situated directly across the harbor from the Royal Palace, and Sergio helping me from the carriage as I stepped out onto the sidewalk and passersby smiled at me. Thinking about our wedding had helped me stay strong as I awaited my hearing, and now I'd been suddenly plunged into uncertainty.

It seemed my whole life was on hold. It never occurred to me that I might stay in GEO for months—and months. At the time, had anyone told me, I wouldn't have believed it possible—and most likely, I would have wanted to crawl into a hole and die. The majority of women cycled out of the jail within three to four months. I didn't want to give in to depression or anger, and I knew that it would help a lot if I just focused on the next key event.

In this case, my mind was on the upcoming decision from the judge even though I had no idea when we'd hear back. I kept thinking it would be "today." I couldn't bring myself to consider that I might still be in jail on Megan's seventh birthday in a few weeks. I spoke to her for five minutes each day (our calls were around noon my time, and bedtime for the girls), and remained noncommittal about whether I'd make it home by July 23. I didn't want to make a promise and break it. I tried to get her to focus on what flavor cake and frosting she wanted, and what games she and her friends would play at the party.

Megan wasn't interested. She said she didn't want to have a party if I wasn't there: My coming home was going to be the best birthday present she could get. Of course I was touched, but it was deeply painful not to be able to promise her that would happen. Sergio had told the girls not to ask me about when I'd be coming home, but she did ask cautiously a few times. I would tell her that I really longed to be there but didn't know yet if I could or not. It crushed my heart and I felt hers breaking as well. Then I would try to steer the conversations to what we would do when I *did* get home, even if we didn't know the exact date. I tried to get her focused on all the fun things we would do. She said she wanted to go to Gröna Lund, the amusement park in Stockholm. I promised I'd take her there. The question of "When?" always hung in the air, but we tried not to talk about it. What would be the point?

Ellen had been right—my initial court hearing at the end of April had been an all-day affair beginning at 3:00 a.m., and in those brief minutes in the courtroom, I was told the hearing was postponed until June, as I said. It was devastating! Still, maybe I'd be home for Megan's birthday in July . . . I had to believe that in order to be able to sleep at all, and to tolerate the limits of my freedom. I just kept chanting my new mantra: *Today is the day I go home.*

Sergio wasn't getting much information out of our Mexican attorney, but he was receiving a lot of assurances that they were gathering all the important evidence I'd need to get my case dropped so I could go home. Every time they offered a few words of encouragement, Sergio shared them with me. I allowed myself to believe in every tiny hopeful sign. It was too upsetting and scary to think about the future, beyond perhaps what might happen this afternoon or maybe tomorrow. My release might happen just as suddenly and unexpectedly as my arrest did, right? And if not, Mike and my Mexican lawyers were going to get me out very soon. I had to believe that and stop asking myself that deeply troubling and simple question: *When?* The wedding had to be my focus.

Meanwhile, Sergio and I were much relieved and thankful that the phone in our office was ringing with calls from new clients who'd been referred to us. Our only means of advertising had been word of mouth and it was still paying off. There was no way Sergio could squeeze marketing the business into his overstuffed days. We had momentum and we consciously decided to believe that momentum would continue until this mess was sorted out.

As for the girls, they were continuing to accept our vague explanation that I had to remain in San Diego on important business involving paperwork. And from what I could tell, they could see how reliable Sergio was and feel his affection for them. They got along with their step siblings and were comforted by the simple rituals of regular family meals and predictable afternoon activities.

Sergio and my correspondence was certainly one of the reasons we stayed so close, because we poured our hearts into our letters and felt our deep connection to each other. The feeling that he would surely leave me and the girls had faded, and that helped me get through each day. The crying spells were fewer, and I felt myself becoming stronger.

I was still routing calls to Sweden through the offices of John Assaraf and of my cousin Rhonda in Connecticut. It was incredibly kind of them to let me run up their bills. I was humbled and grateful. When John's office switched phone services, I had Rhonda firmly in place as my phone angel.

I also had a book angel: my friend, Margaret. She lived in North Carolina, and over the years, we had often shared books with each other. Our tastes were very similar: We both loved to read self-help, but especially self-help books that had spiritual elements. After I'd written to her to let her know where I was, she graciously volunteered to send me some books. It became her personal mission to nourish me with reading that would help me stay optimistic about my predicament. Because of strict rules about inmates receiving packages that could contain contraband, Margaret couldn't simply send me a book off her shelf. She had to buy it through a bookstore and have it sent to me—preferably an online bookstore, because that reduced the possibility of anyone slipping drugs or weapons into the package.

Through her generosity, Margaret offered me unconditional love. She helped me retain my belief that the universe does take care of us by sending us people who give us what we need. Often, people think that to make a real difference in the lives of others, they have to do something grand and showy. Margaret's simple kindness to me was small on the surface, but it had a profound effect on my ability to stay sane. She became like a second mother to me, someone I knew was always rooting for me, praying for me, and sending me love.

As the days rolled on, I kept a firm grasp on my mindset. I knew better than to start thinking, "How could I have been so dumb to trust Leo?" or "What if I'm extradited?" That threat hung over me constantly. But sometimes, emotional agony temporarily overwhelmed me and my thinking turned negative. I constantly reminded myself that I had control over my thoughts, and I was determined to use my self-discipline to avoid spiraling downward into depression. The fear, anger, and resentment would inevitably return, but I wasn't going to feed it by justifying it. There was nothing to be gained by saying, "Damn it, I have a right to be mad! This is so unfair!" All that would do is bring on a new flood of rage-driven tears and leave me feeling powerless, frightened, and beside myself with worry. I *had* to shut down those thoughts and let the emotions be simply sensations I could observe washing through my body. I'd learned that whenever I did that, the emotions wouldn't last long.

Still, I knew they would return, and I needed daily practices that would keep them at bay. I continued silently chanting my affirmation: *Today is the day I go home.* And I spent a lot of time reading inspirational books. I'd read all the ones I had found tucked between the libraries mysteries, ten-year-old cheap paperback romances falling apart at the spine, and ancient Readers' Digest Condensed Books. Margaret's selections for me always seemed to be perfect—and perfectly timed in their arrival.

Whenever my mind started to drift toward "what if"—"What if I don't get out and I'm sent to Mexico?" it was as if I were wading in the ocean and suddenly felt a riptide threatening to sweep me away from shore. I'd pull myself into my head—"Think, Karin, think!"—and remember some specific technique I could use to take my mind off my fear. Yoga, visualization, affirmations, prayers to angels—these I could do any time. Then it was if I were pulling myself back toward shore, away from the danger of my fear and despair.

"This is crazy," he said when my June hearing simply postponed a decision on my release. "If we want to get married, let's get married."

I smiled at Sergio's suggestion. We had set our wedding date for July 13, two weeks after my hearing, on the assumption that my charges would be dropped and I would be freed. What we hadn't counted on is that it can take weeks and even months for judges to come back with a decision. Not like Sergio, who was a man of action and it irked him to have "marry Karin" linger on his To Do list, even if this latest task seemed nearly impossible to accomplish.

"Any thoughts on exactly how to make that happen with you there and me here?"

"I'm the man with a plan. You know that! We'll get married in GEO. I'll bring our officiant, if she agrees. And we'll exchange vows. It'll be official. Don't worry. I'll take care of everything."

Now, Sergio was about to hit up against a formidable obstacle to his plan: In the U.S. penal system, it's possible to get married if you are in *prison*, but not if you're in *jail*. I'm not sure what the reasoning is behind that rule, but because I was in jail, not prison. If we had the wedding, it would have to be kept secret. No problem, Sergio insisted. He'd figure something out.

On July 12, 2006, Sergio came to GEO straight from the airport. When he arrived, he signed in, and then was shown into one of the visitor's rooms. Before they led me out, he says, he stood there awkwardly in his well-heeled leather shoes, new Izod shirt, and chinos that he'd picked up from Nordstrom's as small children ran around the dirty room giggling or crying. They were being scolded or scooped up by grandmothers, uncles, and older sisters, and visitors would suddenly pierce the air with loud voices and obscenities as they bickered and complained, only to have the guards remind them that they held the power to remove anyone who was too unruly. He tried not to be frazzled by the shrieking of children and zealous adults, and the constant clanging of metal doors slammed open and shut.

Seeing him there looking completely out of place, a guard approached Sergio, and in a soft, polite, voice, she directed him to one of the less dirty plastic chairs to wait for my name to be called. When it finally was, the guard explained that she would lead him through the door to the other room, where he'd sit in front of the glass window that separated him from Karin and pick up a phone receiver so the two of them could speak. Sergio thanked her, and as he walked in to the second visiting room, he saw me already sitting down on one of the steel stools on her side of the glass.

I'm sure he was shocked by my appearance, but he did a good job not showing it. I was pale and thin, my hair was dull and my skin was even duller, and I imagine I had dark circles under my eyes. I had no idea what I really looked like because of the lack of mirrors in GEO. He and I sat down quickly, divided by a dirty, thick Plexiglas window. Our eyes welled up and my lip began to quiver. I took a deep breath and placed my hand against the window, and he did the same, pressing his palm against mine. I couldn't feel the heat of his hand, and I choked back tears.

Quickly, he picked up the phone receiver and I followed suit.

"My sweet, sweet Karin."

"I can't believe you're here. I can't believe how long it's been. Are you okay? The girls?"

"We're all fine. Don't worry about us. And don't worry about your situation. I see Mike tomorrow to go over your case, and then the officiant and I will come here during visiting time and we can do the wedding."

Sergio's voice was so strong as he talked that I almost dissolved into tears, but I was determined not to cry. I only had 29 more minutes to talk to Sergio and look into his eyes—and pretend I could feel his palm against mine.

We spoke quickly, without awkwardness despite the strange situation. It was just nice to actually look deeply into each other's eyes now. When our time was up, we said our good-byes to each other softly, and the guard escorted me out of the visiting room. Sergio was guided out of the visitors' area and walked to the outside doors after signing out. He was acutely aware as he stepped out into the warm July breeze that he was free and I was behind bars.

He went back to the hotel and cried.

And in my bunk, under my blanket, I cried too.

"You have a good visit with your man, Volo?" There was compassion in the CO's voice, even though she called me by my surname, as professional protocol demanded. Her kindness broke me and the tears started to flow.

"Yes. This was the first time I've seen him in three-and-a-half months. He'll be back tomorrow." I tried to dry my eyes on the collar of my white t-shirt. I didn't mention the wedding. That was top secret.

"Why didn't you ask for an hour visit?" she asked.

I looked at her incredulously.

"I could have seen him for an hour?"

"Sure. If someone comes from more than 30 miles, you can request a longer visit. He came a long way, right?"

My mouth was dry. "Sweden. He flew in from Sweden."

"Damn! Really? I don't even know where that is!"

"So, you're saying, we could've had an hour together?" My heart was pounding. *What the hell?*

She shrugged. "Yeah. Well, maybe you can ask for an hour tomorrow. You're supposed to ask at least 48 hours before a visit. Talk to Ms. Jeffries, the counselor. But talk to her right away when she comes in cause it's gotta be approved by the warden."

A curl of rage and frustration quivered in my belly, and I felt myself start to shake. I couldn't believe it. Why couldn't anyone have told us? Sergio had to leave in four days. I took some slow, deep breaths to quiet the feeling that threatened to rise up and take over. *What's done is done. Let it go, Karin. Let it go.* All I could do now is talk to Ms. Jeffries and ensure that Sergio and I would get our full sixty minutes for our next visit.

The next morning, I waited in the day room for the counselor to come by on her morning rounds. I begged her to help me get a longer visit approved. She couldn't promise anything but said she'd do her best. For the next several hours, I waited anxiously for the afternoon rounds to hear if I'd get the official approval I needed. Any jitters about saying "I do" again after my first disastrous marriage were replaced by worry that I wouldn't get all the officials to sign off on my "extra long" visit. I needed that full hour. It was going to be my wedding ceremony, after all!

I was elated to hear that Ms. Jeffries had be able to get the paperwork in front of the warden and ask him to sign off. The CO was nice and put Sergio and me in the back visiting room where we could be alone. Still, the glass window stood between us. Because our ceremony was illicit, there would be no conjugal visit—now, or ever. I wouldn't be permitted to kiss or hug my fiancé—and he would not be able to kiss the bride.

I wasn't allowed to have more than one person visiting me at a time, so the officiant had Sergio say his vows outside of the room before coming in to see me. Then she came in to see me; she and I talked a minute in Swedish. "This is one of the most unusual weddings I've performed!" she said. Then, she began the ceremony, leading up to the big question: "Do you take Sergio to be your husband?"

"*Ja! Absolut! För hela mitt liv!*"—"Yes! Absolutely! For the rest of my life!"

Then she got up from her seat and left the room. Sergio came back in and put his hand on the glass and I put mine up against his. His eyes sparkled and I could hear the emotion in his voice as he whispered into the phone, "Now you're my wife!"

"Wow," I whispered. My throat tightened and I felt the first tear make its way down my cheek. I laughed as I wiped it away. The glass was still between

Sergio and me, but all my walls were gone. Sergio and I talked—about our love, about how wonderful it was that the girls were adjusting so well to this bizarre situation, about how we were now truly a family.

The hour ticked away far too quickly, and after saying good-bye to Sergio, I was so excited that I just had to share the news with someone, clandestine though the ceremony had been. I had to walk by the tank where my first bunkie Ellen was now residing after having been arrested again. I motioned to her so she would come right up to the bars and hear me as I walked by and whispered, "I just got married!"

"What? Really?"

I nodded and she pumped her fist in the air. "Yessss!" she said as softly as her enthusiasm would allow her.

Although she was dying to know how I'd pulled off such an incredible feat in a jail where we were constantly watched, she would have to wait for the explanation—until we were together at the library again.

I was glowing from the visit and the only person in my cellblock I was friendly with was Ahalia, who at 19 was one of the youngest inmates. I had to share the secret and when I told her, she could hardly contain her excitement. With her big smile, and pretty round face under chestnut brown hair, she didn't look old enough to drive much less be in a jail. Every time I saw her, I felt I should give her a motherly hug. Ahalia was a romantic at heart, so as soon as she heard my news she gave me a "wedding present": A chocolate Tootsie pop, my favorite, which she'd planned on eating herself. As I savored it, she chirped, "Now I have to make you something!" and fished the wrapper out of the brown paper bag we used for trash where I'd just thrown it. She went back to her cell for a pen, then came back to present me with my only wedding card.

My first wedding, to Leo, had been extravagant but the marriage was hideous. This time, the wedding was hideous but the marriage was wonderful. The ceremony had taken only five minutes, but that's all we'd needed. Now my partner in life was my husband. It was a bittersweet day for both of us, but I was so happy to know that Sergio wanted to be with me, even in these horrible circumstances, even though we had no idea when we would again touch, kiss, make love, live our lives together. It was a "glass act" all the way. No bridesmaids. No rings. No flowers. No music. Nothing. The bride wore forest green scrubs accented with navy blue sneakers.

I sat on my bunk early one morning, and ran my fingertips over the embossed gold title on the fake, blue leather book cover: *A Course in Miracles.* Margaret had sent me this 1,400-page book with its miniscule type and its densely packed pages that were as thin as onionskin. A miracle in 365 days? Well, I definitely needed one. As for the 365 days, I never thought that I might be here in GEO for that long. I determined right then that I would "work" the course as quickly as I could and do the daily exercise faithfully until my miracle arrived and I walked out of GEO and on to the next flight back home.

Although I was impatient and wanted to get on to the work of the exercise, the way the book was written, with its mysterious language and proclamations, forced me to slow down and ponder its passages: "The use of miracles as spectacles to induce belief is a misunderstanding of their purpose." What did that mean? Or, "Miracles are thoughts. Thoughts can represent the lower or bodily level of experience, or the higher or spiritual level of experience." The Course says this world is not real, but whenever I heard those steel gates or doors clang sharply as they shut, and watched the guards ending their shift as they walked out through the corridor that led to the outdoors, to their car, to their kids sitting around the dinner table with them talking about homework and soccer, this world of GEO felt very, very real.

It was challenging at first to take the time to sit quietly with each of these passages and let their meaning sink in, to let my heart inform my understanding. I was tempted to simply allow my head to "figure out" what the Course was trying to tell me, but I knew I wouldn't create my miracle that way. To move through the course rapidly, to take from it the wisdom that might help me remain on the solid shore, I would have to focus intently on this process of drinking in its wisdom and digesting it, and work with the exercises. Often in the past, I'd come across exercises in the self-help books I'd read, and thought, "Oh, that's clever. It might be helpful to do that one." I fully intended to get around to doing them after I'd finished the text. But too often, I'd forget. I retained the ideas in the books, but I didn't always do the *work* they suggested.

Now, I had no distractions from my desire to do all that I could to alter my situation, and no excuses for not making the time to do the work of healing and forgiving.

If I thought about how limited my power was on the physical realm, depression was going to engulf me. Sometimes, when I walked into the day room where women were sitting around watching a familiar *novella* or an episode of Jerry Springer, I felt the pull of the waters around my knees. I was going to bring about my miracle now, whatever it took.

Working the Course began to affect the way I saw my surroundings. I wasn't exactly close to these women who, like me, were stuck here awaiting word on their fate, but at least I wasn't afraid of them anymore and had gotten to know some of them and their stories. Yes, they gossiped and bickered and formed cliques that had everyone whispering, "Well, she said…and then *she* said…" and I had no interest in those dramas. Yet I could see that for some women, bonding with others, even over catty behavior, had its pluses. As the days go by, it becomes harder and harder to keep to yourself when you're staring at the same three dingy grey walls and filthy white steel bars. You yearn for socialization.

So I was friendly but more reserved than I would be on the outside. I didn't feel strong enough to discuss what was happening with my legal situation with the women who asked about it. If someone were to plant a seed of doubt in me, it might grow root, and I couldn't risk that. It seemed better to wave off their inquiries with, "Oh, my lawyer's working on it, so it's just wait-and-see for now." They weren't particularly interested anyway. They were just asking to be polite and to feel some sense of control over what was going on around them. Knowing that this woman was fighting extradition, that woman was in for dealing crystal meth, that one was caught smuggling cocaine over the border—all these little stories helped them to feel they weren't living in total uncertainty. Not knowing how your hearing would go was uncertainty enough.

I can't say I made friends—you don't exactly exchange phone numbers and call each other up after you've been locked up together. But I can say that as the days passed, I was starting to see the value in having positive conversations with the other women. For one thing, it kept my mind off of the pain of being in jail indefinitely. When Megan's seventh birthday arrived in July and all I could do was call her and send her a homemade card drawn on white legal pad paper, I was very depressed. The other women treated me extra kindly, offering hugs and reassuring me that I'd be home with her soon.

The worst days in jail are hidden memories, tucked far away from my conscious mind so that I don't have to relive the pain. Not being with my daughter on her birthday for the first time since she came into the world through me was devastating. I do recall that I cried myself to sleep that night, my head throbbing from the ever-glaring fluorescent lights and my hours of weeping.

I was beginning to realize how badly I needed to talk about my girls—to brag about them, and pass around their pictures, and have someone say to me, "How adorable they are!" and "Wow, so smart!" The funny thing is, I recognized that I also felt a certain comfort in hearing from the other mothers how their kids were doing. I wanted to know that Jose had finally gotten that bully to back off, and Louisa was reading books two grade levels ahead of her. I wanted to reassure Rosalina that her babies knew she loved them even though she hadn't seen them in weeks. It felt good to share our hopes about our children and their futures. We needed to hold each other up when we were scared, or sad, or feeling the weight of guilt pressing down on our hearts. Our kids represented our dreams. I could see that whatever a woman's past was, whatever mistakes she'd made, she could look into the eyes of her children and say, "At least I've done something right." The mothers I met wanted to get clean, get out, get their lives back on track because of their children. And being without their sons and daughters was agony.

There were times when the tears would arise suddenly, and to know that some woman you'd only met a month or two ago would put her arm around you and murmur reassurance—it's hard to explain just how much I needed that, how much we all needed that.

༄ঞ৯ ঞ৯ ঞ৯

I continued to work the Course faithfully, reading the designated text and performing the daily exercise every morning and just before going to sleep as the text suggests. At the same time, I was reading Gary Renaud's *The Disappearance of the Universe,* which reaffirmed my belief that somehow, this experience was meant to be. This situation, like all situations, was impermanent and had a purpose. I would be in GEO for as long as I needed to be. I was so enthralled with Renaud's book and *A Course in Miracles* that I wrote about them in my letters to Sergio, quoting from them, and he would respond to the ideas with his own insights—he even bought *A Course in Miracles* in a Spanish-language edition so he could read a bit of it here and there in his first language so he could better understand why I was finding it so helpful.

Day after day, I worked on letting go of any resentment—especially against Leo. By the time I walked out of the marriage, I had unknowingly programmed a time bomb that would explode years later. Every time I thought about my regrets, I felt weighed down not just by anger but also by my self-judgment. I was embarrassed and humiliated. I was mad at myself for trusting someone I loved who proved completely undeserving of my trust. Leo hadn't cared about the position he was putting me in as he pressed forward with his own plans. He'd taken advantage of me without ever thinking about how easily I could get hurt—without thinking about the consequences of his behavior and how his children would be affected. Whenever I thought of him, I'd feel my muscles stiffen and my heart begin to race. I had long ago stopped beating myself up over what happened, but it was hard not to do it now that my bad decision had landed me in jail a continent and ocean away from home.

How do you forgive someone who has no contrition? Leo had never said he was sorry or acknowledged just how much he had hurt me. In fact, as far as I knew, he was still in denial of all that he did, still blaming me and everyone else in his life for what happened and the choices he made. But Leo's lack of contrition didn't really matter, did it? What mattered was that my anger and shame were tearing me up inside. I had to let those feelings go. Forgiveness was the only way I was going to free myself from the pain of my regrets. I had steel bars all around me; I didn't need bars inside of me, locking me into anger and thoughts about how my life should be, or should've been.

As *You Can Heal Yourself* instructed, I started my forgiveness work by compiling a list of every person who had ever hurt or angered me, everyone I'd ever clashed with, even over something minor. My Bic pen flitted across the white legal pad as I sat on my bunk: I started with Leo, then added the names of several COs who seemed to care more about nitpicky rules than their own humanity. The directions said I should list everyone I could remember, no matter how inconsequential they and their actions might seem to me now. My best friend from third grade went on the list for hurting my feelings, along with the U.S. Marshals who were just doing their job when they arrested me, but who apparently didn't care that I was innocent. My hand started to ache from writing out all the names, but I was determined to dump all my anger and let forgiveness wash over me. Finally, I finished and went down the list one name at a time, saying to them in my head, "The person I need to forgive is _____ and I forgive you for _____." Then I imagined them each saying to me "Thank you, I set you free now."

Then I started using an exercise from *A Course in Miracles* that requires you to go around silently forgiving anyone who irritates or upsets you—or anyone who hurt you in the past and who pops into your mind. I would think, "God is the love in which I forgive you, Leo," or "God is the love in which I forgive you, Ms. Johnson." (She was one of the disrespectful and harsh COs.)

I didn't feel any sense of relief or forgiveness at first, but as I went down the list, silently forgiving every person, and started forgiving people all day long, I felt myself becoming lighter. I knew this new practice of forgiveness wasn't going to smooth out the scars in my heart immediately, or cause me to stop getting upset by the actions of some of the people around me, but it was a beginning.

My forgiveness work continued in the months that followed, as July turned into August. I felt as if I were in a spiritual boot camp of sorts, challenged to not just keep my spirits up but to reconnect with Spirit—and to feel gratitude the manifestation of Spirit, and love, whenever I saw it.

Chapter Seven

· ·

Friends, Bunkies, and Fellow Seekers

Like me, Julie stood out from the rest of the women simply because of how she looked, being tall, blonde, thin, and young. I met her one day after she joined my yoga class on the roof and she came to my bunk to introduce herself.

Before I even met her, I heard through the gossip in the tank that Julie was a heroin addict, which made me feel compassionate toward her since I knew from my brother and previous relationships how hard battling addictions can be for someone. I found it curious that she was strong enough mentally to have made it through basic training and served in the Navy, but not strong enough to overcome her addiction. I couldn't imagine what it would be like to feel trapped by a drug habit that keeps you from having healthy relationships, holding down a job, and staying out of trouble. I knew little about addiction, but I had learned that on the jail totem pole, heroin users are ranked lower than crystal methamphetamine users, because heroin is seen as the more addictive drug. I found it odd that people made these distinctions, but then, it seemed that some of the crystal meth users were in denial of how much control they had over their habit.

Right away, Julie admitted to me that she used heroin, which I thought was brave of her. She was clearly embarrassed, but I think she felt she needed to get that out of the way. She hadn't realized that I already knew. As I said, there are few secrets on the inside because of the close living quarters.

Julie called herself a "functional addict": She had always held down a job after graduating from community college, whether it was serving in the Navy or doing something else, but the casual dabbling in drugs she'd done in her teens just for fun had gotten the better of her. Her parents were divorced and she'd been raised by a struggling, lower middle class single mom who had no idea what to do about her daughter when Julie started to flounder. Now, Julie was paying the price for her experimentation with drugs, facing charges related to the heroin.

One day, Julie came in as she often did and sat on my bunk to talk to me. She said something about how strong a heroin addiction is, and how she had no idea she would get hooked so quickly, or that it would lead her to petty crime and eventually, here to GEO.

"So what's it like to use heroin? Do you snort it or eat it or—" I laughed at my ignorance and so did she.

"Eat it! You're funny! No, I shoot up. Then, it's as if you're instantly floating and all your pain or worry has been carried off downstream."

"Did you do it alone, or—"

"Yeah, I had my little ritual. I kept my stuff in a little black, wooden box—" She started to mime the process of readying herself to inject her drugs. "Then I'd take out the needle and tap it—"

As she worked with the imaginary needle, her voice began to change in an indescribable way, and her eyes seemed to glaze over. I suddenly realized this is what she meant when she told me about "jonesing for her fix." It was as if she'd entered a different reality, one far removed from her cell where I was sitting with her. She was completely engulfed in a powerful memory of her ritual and the feelings it created in her. I felt as if I'd become invisible, a voyeur to this disturbing reenactment.

"Are you okay?" I asked.

She paused for a moment, as if to reorient herself, but didn't meet my eye.

"No," she said quietly.

I began to get up. "Um, well, I'm not really comfortable with where this conversation is going. . . I think I'll just let you go through this on your own, okay?"

She nodded and I slipped away to go to the common room, knowing she'd leave my bunk as soon as her spell broke.

Later, she came up to me and apologized. "I try not to talk about it with people who don't use because it weirds them out. It's better if I'm jonesing with someone like Darlene." Darlene was another heroin addict in our tank.

It hadn't occurred to me that when they were alone together, they would act out this bizarre little scene in an attempt to reconnect with the feeling of being on heroin. It seemed her visualization—or reenactment, really—was incredibly powerful, like my visualizations were. But my visualizations were healthy, while hers brought her back to the experience of being under the influence of narcotics. I could see how that would jeopardize her sobriety.

I reassured Julie I hadn't taken offense. I was glad she'd been honest with me. The two of us had now set a clear boundary that would make it easier for us to remain friendly. In jail, it's really difficult to have any privacy or boundaries, so when someone's willing to say, "Let's not go there, because it makes us both uncomfortable," you feel a little safer with her than you might with someone else. Everyone has so many dramas going on, and if you're not careful, you can get dragged into them.

Although I was 14 years older than Julie was, I was drawn to her. It's a cliché, but in certain ways, she did seem like an old soul. She was so young, but she made no excuses for her bad choices, and so many of the women there did. One drug dealer swore that someone had lent her the shoes she'd been caught wearing at the border, which had heroin in the heels. The excuses could get pretty far fetched, but Julie was very open about the fact that she was guilty of trafficking heroin. The ironic thing was that she and her boyfriend decided to do one more run because they needed to raise money to get into rehab! She believed that everything happens for a reason and there was something she was meant to learn in GEO. That resonated for me and I started spending more time with her.

Julie seemed to be a fellow traveler on my spiritual journey. She liked to read and checked out many of the books I recommended, then we'd sit on my bunk and talk about the ideas. She was the first person to teach me about chakras, the seven energy centers located along the spine that, when not spinning freely and clogged up with energetic toxins, affect our moods and thoughts and can even make us sick.

Julie also knew about something else that was foreign to me: unusual sexual positions and acts. She'd actually engaged in them—it was just her adventurous nature. I felt like a preteen with a big senior high school girl, blushing at how openly Julie would talk about her sexual exploits and why she liked this or that. It was embarrassing, but then I have to admit, I started to take copious notes and making a list, thinking, "I'll have to try that one out on Sergio when I get home!" The time passed more quickly when we could laugh and talk about anything but our legal cases.

One day, Julie and I decided to become meditation partners. The only time it was quiet enough to meditate was during "count." Count happened five times a day: 11:00 a.m., 4:00 p.m., 11:00 p.m., and when we were asleep at 2:00 a.m., and 4:00 a.m. We decided to take advantage of the 11:00 a.m. and 4:00 p.m. count times to meditate. The COs demanded silence as they went through the tanks, mentally counting the "bodies," as they referred to us. For about a half hour, the only sound was the squeaking of their shoes on the cement floor, toilets flushing and the echoes reverberating against the cement walls and metal doors, and the rustling of sheets as women shifted on their bunks, reading or playing cards and waiting for the count to be finished. It was such a relief for my ears to actually hear a bit of silence.

Although we were meditating in cells next to each other, Julie and I would meet afterward and compare notes. One of the meditations we tried was Julie's idea: She taught me how to cleanse my chakras by focusing my attention on each one, from root to crown, and envisioning it spinning freely and sending any dark, heavy energy outward and away from me. Even though it felt like more of mental exercise when I first began doing it, over time, as I sat, I would begin to feel the seven energy centers opening, like a rusty faucet turning that hadn't been used in years. When I reported my breakthrough, Julie got excited as she explained that that I truly was cleansing them and opening them up to receive positive energy.

We also tried a meditation in which we started with the intention of accessing the Akashic records, the place in the energy field we all share that stores all the information about our individual and shared past, present, and future. I wanted to know what that was about, so I relaxed my body fully and set the intention by asking to be shown this energy field. I felt myself float through space and enter a band of golden light that had all sorts of symbols floating around. As I entered this band of light, it felt like a wild roller coaster ride speeding along; I experience the same thrill and sense of movement. Then, the sensation stopped and I felt peaceful. It seemed something was being downloaded into me but I didn't know what. It was a wild experience.

Being able to astral travel like this took time to master, but it was an incredible skill to have when my physical body was stuck in a jail cell. I didn't have a sense of what information was being brought into my energy field and mind, but I trusted, and felt, that it was beneficial and positive and would help me through this ordeal.

Meanwhile, there were emotions and thoughts I had to deal with in order to make it through the many hours when I wasn't meditating. Although I began *A Course in Miracles* mainly to work on forgiving Leo—and myself, for trusting him—I was finding it was helping me to stop being so judgmental. Drug users, I could sympathize with—drugs were so prevalent in their neighborhoods that the taboos I'd grown up with weren't in place to keep them from experimenting. As a young woman, just watching my own brother become caught up in drugs as a result of "innocent" pot smoking, which was really common in the suburbs back then, turned me off from drug use. I understood that if I'd grown up around people shooting up heroin I probably wouldn't think of it as shocking. At the time, my judgmentalism was reserved for women who dealt drugs and who, I felt, were responsible for getting other people hooked, bringing guns and violence into their neighborhoods, and so on.

I really didn't consider that an addict was likely to end up dealing drugs to support her insatiable and expensive habit. It also didn't occur to me that there might be seemingly sound economic reasons for people to sell drugs. One woman I met had been laid off from a bank and was a savvy businesswoman, who saw that dealing, if done properly, could support her and several family members. Until she got to GEO, she had never met anyone whose life was turned upside down by using drugs. It was a huge revelation for her, even if it seemed obvious to me that drug dealing is incredibly destructive. After all, my brother's life was cut short because of his involvement with drugs, and that had made quite an impression on me. Plus, I always felt I had career options. Even after I left Leo, I knew I'd be able to take care of my girls somehow. If I, like this woman, had looked around me and seen only limited choices, and people dependent on me, what would I have done?

The daily exercises I was doing as part of *A Course in Miracles* made me realize that I was judging the drug dealers too harshly, though. I was avoiding them because they scared me when many of them had simply made poor choices, often involving a lover or spouse that landed them in trouble. But really, couldn't someone describe *my* life that way? Who was I to think I was better than they were? Then again, I will say that whenever a mother got bounced back to GEO for making the same mistake again, it angered me. When I thought about how painful it must be for their children to have their mother in jail, when she knew better than to smuggle drugs to make some extra money, it was very hard not to think, "How stupid and selfish!" After all, they had a chance to get out and be with their children, and they blew it by making the same mistake—while I had no idea when I'd see my daughters again. It was definitely a struggle not to judge them.

When Lisa, a new inmate, sat down next to me at lunch, I asked her what her name was, who her cellmates were, and, as always, "What are you in for?" She told me, "Crossing over with coke." That's all I needed to hear. But then Julie began befriending Lisa, and filled me in on the details Lisa had neglected to mention that first day. She had gone to a foot doctor in Mexico because it was less expensive there and, while she was at her appointment, her husband was on his own, apparently filling their car with drugs. When he picked her up after her appointment, Lisa said it was her turn to drive. At the border, they were arbitrarily sent to the secondary station where more thorough checks are done. Her husband got very nervous and said, "No matter what happens, I love you." The words didn't make sense to her until the border guards had them arrested and she learned about the cocaine. As it turns out, her husband was simply trying to make some money for their family and it backfired and put both of them in jail. Since Lisa was driving, she was the main person charged in the case. With both parents in jail awaiting resolution, Lisa's children ended up staying with their grandparents.

That afternoon, as Julie told me Lisa's story, I felt ashamed of myself. I had a life partner who was sacrificing so much in order to take care of my vulnerable little girls, and supporting me in my decision to fight extradition, procuring the best possible lawyers and doing everything possible to keep my spirits up. Meanwhile, Lisa had no one to help her out. And she'd been duped. She'd forgiven her husband for making such a boneheaded mistake, or at least she'd accepted it.

I made a point of saying hello to Lisa later that day at dinner and got to know her a little better. With cheery red-framed glasses and many extra pounds on her petite frame that caused her to walk slowly, she didn't look very scary, and I soon realized she was a sweet and gentle young woman.

"Does the judge know that you had no clue what was in those boxes?" I asked.

"Yes, I told him. I think he believed me," she said, picking at the slimy apple pie they'd slopped onto her plastic tray.

"I don't get it," I said. "If he believed you, why would he accept your guilty plea?"

"Because I told him I had to get back to my babies."

"But you should fight this! You should hire a good lawyer—can you afford to pay someone?"

"I have a little money in the bank from my father's life insurance—he died just after Christmas."

Her story was just getting worse. To lose a parent, and then have your husband get you into such a terrible mess?

"The prosecutor pointed out to the judge that I had the money, and said that it had to be from drug dealing, because I only get paid minimum wage. I can't risk fighting this, even if I do use the money to pay a lawyer. What if I lose, or I get stuck here even longer?"

I grew quiet. Getting stuck in GEO was something I didn't want to think about. How long *would* I be here, fighting extradition, far from Alexa, Megan, and Sergio? If I gave in and took my chances in Mexico . . . No, that was out of the question. It was a fleeting thought. I just wanted quick resolution, like Lisa did. Her choice made sense to me, but her options were bad and worse. And mine? Fighting extradition seemed the only option.

A few days later, when Lisa expressed an interest in yoga, I encouraged her to join us on the roof. She asked me why I never ate dessert, and I explained that the food trays contained more calories than were healthy for women who are mostly sedentary. I told her I ordered diet plates, and had started to save hard-boiled eggs in the cool darkness under my bed so that I'd have something healthy to eat when the foods was inedible. She began to do the same, and began walking with me, too. Lisa was determined to lose weight. Maybe it was the one thing she felt she had any control over.

I stood in the corner of the day room by the bars and rested my knee on the stool from one of the tables. The old-fashioned pay phone was my lifeline to my family and everyone knew that as soon as count ended at 11:30 A.M., that phone was mine. I preferred the one in the corner because I could turn my back to the rest of the crowd that started to gather in anticipation for the lunch trays that would be coming shortly. My fingers pushed the last of the buttons needed to call in to my cousin's office in Connecticut. Her office manager, expecting my call, put me on hold, called Sergio, and patched us together using a conference function. The routine was familiar to him now, and in moments, Sergio was on the line, having waited in our office at our home for me to call at the usual time.

"Anything new from Mike?"

"No, nothing yet. What's wrong?" I could tell immediately from his tone that something was going on.

"I heard from the Mexican attorneys..."

"Good news, I hope?"

His voice lowered and he said in a comforting tone, "No, my sweet. They need more money. A lot of money."

I drew a deep breath. *Just one more obstacle to overcome. It'll be okay.*

"How much?"

"They say for the next payment, $140,000."

"WHAT?!"

I could hardly breathe. We'd scrambled to come up with the $20,000 retainer in April and since then all they'd produced were promises that all was going well.

"Are they *insane?*"

"I know, I know." His voice cracked. "It's impossible. I don't like to think that way, but. . . I asked them why the fee was so high and they said they had papers that could get your case dismissed, but they wouldn't release them until we sent them a check."

My mind raced. Where would we get that sort of money?

"They probably think we're rich because we're from Sweden. Sweden, Switzerland, same thing, right? Everyone has a secret bank account," said Sergio.

I was in complete shock. Our business was successful but the tax rate in Sweden is very high. For a very nice quality of life, we all make do with very little cash for extras. I couldn't imagine how we'd ever scrape together $140,000.

"What...what did you tell them?"

"I said there was no way, that we don't have that kind of money. They said we should borrow it and I said we don't know anyone with that much. Then the lawyer suggested I sell a kidney."

"Oh my God. Seriously? That's like a bad lawyer joke you'd hear in a bar. He didn't really say that!"

Sergio sighed. "I couldn't believe it either. I know. It's madness. But I don't know what we can do. We'll just have to... we'll have to think. Find more people who can help us. Figure out a new strategy." His voice strengthened. I knew he feared I was going to fall apart if he didn't access his own courage and stay positive. "We'll think of something, I promise."

We had no choice but to fire the Mexican legal firm and pray there was some other way to get the extradition case dropped.

Sergio didn't tell me until much, much later that he actually considered selling an organ and researched online what that would involve! He did tell me that he came up with names of people who might help us fight the extradition, perhaps by contacting Mexican officials, or getting some information out of the U.S. State Department that might shed some light on the next path to walk. He sent hundreds of emails, including one to a medium, metaphysical intuitive, and clinical psychologist named Dr. Carmen Harra. Sergio had read her book *Everyday Karma* and thought she might have some insights into our dilemma. Dr. Harra told him she saw me getting out of jail, not going to Mexico. She was quite adamant, and Sergio felt some relief hearing this, especially since another psychic had told him the same thing—but without the specific details Carmen offered, such as that I would get some papers before Christmas that would be key to my release. After these predictions, Sergio felt it was easier to have some faith that I would get out—and by the holiday.

Dr. Harra was so moved by my story that she made a call to a friend of hers, Angela, a well-known defense attorney with strong political connections, to see if she might have some ideas. Every little connection, every thread of hope, became a lifeline for Sergio and me.

There was worse news coming.

In September of 2006, I was suddenly called to court early one morning. I had no idea what it was about, but I was feeling optimistic. I had done my morning affirmations, and I was making good progress with *A Course in Miracles*, sending thoughts of love and forgiveness to everyone I saw while practicing the forgiveness exercises repeatedly. As the CO and I passed the cells full of men, making our way to the courtroom, I noticed there were no catcalls—not one. Was the difference me? It seemed I had stopped attracting a reflection of my discomfort. I felt my courage building.

When I got inside the courtroom, however, it was an unsettling scene like something out of Pink Floyd's *The Wall*. As many as twenty men in prison scrubs and handcuffs were brought up at a time, and then five at a time were lined up in front to the judge who said a few words, which many of the Latino prisoners appeared not to understand. Then all of them were sent back to the holding cells behind the lush chambers. It was like a sinister machine processing bodies. Suddenly, I wasn't feeling very confident.

When I got in front of the judge, I didn't have a chance to speak. Tersely, he told me that I now had a *second* extradition case against me and my lawyer would be contacting me.

Apparently, this is typical in federal cases. As the prosecutors build their case, they find more charges to file. Soon afterward, I was told by a bunkie who was very familiar with the justice system that when you're taken to court in the middle of the day, it's usually because they just want to tell you this bad news.

I was stunned and tried to understand the consequences of having two cases. Mike explained that the first case was being sent up to a higher court, and he was going to have to get more lawyers involved to try to consolidate the two cases and get them both dismissed.

More expenses. More complications. I tried to be brave but it was very hard.

My first hearing on the appeal to the district court was scheduled for October 2006, and Mike, and even more experienced inmates, told me the scheduled judge was a good one. Sergio flew to San Diego, accompanied by Angela, the lawyer who came to us through Dr. Harra, on October 19. Angela came to GEO, and I was allowed to meet with her in a room with a table and chairs instead of the glass wall and phones, but just after we began talking, Mike came in.

"Karin," he said.

He paused, as if measuring his words.

"The hearing had been postponed for a month.

My throat tightened as tears rushed to my eyes. I was absolutely stunned. When Sergio came to visit me a few hours later, we cried together as we talked on the heavy phone receivers and pressed our hands together, the glass wall between them. It was a huge disappointment that we didn't understand. Sergio stayed for a few days; he promised me he would come back in November for the rescheduled hearing to give me moral support.

He did, but once again, the day before the November hearing was to be held, it was cancelled. The district judge had decided he didn't need to hear any verbal arguments and could make his decision from the paperwork. Would this be the pre-Christmas paperwork Dr. Harra had seen as sparing me from any more time spent in GEO? Would these documents get the extradition charges dismissed by the U.S.?

I wanted to be positive, but a huge wave of helplessness washed over us. "There's nothing to do but wait," said Mike.

Christmas was nearing. The girls wanted to know if I was coming home, and I thought maybe it was time Sergio tell them the truth.

"No," he said. "Absolutely not. They're too young. They'll think about their father, and how he was a bad man and went to jail."

"I know. You're right. It's just—I don't know what to say to them."

"You just say what you've been saying. We'll all be okay. But you and I have to be strong for them. I'm with them every day, and I can feel they're not ready for the truth."

"How did I get so lucky to find you?"

"How did I get so lucky to find *you?* And the girls? You know what we're doing tonight?"

"What?"

"Spa night. They're giving me a spa treatment. They're going to massage my scalp and wash my hair. What little I have. I'll smell so good. You'll want to kiss me."

I laughed aloud.

"You have to imagine it tonight, when you go to sleep. Inhale and imagine you're smelling their shampoo. Make it real."

"I will."

"You're coming home."

"I'm coming home."

But when? The question was a whisper in my mind, a whisper I could drown out.

"I'm coming home."

Bright green and red—the colors of Christmas came into my world, breaking up the monotonous grey. It's hard to explain just how deprived I was for color. Everything in my environment was grey, dirty white, black, or dull evergreen. When the COs announced we were having a holiday decoration contest in the tanks, all the women began saving candy wrappers and paper garbage to make crafts. You would think these women were elementary school art teachers on the outside—their ability to spin candy wrappers into festive chains was amazing. One made a little sleigh out of a red graham cracker box, and we took the thin white paper squares that came wrapped around toilet paper rolls and cut them into snowflakes just like back in kindergarten. Cutting was as little difficult because scissors were forbidden, but if you were careful, you could disassemble a disposable razor or a pencil sharpener from the commissary and use the sharp edge—at least, until a CO confiscated it. I made sure to slip the blade back into the tiny plastic pencil sharpener that I kept by my white legal pads and no one was the wiser. I fashioned a Rudolph the Red-Nosed Reindeer out of toilet paper rolls. It did cheer me up a bit, I have to say.

But as the holiday grew closer, it was much harder to stay positive. I usually didn't attend church services, but this particular Wednesday—that was GEO's "Sabbath" day, not Sunday—there was a visiting minister who was known for his great sermons and wonderful singing voice. I thought it might be nice to sing a Christmas carol or two in chapel. The minister reminded us that Jesus said if we have faith as small as a mustard seed, we will be able to enter the kingdom of heaven. Even the tiniest seed has the potential for growth.

I wanted my faith to grow from mustard seed to miracle.

A few days before Christmas, I became very depressed. Although I was talking to Sergio and the girls daily, as always, I felt forgotten by all these lawyers who were trying to help me. They were all thinking about their families, parties, and time off to relax and enjoy their children. I knew that the likelihood of me getting out before all the judges and lawyers took off for the holiday was miniscule. Sergio joked that we should convert to Judaism temporarily so we wouldn't mind so much my being in GEO on December 24 and 25. I wrote in my letter to Sergio on December 21, *Today is just another day. It's not being with the girls that's getting to me. I have kept my spirits and hopes up for so long now. It's hard work! Especially in this place. I don't want to start with another pity party for myself. But in order to mentally maintain, I have to accept the circumstances.*

Julie came to me last night when I was sad, so I ended up crying with her. I'm so grateful she's here!" It was a small blessing, but it was a blessing.

My diary for 2006 has no entry for December 25.

I planted my mustard seed and told myself this was the season of rebirth and renewal, when the dark days begin to give way to the light.

Today is the day I go home.

Chapter Eight

· ·

Ring in the New Uncertainty

I t was New Year's Day, 2007, and if I were at home, I would have celebrated by pressing my lips to Sergio's as the girls, too young to make it to midnight to watch the fireworks, slept soundly. But instead of ringing in the new year with noisemakers and kisses, I was ringing in a new uncertainty, stuck in purgatory trying to keep my spirits buoyant. I was determined not to sink into the darkness that threatened to engulf me. Having finished *A Course in Miracles*, I was still devoting my days to spiritual work and reading inspirational books. I decided to reread the Course as it was intended, taking a lesson each day for 365 days—hoping, of course, that I wouldn't get through all 365 days before being allowed to return home. I'd made my way through everything in the library that was worth reading and was happy and grateful that my book angel friend Margaret continued to bless me with books sent to brighten up my days.

"And their nutritional supplements are *very* high quality," said the grandmotherly woman seated on a metal stool at one of the day room tables. I had just hung up the phone and saw two young women listening politely as Marita made her Amway pitch. Like me, when she first came to GEO, she had been too scared to join in conversations or introduce herself. Now, three weeks later, the dazed and bewildered look in her eyes was gone. Marita had come to learn that the big dramas on the floor were limited to plot twists on the Spanish stories on TV, gossip, and petty arguments.

Several of those shouting matches were started by Chata, the middle-aged matriarch of the drug ring family whose only power here was to rule the remote control and scrub our white underwear clean using her stash of toothpaste. When she wasn't hustling laundress work, Chata was jabbing a chubby finger at another woman who dared to change the channel, or waving the air in front of her nose as she joked about having passed wind again. She was like a big kid who still thought fart jokes were hilarious, and who was used to getting her way and winning all her tiffs with her siblings.

But while I wasn't afraid of the other women anymore, and had gotten used to the routine at GEO, it still took a lot of work to not be in a constant state of high anxiety. Barked orders to move quickly and allow the COs to ransack our belongings or pat us down were far more frequent ever since the new warden had arrived back in October. He showed up a couple times a week to strut down the hall importantly, flanked by a couple of stiff-backed sergeants. Like a grey-haired bulldog in wire-rimmed glasses and a cheap suit, the warden would lift his chin as he surveyed his surroundings, as if sniffing out the potential for trouble. I figured he might be a former military officer because he ran the place like a military base, enforcing every little rule: No clothes left out to dry until after 5:00 p.m. Beds had to be kept tidy all day long unless you were napping at that moment, and then you could only have one blanket on top of you. There was an air conditioning vent by my bunk so I often put on a grey sweatshirt from the commissary to stay warm, but I had to remember to wear my green shirt over it to be in compliance with my uniform. Other women were used to walking around in a T-shirt and jail-issued pants, but they too were forced to wear their complete uniform at all times. It was such a tiny freedom to dress for comfort, but the warden took even that away from us. The COs loosened the rules a bit on weekends and in the evenings when he was gone, but morale was at a low ebb for all of us. It was especially demoralizing when the COs marched into all of our cells, removing the thin flimsy curtains we used to block ourselves from view when we used the toilets. To me, that was the last straw…I thought they were really trying to break us by taking away what little privacy we had. The tears streamed down my face, filled with frustration, anger, and self-pity. We were forced to use our black sheets to create makeshift walls. Luckily, we were able to acquire an extra for that purpose and no one objected. Word got around that they'd taken away the original ones because they were somewhat transparent. No one thought to tell us that or order black sheets for us. To them, it was a small miscommunication—nothing important. But the consequence of them not following through was that we felt humiliated and dehumanized.

Rumors often flew around the tank. Some said that back in the Texas jail, where the warden had worked before, he was pushed out after the powers that be realized he was encouraging COs to bet on which inmates could best each other in a fight. They said the COs instigated conflicts between the men and a couple even died when the fighting got completely out of hand. I have no idea if the stories were true, but his menacing manner made me very nervous from the moment he set foot on the floor.

Week after week, his quasi-military management style sucked more oxygen out of the air. All the COs, eager to please their new boss, had quickly gone stone-faced and stopped being friendly. Worse, he'd hired some new COs who carried out his orders to the very last detail—and he gave all of them the day shift to ensure they'd have plenty of time to terrorize and taunt us. They'd prowl around, stalking us, ready to pounce at any moment and announce a shakedown or room search. No matter what we did, they'd always find something to yell at us about. It was very hard not to be jumpy. I lived for my letters and phone calls and just tried to lay low and stay out of the way as much as I could.

I had taken to envisioning an energy field encasing and containing the warden. Whenever he'd walk through, I'd imagine him surrounded by white light, or inside of a mirrored ball so that his negativity would come right back to him instead of going out to others. Sometimes, I'd cover him with a gossamer drape to contain his heavy, harmful energy. There was probably something in his past that had turned him into a miniature tyrant, and it was powerful enough to dim our mood and raise our fears, so I did a lot of energy work on him. I prayed for him to experience healing and raise his vibration, and asked his angels to bring his vibration up. It gave me a sense of control to work on the situations like this one from another dimension. I didn't know if it would work or not, but I had nothing to lose and everything to gain by trying it out. Working with angels was my newest spiritual practice, and I was devouring Doreen Virtue's books. In fact, I had her newest one in my hands.

I looked up for a moment and Marita, catching my eye, smiled and winked at me, as if to remind me that the Amway opportunity was open to me, too, any time. I smiled back. Marita had tried to sell me on being a distributor. I told her it really wasn't something I was interested in, but we talked about how it made sense for a homemaker like her, kept out of good jobs by ageism, to sell products from Amway, Mary Kay, or Avon out of her home or car. Julie had sold Mary Kay cosmetics, even though she never wore makeup before. She told me she had mastered the art of applying eyeshadow in the hopes that she would inspire more sales. If only that business had taken off, maybe she wouldn't have been tempted to smuggle heroin again to pay for rehab.

I'd heard Marita's story and knew she worried about how she would be able to afford a car again to get around to customers. The beater she drove had been impounded when she was arrested. She said she'd bought it used for a good price down in Mexico, only to learn later that a large bag of marijuana had been stashed in it. The discovery was made by a police officer after Marita was stopped for a minor traffic infraction.

"It must've been there when I bought it. How am I supposed to know? The officer starts poking around and suddenly, he pulls out this huge bag of old, brown weeds! And I'm like, whaaaaa?" she said, her eyes wide. "Where'd that come from?"

"It was probably there when you bought the car," explained another woman in a knowing voice. "The dealers know they can get their stuff across the border that way. Everything's good, then one day, you come out to street and it's gone. Whoosh! All your money. They steal it to get the dope back and you're there trying to find change for the bus."

"You get your transmission fixed cheap down there, but the mechanics work with the drug dealers. They put in new parts and bags of Mexican gold!" said another woman. "You never know but then one day you're like, 'I know I parked it there!' Where'd it go? *Oye!*"

Some of the women laughed, but poor Marita looked dejected as she realized she had been set up. I believed her when she said she'd never been in trouble with the law before. We were both getting an education in the ways of criminality—and in how innocent people can become caught up in someone else's underhanded schemes.

Some of the women were defensive and in denial about what they had done that landed them here, but many were frank about their own role in their troubles. They admitted to their drug use and addiction, and to selling drugs to make ends meet. Ellen had told me how she faked a urine test when she was on probation, secretly piercing a foil covered vial she has hidden inside her vagina with another woman's urine who she knew was clean. The other woman's urine would go into the specimen cup while she peed into the toilet. She was busted when a random blood test revealed she'd been using meth again.

There was drug use in GEO, but I didn't see it. I heard they found ingenious ways to smuggle in contraband. When I wondered why they wouldn't let me have the girls' letters to me that they had decorated so carefully, Chata explained you can distill drugs into liquid form and paint them onto a card that can be licked—so we were only allowed to receive mail that had no paint, glue, or glitter. We had learned this the hard way early on when Alexa's and Megan's letters to me were whisked away by the mail room staff if they weren't on plain paper inside those Federal Express envelopes from Sweden.

Sometimes, Ellen said, someone on the outside would paint the drugs onto the upper right hand corner of envelopes where the stamp would cover the spot, so our letters arrived not just opened (from having been read) but with the stamps removed. The creativity that showed was remarkable, but I could see from talking to Ellen that addiction was no joke. Addicts had to find a way to get their fix. What I learned! Ellen, who had cycled back in on her second violation, loved to tease me about my naiveté.

If there was anything positive about jail, it was that it had already made me less judgmental. Many of these women's lives were much tougher than I had ever imagined possible. I had never thought about what it was like to be poor and desperate, or to have to pay for bad choices in men by sitting in a jail cell awaiting word of your fate. But here I was, in the same situation they were, having made bad, foolish choices. The inmates who were selling drugs knew they were doing something wrong before they were caught, but what other options did they have making enough money to pay for cars and fuel and repairs, their children's school uniforms, health care, day care—all the things I could have paid for easily when I was on the outside?

Now, as I sat in the day room watching Marita, I thought about what would happen when I got out. I would be free to come home and resume my career as if nothing had happened. But many of these women, like Ellen, were caught in a cycle of poverty, drug use or drug trafficking, jail, court, prison, and probation. What would happen to them? How would they break free of the cycle, and reinvent their lives? In the months I'd been here, I'd come to realize that a criminal record was a permanent scar, like the ones left on my legs after just a couple of weeks of using the jail-issued

116

single-blade razors before I started purchasing the double-bladed ones. I was coming to realize how much I had taken for granted before, and said a prayer of gratitude for Sergio, for my business—and for double-edged razors that don't cut up your legs!

As for my scars, the emotional ones were healing because of my reading and my spiritual practices. But how would these women overcome the scars of felony convictions? I had an emotionally supportive husband and a thriving business to return to when I came home. How would these women get back on their feet, having lost jobs when they were arrested and incarcerated for days or weeks?

The thought of their struggles suddenly weighed me down. I took a deep breath, closed my eyes, and said my affirmations silently. I envisioned a protective blue light around me, holding me safely like the shell of an egg. And then I played my movie in my mind again: My charges are dropped, I walk out of GEO with my beloved books, and I board a plane to return home to my family where I belonged. I sympathized with Marita and the rest of them, but taking on their troubles and being empathetic was more than I could handle right now. I had to create some emotional distance from the problems they talked about, cried about, and worried about day after day. After all, my own situation was fraught with uncertainty. Unlike prison, where you count the days until your release, jail is a temporary place to hold people. I could count the days to my next hearing, and refuse to think about whether it might be postponed or turn out badly, but I didn't have the security of knowing when this nightmare would end. I'd been here for nearly nine months already, long enough to give birth—but my "due date" for my freedom couldn't be predicted. I felt I had no choice but to convince myself that I'd actually walk out of GEO on my hearing day.

There was lots of murmuring all around after Marita told her story of how she got arrested, and she gratefully accepted one of the women's hugs. Marita was a big hugger herself. She had that warm, comforting grandma energy, and she'd make her rounds hugging several of us to say good night. The only touch I got these days was the feel of a CO patting me down or placing handcuffs on my hands, which wasn't exactly comforting. Julie joked about how a girl had to try to appreciate the COs copping a feel when they patted us down roughly and accidentally brushed against our breasts. We had to laugh about these things. If you let yourself feel the full brunt of your anger and powerlessness, it could really wear on you.

117

How I missed kissing Sergio, and—well, the rest of it! I couldn't talk to Sergio or write about sex. It felt incredibly strange to be married and celibate, to be sleeping in a cold cement cell on a hard metal bed and listening to the snoring of a woman in drab socks and prison greens instead of lying next to my husband!

Each time a judge pushed back the decision about my freedom, I was devastated. And it seemed to happen in three-month cycles. What was that about? I held in my tears as I talked to Sergio those days after receiving horrible letdowns. Later, I would sob as I showered or quietly weep as I lay in my bunk, my head under my blanket.

Meanwhile, the shakedowns, patdowns, verbal harassment, and small-minded cruelty continued and the tension increased for everyone. Prayer and meditation became more important than ever. The prayer circle that had been started by some women long before I had arrived could no longer meet. We were given some sort of flimsy reason why it was a threat to security to have women sit together in a group of ten or twenty to pray. It was such a clear violation of our rights, but there were so many violations—and so many women who simply put up with it because they would be out of there soon. The prayer group meetings got moved into one cell or another, but even it was impossible to get that many women into such a small space comfortably. The prayer circle broke into smaller groups and eventually fizzled out after more and more women who had been participating left.

The COs continued to terrorize us, and there was a new CO—I'll call her Rottweiler—who was bent on making us miserable. She took advantage of a spat between Lisa and Chata, who were bunkies, to amuse herself, arranging for Chata's daughters to attack Lisa in the holding area between the tanks that was out of view of the security cameras. It all started when Lisa came back from the laundry where she worked and noticed that the ink in her pens was gone. She had just bought some new pens, and was sure that Chata had drained them to use the ink for her paintings. Chata's daughters, who were involved in her family drug ring, were incarcerated with us at the time, and Rottweiler decided to "create the opportunity" for the daughters to beat up Lisa. The next thing I knew, Lisa didn't come back from her job at the laundry for several hours and no one knew where she was. When Lisa finally returned a few hours afterward, she didn't want to talk at first, but we made her tell us what had happened. She told me she'd gotten punched in the face and then fell to the ground, and that Chata and her daughter had proceeded to kick her, while Rottweiler "disappeared" from the area. Finally, Rottweiler came back and ended it, declaring Chata's daughters the winners.

"Are you okay?" I asked Lisa.

"Oh yeah. I'm good. But get this—my dad told me just before he died that if I ever needed him, I could call on him and he'd protect me, right?"

I remembered that back when I first met her, Lisa had told me that her father, a former Catholic priest, had recently died.

"So I called out to my dad when the sister punched me," she explained. "I felt it, hard. But as I fell to the ground, I felt a warm, white light surrounding me. I didn't even feel myself being kicked after that, and I'm sure they kicked me hard. The nurse and doctor up in Medical didn't believe me when I said it didn't hurt. Karin, look at me. I'm not even *bruised*. No wonder they thought I was lying!"

I stared at her. She was right—there wasn't a mark on her face or her harms, and she even showed me her back and legs to prove her point. I got goosebumps!

I couldn't help thinking about the contrast between her spiritual work that had protected her in such an astonishing way and the harshness of her life in GEO and on the outside. Did her suffering have meaning? We were obviously receiving spiritual protection, but that power would not release us from confinement. More than ever, I thought there must be a plan for my presence in GEO. I had to trust my angels and God.

As the weeks passed, I continued to do my own spiritual practices in my cell. So far, I had learned to clear my energy, repair my aura, put on protective light shields, and send love bombs at the warden and COs. I even called upon Archangel Michael, with his powerful presence and sword of intense blue light, to cut the cords that energetically connected me to others, and my ex in particular—so that I would be freed from all emotional and spiritual ties. All of them helped me get through this particularly dark time.

Lockdown was an omnipresent threat, and though I only went through three the whole time I was in GEO, they were terrifying. Marita even had heart palpitations the first time she went through one. The entire tank would get in trouble for somebody's infraction. Everyone would be locked in their cells after the COs had screamed at us to hurry and get back to our bunks.

The first time we had a lockdown, it started with a problem with the counting of the inmates. They had called an emergency count two hours earlier than usual, and the numbers were off. Of course, in theory, it was possible someone was missing, but they knew it was far more likely that they'd simply miscounted. They locked the bars to do the count again, as if we were suddenly going to wander off! In protest, we started making animal noises: meows, barks, ape sounds, donkey brays, cow moos. The zoo sounds grew louder and louder, spreading from our tank to the other tanks, and many of us began to laugh at how ridiculous this was. If they were going to make us feel like caged animals, we were going to enjoy our little rebellion. The COs became angry because they couldn't concentrate, so afterward, one of them returned to the floor with a sergeant and sneered, "Since you've been so loud and thought you were being so funny, you can all stay locked down until further notice."

She explained this meant no talking with friends in the day room, or going out into the hall, no watching television, and no taking showers until further notice. And most importantly to me—no phone calls! Although we all had a black sheet to hang up between the top bunks that shielded us from view when we used the toilet, we normally had privacy because the others would leave the cell so you could be alone to do what you had to do. For hours, we put off using the toilet to avoid embarrassment, hoping the lockdown would end.

They brought the meal cart into the cells instead of the day room, and handed out trays before locking the bars again. By the second lockdown, I knew the drill: We would put two of our boxes in the middle of the cell, one on top of the other, to serve as a table and sit on the lower bunks to eat instead of eating in the day room.

The actual lockdown didn't bother me as much as it did some of the others who were used to running around and visiting. But I was extremely distressed over losing the ability to get to the phone. I worried what my family would think had happened because I wasn't calling. I was used to spending a lot of time in my cell meditating, writing, studying—solitary things, so that part wouldn't have bothered me. It was being in such confined quarters with three other people without a break from it that was hard. And the lockdowns lasted for two or three days.

We had other lockdowns after a couple of women got into fistfights— one lasted an entire weekend. It could have been worse. We could tell from the sounds coming from the men's floor above us that they had a lockdown that lasted a month! Word went around that it was punishment for some inmates accidentally starting a fire when trying to heat up some water for soup. The water was always lukewarm, but the salty, sticky Ramen noodles couldn't have been worth a month's confinement in a cell—and of course, all the inmates were stuck in lockdown even though there were only a couple of culprits.

During a lockdown, we had to beg the COs to let us take quickie showers one at a time. It was a relief to get clean, but the showers were beyond disgusting. Black mildew grew all over the cement walls, which were in a constantly damp state. I was grateful for the plastic flip-flops we got so our bare feet didn't have to touch the floor. The very first shower I had in GEO, I took them off, not knowing I should keep them on for hygiene. Ellen told me I should to wear them in there or I'd end up with athlete's foot, warts, and who knows what. I believed her because over time, the sanitation got much worse, so the number of virus and bacteria on the floors and walls had to be astronomical.

I began to complain about the conditions and soon became very assertive. I took on a mission to be the "Comet bitch," demanding that we get Comet scrubbing powder to clean the showers. They finally relented and gave us some to use, but our allotted one can per week for the entire floor quickly ran out. As a "senior" inmate compared to most women, I appointed myself to the job of advocating for even more to be done, like the application of bleach and a coat of paint. Again and again, I went up against the COs about this until finally, the warden gave in and we got action. Really, how much is it to ask that you can get clean in a clean space?

Back in Sweden, Sergio continued to be my advocate. He told me he had sent letters to over 200 U.S. Senators and 450 Representatives, begging for them to intervene on my behalf. I didn't know he had also called several abuse hotlines to see if they could help recommend any good attorneys or offer any help. I clearly had been the victim of Leo's psychological and verbal abuse, so it seemed to him that anyone whose mission was to help women in abusive situations would help him somehow. To his shock, one of the women who answered a hotline phone told him, "If she's already been arrested by the U.S. Marshals, she must be guilty. She's probably conning you about what happened back in Mexico." Maybe to her, it seemed impossible that an educated woman could possibly be in an abusive relationship or could be so easily oppressed and manipulated by a man. When she warned Sergio, "You should stay away from her," he didn't explain that he was very far away from the woman he loved—and that he completely believed in me. He just stammered and tried the next phone number, but every time, he found the people running the hotlines expressed no sympathy for our situation or me.

As I did my forgiveness work alone in my cell, I continued to work on forgiving myself for having stayed with Leo for so long. I read about soul contracts in Neale Donald Walsh's books, and began to believe that Leo and I must have made one with each other when we were souls on the other side. A promise to help each other learn about forgiveness made sense: I *was* learning forgiveness and patience as a result of being in jail, and I wouldn't be here if it wasn't for what he did. Maybe my soul yearned to have the experience of being betrayed in order to learn to forgive. Maybe his soul had agreed to help me with that lesson, even though learning it would cause me pain. I was here for my soul's growth; that much I was sure about. I was in spiritual boot camp and I was not going to crack—or waste any time feeling sorry for myself.

I had read about doing a past life meditation in one of my spiritual books and tried it. What I saw was that Leo and I had shared a life together back in ancient Egypt, where I was a slave and he owned me and regularly beat me. I wasn't sure what to make of that, but years later, in a conversation with Carmen Harra, one of the intuitive counselors Sergio and I had consulted, she described to me a very similar scene to what I had seen. And I'd never told her anything about it! That definitely blew my mind. In fact, she told me I had shared many lifetimes with Leo and in each, I was the victim of his bullying and abuse. She told me my lesson in this life was to claim my own power—and that his was to recognize the damage he was doing to others and take responsibility for it.

I was willing to learn my lesson. I was working on it daily! When would the universe be satisfied? Being incarcerated in a jail, never knowing when I would get out or whether I would be sent to a Mexican jail and possibly prison, was definitely stretching my tolerance for uncertainty and forcing me to be patient. My hope for resolution was like a dream that slips back into the forgotten corners of the mind when you wake up. I knew I had to hold on to the feeling. The more I believed in a positive resolution and outcome, the more likely it was that the universe would respond accordingly, aligning with the emotion of peace I felt whenever I held hope in my heart.

From my books, I was learning all about the intuition and connecting with spirits and guides. I had begun a meditation practice, sitting to focus on my breathing whenever they did count. It was the only time the floor was truly quiet, with no one but the COs walking around and silently eyeballing us as we sat on our beds—and it took about a half hour, which was perfect for a meditation. I always pretended to be sleeping as it brought less attention to what I was really doing.

It felt *so* good not to be interrupted. I was proud that my mind was able to stay focused for longer and longer periods. When you're incarcerated, it's nearly impossible to maintain a train of thought for very long. You're constantly interrupted by a harsh reminder that you're subject to someone else's rules and authority. You can't even sleep without being jolted awakened by the shouting for someone to roll out.

In the beginning, I started to feel what I thought were shivers and wondered why I was getting goosebumps when I wasn't cold. I understood later that goosebumps are a way that my body receives waves of energy from the energy field we share with Spirit—and that I had opened up the energy channels to connect to a greater Source. The more I meditated, the more I felt the presence of love around me as I sat there focused on my breathing. The love was coming from my guardian angels and spirit guides. I believed, and believe today, that these souls were assigned to look out for me and remain with me however dark my circumstances. I trusted that they would be there, helping me and expressing love to me. I couldn't identify how many there were, or if they had names, or even what gender they were, but I believed in them. I could feel their presence when I was still, and more often, I could feel it even when I wasn't meditating.

Every morning, I did a meditation in which I surrounded myself with protective layers of light from my angels—a golden ray from Christ, rays of purple and royal blue from Archangel Michael (the protector—I worked with him *a lot!*), and a ray of emerald green from Archangel Raphael (the healer). As I meditated more, my intuition grew and I kept seeing signs that I was not alone, that I was being supported by forces unseen who were watching over me and the other women. I came to realize that I must be a part of a bigger plan, something beyond what I could see from my current perspective. Why else would I end up with a life partner who lived in Sweden but spoke Spanish fluently, and who would never leave his kids (or mine!) because he was such a family man? I just couldn't believe I was that lucky. It seemed like fate—or a soul contract—had brought him to me. And why would clients continue to contact us and hire us when Sergio wasn't putting any effort into marketing our business? Why did I have an inner circle of distant friends who gave the support and hope we needed? I couldn't think of a logical reason for any of this—and my gut told me it wasn't luck. I decided to remain open to messages from the universe about my purpose here in GEO. I had faith that the answer to the nagging question "Why?" would come to me someday.

Meditation is said to change your vibration and open you up to souls who are unattached to physical bodies, and vibrating at a higher frequency than most people's energy fields are vibrating. One day while sitting on my bed, I had an inner knowing and a feeling that my father, my brother, and my grandfather were sitting there with me, wordlessly giving me their support and protecting me. I'd learned from *Divine Guidance* that there are many forms of intuition, and not to get hung up on whether I heard words in my mind, or received visions, or felt sensations that made no sense to the rational mind. In my case, I simply felt the presence of my family's spirits and knew, without a doubt, who was with me and even exactly where they were sitting. I felt comforted, no longer so alone—and more determined to continue my meditation practice. And ever since the new warden had arrived, the meditation to raise my vibration felt even more necessary.

Sergio flew to New York in February to meet with Angela, the attorney handling the political angle. Together, they prepared a package about my situation that they would send to influential politicians with the hope that it would get attention somewhere. They received a handful of vague promises to look into my case—that is, my cases, plural, now that I had two pending. They even spoke to someone in Secretary of State Condoleezza Rice's office. Surely, someone would see the need to intervene on my behalf given that I had been sitting in jail so very long. Angela was telling us that presenting my dilemma to them couldn't hurt, which was true. Later, we would realize that people working in government are often very reluctant to intervene in legal cases. Maybe not knowing that was a good thing in a way. We needed to grasp hope wherever we could find it.

Sergio and I were both trying to keep each other's spirits up. Whenever one of us sensed the other was losing faith, we'd zero in on some sign, however small, that a judge would send me home soon. We expressed love and support to each other daily—but we also were judicious about what we told each other. It really wasn't until I got home that we learned that we'd each kept some secrets in order to protect the one we loved.

Before returning to Sweden from the east coast, Sergio was going to fly out to San Diego to visit me for a few days. His presence always strengthened me even though of course I couldn't kiss him, hug him, or even touch him through the glass that divided us. We would talk about the girls and what they were doing, and I even managed to laugh a couple of times at his stories. Each time I looked at photos of the girls, they looked so much older. My heart ached as I saw in their faces the clear evidence of time passing quickly even though the days were agonizingly slow for me.

As the days went by in GEO, had I let myself ponder the possibility that the girls were crying, or angry, or resentful, it would have taken me down a deep, dark hole. I just couldn't go there. Sergio knew it, and on some level, young as they were, Alexa and Megan did too. Instinctively, they knew to focus on and share all that was positive in their lives and not devote their attention to the fact that I was gone, that they had no way of truly knowing when I would return, and Sergio would have to fill in for me as much as he could.

They weren't the only ones keeping a secret. I didn't want to tell them about my run-in with an inmate named Vero. I was afraid to add to their worries. I would remain silent about the incident until that day when I was home again, safe in Sergio's arms.

Chapter Nine

· ·

Hoping and Coping

During the zoo-like lockdown, Vero, my new bunkie, had amused all of us with her monkey calls. For our first two weeks together, she and I got along very well. But our cell was very small, and fellow inmates attached to Vero like fuzz to Velcro, congregating in our cell and sitting on my bed despite my polite requests for them to respect my space. I'd had so much taken away from me that I treasured my privacy. In fact, I usually left the cell only to eat, walk, or go to recreation. Otherwise, I pretty much kept to myself and read my books while sitting on my bunk. Vero had a need to fill any silence with talk, and even though she mostly spoke in Spanish, it was hard to tune out the voices of Vero and her chatty companions, especially during the daily count, which was the only quiet time I had to meditate. Our other two bunkies didn't mind, because like most of the women, they spent a lot of time in the dayroom or other people's cells. But I minded—a lot.

No matter how often I asked Vero to not talk during the count, it was clear she didn't care about my feelings. Soon, Vero became very angry with me for pressuring her to take her long conversations elsewhere. She turned my other bunkies against me and complained about me to one of the COs. The CO confronted me, and seemed to think I felt entitled to special treatment and full of myself because I'd been in GEO for so long. She just couldn't appreciate my perspective. Vero told me I had to stop "policing" the tank as if I were a CO, and wouldn't listen to my reasoning.

One night just before Sergio came to see me in March of 2007, Vero got really angry at me and yelled about what a bitch I was. The other women were able to calm her down, but I was shaken up. I'd never been in a fight and I wanted to keep it that way. After midnight, I went to bed, but soon Vero returned with a new friend and sat on her bunk less than four feet away from me. Throughout the entire night, our cell was filled with the sounds of the two of them talking. They thought I had already fallen asleep and I could tell—from the few words of Spanish I'd picked up in my time at GEO as well as from their tone—that they were ridiculing me and talking about what they might do to me. It was deeply unnerving, and I didn't sleep at all. The next morning at breakfast, the CO I was friendly with could tell something was wrong. I was completely exhausted. I quietly confided to her what was happening with Vero and that I needed to move out of my cell ASAP.

"You can't just move, and I can't move you. Ya gotta go through the procedures. File a complaint and request to get moved."

"I did that yesterday," I said quietly through the bars in the dayroom, concerned that our voices would carry when everyone had returned to bed. I didn't want Vero, who was back in our cell, to hear. "But this is escalating too fast. They said they won't even look at the papers until Monday at the earliest. Isn't there *something* you can do to help me? I'm seriously worried about my safety!"

"Sorry, hon. I got no authority to do anything. Talk to the sergeant when they come by later on today then."

I returned to my cell, hoping that Vero had already gone back to sleep. But she *had* overheard the conversation and was livid.

"I'm this close to beating the fuck out of you! I can't believe you'd sit there and talk to a CO like I'm not even here!"

"You need to calm down. We have nothing to talk about," I said calmly although I was quaking inside. Vero stormed off to the dayroom with my other bunkies who were sticking by her.

I had no one on my side. Since I definitely feared for my safety and could not wait for the bureaucracy of GEO to move me, I went to Lisa's cell two "doors" down and woke her up. She was the only friendly face in the tank at the time, and since they'd done a big roll out that week, there were three empty bunks in her cell. I told her what was going on and asked if I could move in right away. Fortunately, she agreed.

I didn't want to get in trouble with the COs, but I was too scared of Vero to wait until I got official approval. I walked back to my cell, quickly gathered my mattress, put it on top of my storage box, and very quietly pushed it over to Lisa's cell two "doors" down. I began to set myself up there, thinking it felt very strange to move after being in the same bunk for almost a year.

When I was finished, I was so exhausted from lack of sleep that I crawled into my new bunk. Shortly afterward, I woke up and heard my former bunkies returning to my cell. I could tell they were pleasantly surprised that I was gone. They had won and were now rid of me! Much relieved, I soon dozed off. But a couple of hours later, the COs entered the tank for one of their cell searches—and wouldn't you know they wanted to search Lisa's cell?

"What are you doing here, Volo? You're in the wrong cell!" said the CO. She was one of the nicer ones, but I knew she wouldn't want to get in trouble—and that was very possible if I didn't follow the rules.

I drew myself up for courage. "I had to move because I was concerned for my safety."

"Well, move yourself back until you get it approved. You can't stay here."

"Sorry, but that's not going to happen. I am not leaving this cell. You can write me up. But I'm not moving back."

The CO got very nervous and clearly didn't know what to do. As she took me out into the hallway to talk to me, I could hear Vero laughing from the doorway of my old cell.

I looked at the CO and asked quietly, "Do you see that we have a problem here?"

"Yeah," she said. "I'm going to take note of all of it."

I waited with her by the elevators in the hallway until a sergeant came to talk to us. I didn't know any of the sergeants at this point because I'd never been in trouble. After I explained the situation, he said, "Well, you can't move, or we'll have to write you up."

"You can do what you want," I said evenly, "but I'm not moving out of the new room. Isn't safety your highest priority in your mission statement?" It hung on the wall of the library, so I remembered it well and decided it might help me here. "I refuse to move."

He said he needed to get Vero's side of the story. When he returned, he said, "Yes, we'll make the change. But if I hear one little peep out of either of you, you're both going into isolation for two weeks."

I said that was fine, and we wouldn't have any problems. I was officially moved into Lisa's room.

I knew that in GEO, fights were settled with fists, so if Vero was still angry, she might challenge me. I'd never seen anyone back down from a fight—and that seemed like a big risk considering how tough Vero was. It was almost like a badge of courage for a woman like her to have been in a fight. I would only offer to fight her if I felt it might somehow make me safer. Proving you're willing to fight seemed to calm down the other person, at least in some cases.

What was I thinking? Even if I thought I could come away unscathed from a tussle with Vero, I couldn't take the risk. I'd seen several fights while in GEO, and I was not up for the first fight of my life! I really hoped I could strategize and talk my way out of this conflict. Besides, if I did get into a fistfight with Vero, I'd lose my ability to make phone calls home and get sent into isolation for two weeks. And Sergio was flying in that afternoon to see me!

When I saw Sergio later, I mentioned the situation with Vero but downplayed it because I didn't want him to worry. I was so relieved to see him, to be able to look into his eyes, that I focused on the good in my life and thanked God and my angels that I was okay. We focused on the hope of our breakthrough, our vision that I was released, and that I would be coming home soon. In retrospect, scary as that incident was, I'm glad I kept my wits and protected Sergio from the frightening truth of what was really going on while de-escalating the situation. And thank heaven for Lisa and the understanding sergeant!

Over the next few weeks, Vero glared at me and murmured here and there, but I didn't hear any more threats. But because she was badmouthing me right and left, even inviting newbies into her cell to give them a cup of coffee and tell them how horrible I was, almost everyone in the tank turned against me. No one spoke to me or would have anything to do with me except Lisa, and even she was keeping her distance. I can't blame her. It's safer to avoid dramas and conflicting loyalties when you're in jail

One month later, Vero was still ignoring me. The tension between us had to end. Besides, enough time had passed to give peace a chance. I made an iced coffee mocha and split it into two cups, and then carried them to Vero's cell. I stood in her "doorway" and began the little speech I'd prepared.

"If we were Indians, this would be a peace pipe. But we're not Indians; we're in jail. And all I can offer you is an iced mocha as a peace offering."

Vero laughed. Progress!

"I don't want to have problems with anybody," I said. "Let's just put all this in the past and be civil to each other from this day forward. What do you say?"

"Yeah … Okay." I knew she wouldn't turn down an iced coffee.

We shared the ice coffee and she stopped trying to turn everyone against me from that point on. In time, she took me aside to tell me admired me for using "all that spiritual stuff" to handle the stress of being in GEO. "When I first got here, I into some dark stuff," she confided. "Curses, and thinking about how I could hurt people and all that. It was like some dark energy just came over me. And then I said, no! I hated feeling that way. So I imagined the dark energy going away like a cloud of smoke. Then I tried meditating, like you do. It helps."

"That's great!"

"You know, I could really learn from you. Everyone says you know so much about how not to go crazy in here."

"Yes, well, I picked up a lot from the books I've read. I donated some of them to the library. You should read some of them."

I wanted to be encouraging, but I didn't want to be friends with her. Not being enemies with Vero was enough for me. After "clearing the air", I was polite but let her friendly gestures float to the ground gently rather than picking up on them. I had a reputation as reserved, so she didn't push it—and that worked for me. It was easier to let my guard down with women who were there for a long time and shared a bunk, or shared stories of their vulnerability without drawing me into their dramas. I had enough drama going on with the roller coaster of hopes raised and dashed.

Spring was coming and the sky through the chain link fencing on the roof was so blue it looked as if it had been drawn with a crayon. The clouds accumulated in puffs and sweeps that in another lifetime, I would have taken the time to stare at as I lay on a beach or in our backyard with the girls.

If only I could occasionally see a sunset or sunrise or a star lit night! That was another thing I missed—those beautiful moments of heavenly artistry we so often take for granted.

With only forty minutes or so outdoors, I couldn't spend much time looking at the sky. After all, it was my one chance each day to do yoga, and many women continued to join me. One morning, just before I was about to join them to be taken down to the tank, I spotted a dying bee. I was temped to scoop it into my breast pocket and smuggle it downstairs. The poor little thing was clearly was too near death to fly again, but I could gently transport it to my cell and, for a little while at least, have this tiny creature share my space. Plus, I had some honey from the commissary—that might revitalize it. The little bee was the closest thing I could have to a pet. Insects, animals, plants, trees, and grass—all of it was now something I only could appreciate in two dimensions in photographs that appeared in my yoga magazines or books. At one point, there had been a little black fly that lived in our cell. I refused to kill it, as it was another living thing that was new to see. One of my bunkies told me the flies came from the sewer system, but I didn't care. I called it Charlie and said he could stay.

San Diego's nice weather seems to have no seasons, so I marked them by the holidays I missed—like Alexa's and my birthday. I couldn't let it demoralize me. Sergio and the girls sang to me when I called, which was sweet, but no one else wished me a happy birthday because it wasn't something I had mentioned to anyone. Birthdays were days to be with family and friends, so the women in jail didn't talk about them or celebrate them.

Sergio and I continued to cling to any sign of hope that there would be a break in my case—any sign, no matter how small, had the potential to keep us optimistic. We just had to believe there was something in the papers that would set me free.

It was the start of the Easter season and my eggs were all in one basket—under my bunk. The spot was cold enough to store hard-boiled eggs that came for breakfast once or twice a month if we were lucky. I could always collect more than my two eggs from all the ladies who didn't like them. The frequent searches ordered by the warden were sure to expose them, but I kept them anyway. I prayed to my angels to protect those eggs—and wouldn't you know that the guards somehow completely overlooked them? There were many moments like these when again and again, my little prayers were answered. I made decent egg salad sandwiches with the eggs, using mayonnaise bought from commissary and two slices of wheat bread from my diet tray. Those sandwiches filled my stomach when I couldn't eat a meal that was served, and it gave me a sense of power and comfort to know I had those eggs all to myself. They were my secret and my angels wrapped their wings around them as if to say, "You see? We protect your eggs like God protects the lilies of the field. We've got our wings wrapped around you too!" I imagined their soft, white, feathering wings around me each time I peeked at my eggs or took one out for a meal of my own making.

Soon, there was a new reason for me to be hopeful. Through a friend of a friend, Sergio had found me a Mexican attorney who was confident he could get both of my cases dismissed based on the premise that my human rights had been violated as result of how long I had been in jail and the lack of due process. Sergio put a great deal of faith in this fellow and in Mike. I had to as well. Otherwise, I would have gone crazy.

Almost immediately after the new Mexican attorney was hired in May, he told Sergio that he was getting the Mexican cases closed and all the paperwork would be in order so quickly that Sergio needed to prepare to fly to San Diego as soon as possible to pick me up! And then, we received the fantastic news that all the papers were being sent to us. Well, he did need one more official signature to set me free, but at least we had proof that Mexico was no longer going to claim me—and he promised that the signature would come shortly.

My heart soared on eagle's wings. I didn't worry about the details or what specific date I would be released on. I simply trusted in the larger plan for me, whatever it was. "As You will," I prayed.

In a moment of doubt, I remembered the psychic's prediction that I'd be out around Christmas time, but I decided she must have gotten the timing wrong by a year. What was important, I decided, is that she said there would be papers releasing me—surely it was these papers from Mexico! I was not going to be in a Mexican jail. I had to believe that. I just kept envisioning that wonderful moment when I would walk into Sergio's arms. Mike would file the papers and I'd hear that I was free to go home!

Sergio waited with reserved excitement to get the call that he should go pick me up. It came in early June. He bought a ticket, booked a hotel, and was back in San Diego within 48 hours. I wanted to look my best when he visited so I was going to buy some makeup at the commissary, but one of the women showed me how to make my own by grinding the tips of the colored pencils they sold and using that for blush and eye shadow. And if you added baby powder to ground up coffee crystals, she explained, you could make foundation powder. I sharpened a maroon pencil, separated out the wood shaving, used the end of the pencil to grind up the maroon wax, and added it to some petroleum jelly to make lipstick. It didn't give me a lot of color, but it was something. It would be the fifth time I had seen my husband in fifteen months.

We were floating with excitement and joy to be with each other again, even if we couldn't touch and I was locked up. Sergio spent his days walking around the city and his evenings coming to GEO to talk to me for our hour-long visits. On the second day, the Mexican attorney, who had reassured us that I really was getting out, stopped answering his phone. Sergio didn't tell me, but he felt panicked. What could have happened? He kept everything positive and didn't let on that he was completely out of touch with the man who supposedly had papers to free me. Finally, a few days later, Sergio learned from the man's wife that he'd been kidnapped! She was desperately trying to free him and asked Sergio if he could help out. We didn't have a lot of cash reserves, so Sergio took a cash advance from his credit card and sent the money via Western Union, praying this wasn't some sort of fraud, knowing that having this attorney follow through on his promise to get the extradition orders dismissed was the only chance we had. The next day he did talk to the attorney, who was now in the hospital because he'd been severely beaten up and was being released soon. He reassured Sergio over and over that everything would be fine, and apologized for being out of touch.

Sergio didn't tell me any of this, however. Thank goodness, because I would have been a total wreck. He was trying to be strong for me. Having so little power to fix our situation made it incredibly difficult for him, but he was determined to show up at GEO looking calm and confident for my sake.

Days passed as we waited for the promised signature on the papers. A week went by. Apparently, there were some "administrative issues," and it was going to take more time, or so the Mexican attorney said. Then, after almost two weeks—several days past when we thought we would be home—we realized Sergio really needed to go back and take care of the girls. His mother came from Spain to live with the three of them in the house near his own children's. I was grateful that she could help out until I got back. How long would it take? I couldn't let myself think about it. Even though Sergio had not said anything to the girls about me coming home, they too were filled with hope that Daddy would bring Mommy home and their hearts were crushed to not see me there.

We both cried when Sergio left, but continued to pray and envision that we would be back together again soon. Each day, I waited eagerly for my name to be called when the mail was passed out, and my daughters continued to follow Sergio's instructions to write to me about their days. The mail was always a boost for me. It was the biggest highlight each week besides the phone calls. My mother was a poor correspondent, but she would take snapshots of the girls regularly to send to me. And of course, Sergio's letters continued to give me strength. He used them to say all that he couldn't say to me on the phone. It was like stepping back in time to another era to have a relationship that wasn't just long distance but dependent on written correspondence delivered by snail mail.

Sergio's letters were romantic, funny, and full of information but also packed with encouragement. We knew they would be read by people who worked for GEO and were assigned to make sure that any letters going back and forth weren't communicating plans about illegal activities. Still, we confided in each other. Sergio, who had been raised Catholic, told me that he was praying every morning, using the prayers he'd learned as a child and rediscovering how they made him feel a sense of peace and hope. Because of our correspondence, we were getting to know each other even more as we wrote about our inner feelings and what was going on with the girls.

What he didn't share with me was that Alexa and he were clashing more often. She's slow to move, taking her time to get around to doing what you ask her to do. Of course, that can be a strength when reflection is called for, but when Sergio wanted her to follow his routine and tight schedule, there would be a conflict. It was hard for her to understand how important it was for him to delegate some task to her and rely on her to get it done without lots of prompting and supervision. He was on overload, and Alexa was having to grow up too soon, taking on responsibilities beyond her years. Both girls were.

And Alexa naturally had difficulty adjusting to this strange situation of Mom being away in America indefinitely, month after month, with no one ever explaining to her exactly what was going on. Even though she wasn't in a jail cell as I was, her freedom was constricted by not having a mother around to talk to when she felt like talking—to spend time with when she felt like just being near Mom and resting her head on my shoulder. This is a cost of jailing mothers that is rarely talked about: the price their children pay. They should have the freedom to be kids, to not have to worry so much about supporting the family's need to keep everything together. When I talked to other mothers, they showed pride in how their children were stepping up and doing more chores back home, taking care of younger siblings and applying themselves at school. I wondered sometimes how Alexa and Megan were holding up, but they and Sergio reassured me everything was going well.

The brave face each wore was meant to keep me from worrying about their relationship during the long days when I was away from them. It's horrible to think of the pressures on my girls at that time. It's very hard not to sink into guilt over what they went through that I was, in many ways, responsible—but I also know it would have been deeply upsetting for me to hear back then about Alexa's unhappiness and her spats with Sergio, the only father she ever knew. Her feelings were fleeting, because she and Sergio did love and trust each other, but week after week and month after month, she couldn't simply say, "Mom, I'm just so mad at him today." I couldn't be there for her. I couldn't be the loving, compassionate listener I wanted to be, the mother she and Megan deserved over those many months when I was in jail. I could only do my best within my circumstances.

Fortunately, my two little girls had each other. I found out later that very often after Sergio had said goodnight to them, Alexa would sneak into each Megan's room so they could lie together snuggling and give each other the comfort they needed, the comfort they weren't getting from me. Both of them showed a strong front to the outside world and only in the dark nights could they share the fear, sadness, and uncertainty that was deep within them.

I continued to have faith that something in the legal papers would set me free, and Mike sent an intern to go over papers with me to look for discrepancies, as any one might be the key to remanding my case to a lower court or throwing it out altogether, denying Mexico the right to seize me. We found all sorts of anomalies, and told Sergio that much as I wanted to tell my side of the story of what happened between me and Leo, I did think we could get the extradition orders dismissed on a technicality. In the meantime, I just had to keep hoping and coping.

The sense of violation is incredibly strong when you're in jail, and people respond to it differently. I understood Vero's threatening people, or trying to form cliques. Many women found God and began to pray for the first time—or started reading the Bible.

All of my spiritual practices helped me feel stronger. One of the books I was reading in 2007 really clicked for me because it talked about feeling as if you have no boundaries, and anyone can invade your space at any time. That was true for me literally! In Colette Baron-Reid's book *The Future*, she writes about how her psychic/medium abilities suddenly were awakened the night she was raped by three men, and how she wrestled with controlling her intuitive gifts as other people's emotional energy and pain came into her own energy field. Being forced to live as I had lived at GEO and being lost in a legal maze felt similar in so many ways to her experience!

My waiting game carried on through the spring, summer, and fall. Sergio's visit when my release seemed imminent, the discovery that the Mexican lawyer had falsified the papers—it was up and down, up and down. I couldn't help wondering why we were going through this roller coaster of hope and despair. My friend, Margaret, who is very intuitive, had told me that she sensed there was a higher purpose for my incarceration, but what could it possibly be? How was my being here, my heart torn open and slammed shut again and again, helpful to me or anyone else?

I thought about a teaching story I'd once heard. An old farmer had a very old mule that had fallen into an old dry well. He wasn't moving and he wasn't making any noise, so the farmer assumed the animal had died in the fall. The farmer called a few friends and they began shoveling dirt on top of the mule to bury him and fill in the dry well. After a tremendous amount of shoveling by the men, the tips of the mule's ears made an appearance at the top of the well. He wasn't dead after all! He had come out of his stupor and when the dirt hit his back, he just shook it off and stepped up on top of the pile. The men hadn't been aware of what was happening, so they kept shoveling, while the mule kept shaking off the dirt and stepping on top of it. Eventually, he made it to the top of the well and was able to step out onto the ground and walk away, leaving the men to slap each other on the back and laugh heartily.

That old mule's attitude was exactly the same attitude I needed to survive whatever jail life and the legal system threw at me. I learned to just shake it off and use it as a stepping stool to higher ground. Every time Sergio and got our hopes up that I would be released, it was as if we were the mule having piles and piles of dirt thrown on top of us. And like stubborn mules, we would have to climb to the top of the piles, shaking off the discouragement and disillusionment. We'd say to ourselves, "Okay, what positive thing can we look at?" There was always something, no matter how small, to hang our hopes on.

And frankly, my situation could be worse. I was reminded of that at times. I met a woman named Renee, who became my bunkie for almost nine months, and watched her take a big gamble in the getting back to her children as quickly as possible. Renee was in her early thirties and a single mom. She'd had her car worked on by a mechanic in Mexico—which by now I knew was mistake number one—and traveled across the border by bus with a neighbor who would help her drive it back. Both became victims of a dealer who secretly stashed drugs in the vehicle that were found when they got to a border checkpoint. Then again, maybe the neighbor, who had been driving, knew all along. . .

The neighbor wanted the case taken to trial, but that choice left Renee sitting in jail awaiting trial for a total of nine months. She had wanted to plead guilty so she could go home after just three or four months, but her lawyer told her that wasn't an option given her neighbor's plea of "not guilty." Renee didn't care about having a felony on her record. She didn't care that she would be pleading guilty even though she hadn't had any knowledge of the drugs. Her concern was getting home to take care of her kids, who were being taken care of by her ailing mom for the time being. I could understand that, and told her how scared I was about my own children when I was arrested. I wished she'd had a man like Sergio to step in and care for her little ones!

For months, Renee and I bunked together, and I taught her to do angel work, which she eagerly embraced. Finally, the day came for her to go to court. Her co-defendant ended up not being able to testify and Renee, who hadn't been prepared by her lawyer to get on the stand, had to go up there unprepared. As a result, they lost—and Renee was devastated. The drug charges carried an 18-month minimum mandatory sentence. If she had been allowed to sign a deal, she would have been home months beforehand. When she told me, her face was ashen. I felt sick to my stomach.

I tried to comfort her, and she vowed to continue working with Archangel Michael and Archangel Raphael. "There must be a reason for this," she told me, "And I have to trust in the angels and God."

"They'll be with you," I assured her.

"Yes, but they'll have to crouch down to fit in my new cell like they did here!"

The two of us smiled, remembering the time she said she actually saw the tall beings of light bending their knees, necks, shoulders, and wings to scrunch into our cell after we'd called upon them for healing and protection!

As the saying goes, better to laugh than to cry. I'd experienced firsthand that one of the most important spiritual techniques for coping is to create levity. Laughter raises your energy level very high and replenishes you. I always liked it when someone with a good sense of humor came through because humor helped so much. Back home, Sergio told me that he and his mother had taken to watching the Ellen DeGeneres show to get a break from the stress of all they had to deal with. Although Sergio's mother didn't speak English or Swedish, just Spanish, Ellen's facial expressions, funny little dances, and oddball and amusing phone conversations with the elderly lady named Gladys made them laugh out loud. Plus, the show had so much positive energy, with feel-good stories that even Sergio's mom could understand with just a bit of translation from her son.

At GEO, the humor was a bit cruder sometimes—because after all, all of us women were sharing close quarters. Bodily functions couldn't be hidden. Once, a woman who had depression was put on some new medications shortly after arrival and they made her just a bit too uninhibited. Several women were in the dayroom when the woman—let's call her Sandy— decided to take a shower. Over the sounds of the Spanish novella everyone had gathered to watch, they heard the water, and then, her singing—and then the singing started to turn into noises of a more intimate nature.

One of the women, Irma, just loved her television "stories," as the women called them. Disturbed by my bunkie's vocalizing, she left the dayroom and came to my bunk to ask me if I could do something.

I looked up from my book and said, "I'm not going to interrupt her in the middle of it!" I had no interest in being the den mother in this situation!

Later, when Sandy returned to our cell, she told me she'd had a *wonderful* shower session.

"So we heard," I said. "I think everyone knows what was going on."

Sandy wasn't embarrassed in the least. I was amused, and told her she might want to schedule her showers for a time when the dayroom wasn't packed with women obsessed with their Spanish stories. They had clearly been irritated, although Sandy didn't seem to care very much. I don't know what bothered them more: the intimacy of overhearing her, or the fact that she made it difficult to focus on their show!

Later, Sandy's attorney insisted that her medications be adjusted because she was experiencing a strong personality change as a result of them. They acquiesced. I found that in general, at GEO, they pushed medications on people. I couldn't help but wonder if this was a way to test medications on unwitting population. I refused to take anything other than my migraine pills.

One of the other funny stories came about when I was using a bit of BENGAY pain relieving cream that would give you a warm sensation when you had sore muscles. There was a small paper cup with the cream, retrieved from the medicine cart, sitting on the sink next to the toilet. I used the toilet as one of my bunkies, Lola, a frail Mexican woman who slept all the time because of her diabetes and high blood pressure, was sleeping in her bunk and thought to rub some of the cream on my sore back, thinking, "This might feel good." In doing so, I got a little on a piece of tissue I guess. I finished my business, stood up, and suddenly felt a deep warm tingling sensation burning in a place where I hadn't had *any* action since I'd been home. Apparently, some of the Bengay had transferred from my hand to the toilet paper, which had transferred elsewhere.

I started laughing as the warm, tingly feeling spread. "Oh, my goodness!" I cried, and I started to laugh with embarrassment as I grabbed the side of the sink. In fact, I started laughing so hard it woke up Lola. I just had to tell her what was going on—it was too funny. She thought it was hysterical, and started laughing too. I swear, the sensation lasted about 15 minutes! Then another bunkie, Cale, came in. I told her what was happening, still laughing and STILL enjoying the sensations, and said, "You two are *sworn* to secrecy! But it feels fabulous!"

"Well, I guess Ben's not gay anymore!" said Cale.

"He sure isn't!" I said.

Now I'm not advocating that anyone go out and buy a tube of BENGAY and apply it to their personal areas—I had only transferred a little bit onto myself via the toilet paper! So here's my disclaimer: I'm *not* going to be responsible if you hurt yourself with Ben. You've been warned: Ben can be potent!

So with humor, spiritual techniques done alone or shared with other women, and calls and letters that kept me connected to the girls and Sergio, I was managing to keep my spirits up to the point where I was coping reasonably well considering my roller coaster. A hearing would be set, the judge would decide he needed more information, and the roller coaster car would take off again. All I could do was wait while Sergio, Angela, and Mike did whatever they could to set me free.

The boredom could drive you crazy, and I did allow myself the treat of a couple of hours of TV a week—mostly musical shows like American Idol, So You Think You Can Dance, and Glee. Music helped lift my spirits, and we didn't have any music to listen to except what came from the TV. There were inevitably spats about TV watching—not just about the programs but about whether to tune in to Spanish- or English-language channels. I tried to stay out of the fray and keep myself occupied in other ways.

Some women got into cooking. For instance, they would make a larger cake out of several pieces placed together and served on a piece of cardboard that had been connected to a pad of writing paper. Others made arts and crafts by kneading the white bread until it had the consistency of soft dough, then adding ground up tips of colored pencils to make colored sculpting material. From that, they made religious figures, rosaries, flowers—all sorts of things. One woman showed me how she wove baskets from magazine pages. I became quite skilled at it and even figured out how to make eyeglass cases out of the woven paper. Another bunkie I had made white strings out of plastic garbage bags by pulling and twisting them into long strips. Then, with the plastic string, she could cover pens. She'd also make strings out of candy wrappers and use those to write names on the pens, weaving in the colored material that contrasted against the white plastic. She could make bracelets and rings with names on them too. Her husband, who was also incarcerated, managed to smuggle all sorts of beautiful rosaries, rings, necklaces, and bracelets to her whenever they saw each other at court. I was amazed how they were able to get away with it considering all the patdowns and strip searches. The creativity the inmates displayed was incredible.

As the second Christmas was approaching, the tank-decorating contest was on again. This time, we were given only limited materials to use—none of the candy wrappers and commissary trash we had used the previous year. With the red and green streamers, we were able to decorate the bars so they looked a bit like candy canes. And the creativity abounded again with colored construction paper. Although we weren't supposed to, we used the toilet paper wrappers again because they made such nice snowflakes. The colors brightened the drab environment, but once again, there was a collective feeling of deeper depression, as everyone wanted to be anywhere else at Christmas time.

I was crying more, even despite doing all of my meditations and angel work and talking to Sergio and the girls daily. A second Christmas in jail? I prayed silently but passionately. One day, my blanket pulled over my head as I lay in my bed, I sobbed quietly, praying, "God, please. I can't take it anymore! What kind of a mother isn't home for Christmas with her kids? Please help me with this! I can't handle it! Angels, can't you help me?"

Suddenly, all the desperation was lifted out of me and I felt peace flooding in. The shift in my energy was so dramatic I sat up and simply remained present with the feeling of having experienced the loving embrace of God and the angels. In that moment, I accepted that I would be in GEO for another Christmas. I spoke silently to God: "If I have to be here, I'm going to give it to you, God, and I'm going to study the life of Jesus. That will be my Christmas."

I had finished the entire yearlong *A Course in Miracles.* Now, I would tackle the Bible. I began with the New Testament to study the life of Jesus. Simultaneously, I read some supplementary books, including the gnostic gospels. I'd been raised Episcopalian but didn't have strong religious beliefs, so I was open minded about what others had written about Jesus—and about what was written in the gnostic gospels about reincarnation, meditation, and Jesus's relationship with Mary Magdalene.

Once again, Christmas day passed without an entry in my journal. It was easier to treat holidays as any other day rather than think about what they would be like on the outside. The only decent thing is that because of the high population of Mexicans in GEO, we got very tasty tamales each Christmas. They also gave out bags of commissary food as presents, which included chips, popcorn, candy, and cookies. It was a nice gesture...but I also noticed that all the bags had expired dates so I guess it was a way for the commissary to clear out the excess outdated stock instead of throwing it away.

Then, winter turned to spring, and I started assisting the GEO librarian. It meant missing yoga once a week, but I was bored and needed some stimulation. One day, the librarian received a bouquet of flowers and placed them in a vase. I saw them and, calculating that I couldn't be seen from the COs' office if I stood "just so," the librarian beckoned me to come and check them out. The colors alone—soft pink, sunny yellow, the bright green of the stems—were enough to dazzle me. But then I bent over the blossoms and drew in their scent. It was probably faint, knowing how cut flowers tend not to be pungent, but I remember that I'd missed the smell of flowers for so long that I felt transported to a lush garden. I closed my eyes and relished the incredible fragrance.

Consider the lilies of the field. I wasn't toiling. I wasn't spinning. I wasn't "arrayed in splendor"—just dressed in a drab, dark green uniform. But I knew God was here, watching me and counting the hairs on my head, as Jesus said. Sometimes, it didn't feel that way. On those days when I felt lost and forgotten, I forced myself to read, write letters, do yoga poses— anything to keep my mind off the feeling that I'd been abandoned. But now, in this moment, I was fully present as I took deep pleasure in that simple bouquet.

"Don't tell anyone," the CO working in the library whispered. I nodded. I knew better than to let anyone know of a CO's kindness. They needed to appear tough and professional, unmoved by the inmates or their stories. Even so, some of them couldn't help but reveal their human sides. The best birthday present I got while I was incarcerated was a real tea bag, slipped to me by a CO who knew I drank a cup of hot water with honey in the mornings—the only time we had hot water. I didn't drink coffee, so my ritual was to wrap my hands around my white plastic cup with warm honey water, close my eyes, and pretend it was tea. Finally having a tea bag to flavor it made for a wonderful treat. It was such a small gesture to sneak in a tea bag for me, but it meant so much when I had so little.

I had to be grateful for these little luxuries. I'd say a special prayer of gratitude if my meal tray had a piece of fresh fruit that was especially tasty. And of course, I said prayers of gratitude for the books that were sent to me by my book angel, Margaret. Once, I got to taste a piece of home-baked apple pie. To think that I used to eat an entire piece! I remember Thanksgivings in America when I was a kid—pumpkin pie *and* apple pie, one slice of each. Talk about indulgence!

But when it came to the COs taking pity on us and being unexpectedly compassionate and kind, I really didn't need treats or special privileges. A genuine smile, a joke that made me laugh—these small acts could make a day more bearable. I wondered if they had any idea how much of a difference just a brief moment of being treated like a person instead of "body" made for me?

One day, I found myself talking to a CO named Jones. She was stout and tough looking, with thick lenses in her plain plastic glasses. Jones was always yelling, as if she were still in the military. They had set up competitions for cleanest tank and best behavior and, having won, all the women in my tank were preparing to go to the first floor to enjoy our reward of a movie and popcorn. Jones was filling me in on the details. I mentioned that life in GEO had become less stressful than it had been in the past. She nodded, and neither of us spoke about the previous warden who had unnecessarily set the tone that had everyone on edge for many months. He was gone like a bad smell!

Somehow, our conversation turned to nicknames and, having known CO Jones for two years by this point, I ventured to let her in on a secret.

"You know, everyone has a nickname for you."

"Really?" She seemed please that she made a special impression on the inmates.

"Yeah. Two-Hole Jones."

She scrunched her face. "Whhaaaa? What does that mean?"

"Well, once, when you were doing a strip search of a newbie, she bent over and you said, 'That's not far enough. I need to see *two* holes!' She was so embarrassed! She told the rest of us, and someone decided your name should be Two-Hole Jones."

To her credit, Jones laughed heartily. "You're kidding me? I don't remember saying that! 'Two-Hole Jones.' That's a good one!"

Not everyone has a sense of humor about herself, and I was glad I hadn't misjudged her. But it just goes to show that what's no big deal to a CO with a life on the outside—an event that happens and is quickly forgotten by the end of the day—can be huge to a woman who goes to sleep at night looking out at metal bars.

Hoping and coping, laughing and praying—that's what got me through day after day.

Chapter Ten

• •

Dreams, Home, and Hope for Change

Some mornings, I would wake up and realize that I'd been dreaming of home. I tried to hold on to that feeling as long as I could before bringing myself back to my cell, the fluorescent lights, and the sound of my bunkies pulling on their prison greens. Had it really been two years since I'd slept in my own bed?

As the winter of 2008 turned to spring, our waiting game continued. Every time I called Mike to hear if there was any news, he said no, and told me yet again that there was nothing we could do but continue to wait. The longer it took, the more forgotten I felt. Did anyone even care? My daughters were growing up without me! For Mike, I was one of many cases so his days were hectic and there was always a new case to manage. For me, it was day-to-day survival as I hoped and prayed someone somewhere with some power would make a decision to release me.

In the meantime, here in this boot camp, my job was to become a soldier of the spirit. My enemies were fear, depression, and anger that would arrive whenever I thought, "Why can't they just let me go home?" I was determined to be the master of my mindset and emotions and use this opportunity to connect with Spirit and my own spirit through all the techniques I was learning about. Most people have the leisure to work through the exercises in books by inspirational authors at their own pace. If only! As soon as my eyes opened each morning, I set my intention to do my work and learn my lessons. If I had to be here even one day longer, then my sole purpose was to do soul work. I had to get through this one day at a time and not think about how many more days it would be before I could go home.

Back in Uppsala, Sergio's mother, who had been living with him and the girls for almost two years now, decided it was time to return to her own home in Spain. The winters in Sweden can be brutal, especially if you're used to a warm climate. Besides, my mother-in-law didn't speak the language of Sergio's adopted country. Her mother, Sergio's grandmother, had passed but Sergio's mom felt she could not leave our family in this time of need, especially since my own grandmother had just died. Then, when Sergio's mother's beloved Yorkshire terrier died, she realized she really felt too isolated, needed to get home to take care of matters, and decided it was time to return to the life she'd known back in Spain. Bless her for devoting two years of her life to helping out our family!

Sergio and I completely understood her feelings, and we were very grateful for the sacrifices she made. But I couldn't help thinking about how badly I, too, wanted to return to my normal life.

I had come to realize that there would be no magic hearing where I would be unshackled and freed. That's not how extradition cases work. Even so, every time they put me in handcuffs and shackles for a court appearance, I envisioned the judge dismissing my case. There was always something to encourage Sergio and me. We refused to give up hope no matter how often we received bad news! The case had been sent to a higher court and we were just playing the waiting game.

Alexa's and my birthday, Sergio and my wedding anniversary, and then Megan's birthday all passed. Time had a different quality in GEO, marked solely by the passage of holidays. The only joy on those days was my twenty minutes on my phone call back home, but at least I could dull the pain of the rest of the day by sleeping, meditating, praying, and mentally escaping through reading books. The contrast between where I wanted to be and where I was at that moment was too hard for me to handle, so I made a point of distracting myself on those days.

One of my tricks was creating an imaginary memory. I would write letters to Sergio, or to the girls, about adventures we might have, but I'd put everything in the past tense, as if we'd already experienced them and I was reminiscing. It was a technique I had learned from one of the many books I'd read. The pretending made these false memories feel real. I believed that by writing about these wonderful experiences that I might actually have someday, and experiencing them in my mind, it would signal to the universe that we were all ready to have them in real life. To this day, I believe in the Law of Attraction, which works in conjunction with Spirit's plan for us and our soul contracts.

Often, I would take time on a holiday or other day to imagine the sounds and sights in every detail. For Sergio's birthday present, I gave him a new memory... I wrote to him about our wonderful "trip" to the romantic Italian seaside town of Positano where we strolled the sidewalks breathing in the salty air—we'd never been there, but wouldn't it be lovely to go someday and have that very experience? Or I'd imagine my girls screaming as the roller coaster at the big amusement park raced down the first hill, and Sergio and I laughing as we stood there with the other parents watching them. When I writing descriptions of these sensory "memories," I truly felt I was changing my vibration and what I was attracting. And I felt that in reading them, Sergio, Alexa and Megan would raise their vibrations, too, and help us all to attract the situations I was describing in detail.

I was still calling Sergio and the girls almost daily, and in July 2008, I received a long letter from my sister, Sue. She wasn't much of a writer, so I especially treasured her words on paper. She wrote about our childhood, and how she wished we had been closer—and how she wanted to spend more time with me when I came home at last. I wrote back, happy that if one good thing could come out of my time in jail, it was that it somehow rekindled communication between Sue and me to bring us closer again. My time away during these years I was incarcerated had put a distance between us, as we were leading separate lives and didn't share the details of what we were experiencing.

By now, I was also talking to my mother once a week using money my mom sent to call her. Often, Sue would make a point of being there so she could talk to me, too.

"I've been tired a lot lately," Sue told me one day, but I wasn't prepared for her next words. "It's the cancer. It's back. The tests just confirmed it."

"Oh Sue. I'm so sorry."

"But I'll beat it. I did it once. I can do it again."

It was the very same cancer Sue had survived twenty-five years before, and that our aunt had beaten three times.

"You know, there's a lot you can do with nutrition and visualization and other things I've been reading about," I said.

147

"Oh, I know. But I have a great team of doctors here. I totally trust them. So don't worry about me."

I tried to be positive. She had to fight her battle in her way, but I was afraid that the stressors in her life had triggered and were contributing to the cancer. I made a commitment to pray for her and send her healing light through Archangel Raphael, the angel who intercedes when we have problems with our health. I would imagine an emerald green light surrounding and healing her body.

Sue began chemotherapy, and soon, my mother sent me some photos of a visit Sue had with the girls. They adored her, and I could see they were having fun goofing around with her. One was a photo of Alexa playfully modeling a wig Sue had bought to wear after chemo made her hair fall out. It was hard to smile at that—a reminder both of Sue's cancer and Alexa growing older, as she looked so tall compared to the last time I had seen her. There was no photograph of Sue—only later would I see she had gained a lot of weight from overeating, so much I hardly recognized her. I felt bad for her, because even though she would always be beautiful to me, I knew the obesity was a sign that she wasn't taking care of herself properly. I wanted her to be healthy and happy, and yet there was nothing I could do for her. And surely, the stress of having me in jail must have added to her own stress. It was hard to think about how much stress my situation was causing everyone in our family.

On September 16, 2008 the Ninth Circuit Court panel of judges remanded my case, which meant they were sending it to the lower court to look at again because of discrepancies in how it was filed. This was an excellent break, Mike explained to me when he came to see me in a private room at GEO set aside for meetings with defense lawyers.

"That's great," I said, trying to muster enthusiasm. I didn't quite understand why this was good news, so Mike told me about how remands work and why I should be glad the judges issued one. But Mike couldn't give me any idea of how long it would take for the case to come up again, offering new hope of it being dismissed with the pounding of a gavel.

Before leaving, Mike told me about his new son, who was already a year old.

"He sounds adorable," I said. "You know, you haven't been to see me in over eighteen months."

"Has it been that long? That doesn't seem possible." he asked.

"The last time I actually saw you was in March of 2007."

"Wow. I hadn't realized." He looked a little shocked, and maybe even guilty. I reassured him that I knew he was doing all he could. The truth was that in the long stretches between court dates, my case and situation naturally wasn't in the front of his mind. There simply wasn't anything more he could do. In the hope of swaying a judge's decision at some point, I had collected over thirty letters of recommendation from friends and family, all vouching for my character, as well as letters from Leo's ex wives explaining that they, like me, had been completely conned by his lies and abused by him. But I was still waiting to be allowed a chance to tell my side of the story to the court. Also, working in the library, I was able to research human rights. The more I learned, the more I realized that several of my rights were being violated. I wrote a letter to the UN commission about it, hoping that would help. Sergio and Angela continued to do what they could, too—but Mike had plenty of other clients and a wife and baby to focus on.

While Mike had always been sympathetic to my plight, I sensed that being a new dad, he understood for the first time—at a heart level—how hard it was for me to be away from my children for so long, with no certainty about when I would see them again.

Back in Sweden, Alexa and Megan wrote me letters about how much they loved reading the stories I'd written and sent to them: *Bringing Joy to Hope, Bringing Joy to Forgiveness, Bringing Joy to Appreciation*, and others. I'd written them in the most magical way: They seemed to come right from the creative well of the universe, into my brain and my hand as I wrote the words and used my set of twelve colored pencils to sketch out illustrations. Joy was an enlightened girl who taught all about spirituality and the power of raising your vibration to attract all that is nourishing to our souls. The first story had come to me about five months into this ordeal, and then another and another came. Sometimes, weeks or even months would go by and I'd think I had stopped channeling these children's books, but then another one would show up in my consciousness and flow forth from my pen. Through the Joy stories, my girls learned about love, hope, faith, forgiveness, the Law of Attraction, Law of Abundance, the Law of Giving, peace, prayer and meditation, affirmations, and visualizations. Sergio and I urged them to follow Joy's example and replace their fears with hope, joy, and other higher emotions.

"Have you written another story about Joy?" they would eagerly ask me again and again. The books became a lifeline for our family, helping weave stronger bonds of hope that connected us across an ocean and a continent. I loved being able to slip the text and sketches for a new Joy book into a mailing envelope.

Margaret continued to send me spiritual and inspirational books, and my cell became like a second library in GEO as I lent them out after reading them. In jail, people really need uplifting material that can help them be strong and reconnect with Spirit. In my time in GEO, I saw that many women who had never been religious began to open up to a relationship with God or a Higher Power once they were locked up—just as you might expect. I lent out books like *Conversations with God* by Neale Donald Walsch more than once, including to a delightfully upbeat woman named Denise who was an admitted high class escort, better known as a prostitute.

The day Denise came in, I visited her in her cell to bring her small bottles of shampoo, conditioner, and lotion I kept on hand for newbies. I remembered how terrified I was when I first got to GEO, and how comforting it was when Ellen reached out to me. Having some toiletries to hand out right away gave me a good excuse to say hello and offer some support to women who had just arrived. Denise, like me, was in the minority, being a white girl. Her face was covered with freckles, and she had a bit of an Irish look to her with her auburn shoulder-length hair and blue eyes. She was thin with long legs and quite proud of her silicone-endowed chest—clearly an asset in her line of work.

Denise, like so many at GEO, was facing drug trafficking charges. She told me she was under a lot of pressure to turn in people higher up in the drug ring, but she knew better than to risk betraying them. The prosecutor kept coming in with books of mug shots and point out men he thought might be involved to see if she could identify them. Denise would say, "Oh yeah, I know him!" He'd get excited, but then she'd disappoint him by explaining that she knew nothing about the man's drug use or criminal ties—just what sexual positions he liked or what kinky things he'd ask a prostitute to do. The attorney would get his hopes up again and again only to go through the same ritual with Denise. Apparently, she had quite a lengthy list of dubious clients and never forgot a face—or a sexual perversion!

"I have to start thinking about what's next," she told me one day. "I had endometriosis. Which is what got me into this mess. I couldn't do my usual work after my surgery for six weeks! I had to make money for the rent and this seemed like an easy option. Boy, was that a mistake!"

I laughed. Denise oozed sex appeal and made all the men at GEO nervous. For fun, she'd flirt with a sergeant or a member of the laundry staff, and they'd always end up dropping something or stuttering. One day, when she was called to the courthouse for a hearing, she flashed the men in the holding cells from across the hallway. I'm not sure how she managed to pull it off without the guards seeing her. Denise had life force! She just needed to channel that in a new direction.

"You know what you should do, Denise? Become like the Dear Abby of sexual advice. You could have a column and answer people's questions. Post it on the internet. No one knows as much about sex as you do. You could make money sharing all your secrets! And then someday, you can write a book."

"Yeah . . . I like that! Become a writer. My name on a book. Imagine that!"

"It can be your legacy."

She was quiet for a moment.

"I always thought I'd have kids. Just figured it would happen. But now . . . "

I felt for her. I'd always taken for granted I could have children, and as soon as I got off the birth control, boom, the little line on the stick turned blue. I couldn't imagine not having Alexa and Megan. Being their mother was central to my life. I had missed too many birthdays, too many vacations and tuck-ins at bedtime, and yet I would always have them and be their mom. I said a silent prayer of gratitude, and asked God to comfort Denise. Then, my eyes started to tear up, and I brushed away the sadness quickly, before it could overtake me.

Sitting in my cell, I took out of my growing collection of photos of the girls, frozen in a moment of time that had already passed. I went through the stack. One moment, then another, than another—all of them existing only in a snapshot now. While I was here, trying to remain in the present, hopeful about the future, the present was becoming the past. Moments, days, years. The time I had lost could never be recovered. And so I created memories and hoped they would transform from dreams to reality someday.

I closed my eyes and imagined Sergio, Alexa, Megan, and myself in a movie filled with moments of happiness, affection, and laughter. I made it

151

as real as possible. I knew when I opened my eyes, the pain of separation wouldn't be gone, but its edges would be dulled enough for me to make it through another day.

The sharp edges of pain were also softened by the books I was reading, and at this point, it was Brian Weiss's books on reincarnation and memoirs about near-death experiences that I was absorbed in. Death was on my mind also because Alexa's best friend's father, who was exactly my age, had died while I was in GEO. And Reje, a very good friend of the family I'd lived with many years ago after my split from Aaron, and a father figure to me, passed, as did Leo's father. I had never had a chance to meet Leo's dad. I only talked on the phone with him. And of course, I feared losing Sue to cancer, although I didn't allow myself to think about it. I couldn't.

The books reminded that we never really die; we only change form. I had no doubt that spirits survive the death of the body. The visit in my dream from my father those many years ago, and the experience of feeling him, my brother, and my grandfather near me in my jail cell during meditation one day had further cemented my faith in the afterlife. But I had lots of curiosity about our souls' travels from lifetime to lifetime. Why do our memories of past lives become deeply buried in our unconscious minds? I wondered what it would be like to actually remember them.

In meditation, I recovered a memory of being killed in World War II while running across a bridge. Was it real? When I was younger, I used to love spy and war stories, which was pretty odd reading for a teenage American girl! I grew up in the 1980s but in those years, I used to think it would have been nicer if I'd grown up in the 1940s. Could a past life explain my unusual interests back in my teens and twenties? Could my past lives with Leo have led me to the experiences in this life, as I'd been told? If so, I was going to resolve my karma with him for good.

But I felt I had done that! So why did I still have to be here? The question gnawed at me.

Then, Bernice arrived, and I started to think that maybe I truly was meant to be here to help others as part of my life's purpose.

Bernice was a young mother who had to leave her one-and-a-half-year-old daughter with her husband when she was placed in GEO, having been arrested for transporting drugs or "pollos" (illegal immigrants across the border). I can't remember what the charges were, because they were overshadowed by what happened to her while incarcerated. She was five

152

months pregnant when she was brought to the tank. All of us were especially kind and gentle with her. It was an unspoken rule that even the most cynical, callous CO followed: Be nice to pregnant women. Bernice's shy brown eyes were often hidden behind her long, wavy hair.

She had been at GEO for two months when she took a call in the dayroom and suddenly began to wail so piteously that the entire tank seemed to be filled with the sheer volume of her pain. Her cry came from a place deep inside her, a primal place.

It was her husband on the phone. Their baby had died.

A CO took Bernice up to the medical wing to sedate her, half carrying her, as the weight of Bernice's loss was so great she could barely walk. The sobs came in waves, the wails rolling and breaking as we all sat helplessly, numb with the shock of seeing her broken by the loss, or sitting there with tears streaming down our faces. Bernice had just experienced our worst fear. *What if something happens to my babies while I'm in here?*

"Lord Jesus, have mercy on Bernice and her baby. Jesus, welcome that little baby's soul into your loving arms," a woman began to pray. Heads bowed as the heartfelt words broke the silence left in the wake of Bernice's departure to the infirmary.

The whole day, a cloud of sadness lingered over the tank. When Bernice returned, she crawled into her bunk and cried and cried, refusing all food. That night, over the buzz of the dim fluorescent lights, we could hear her quiet sobs, which didn't cease even when we were called to breakfast the next morning.

Her bunkies gathered in the dayroom, trying to figure out what to do for their cellmate. One came to me and asked me to go to Bernice. They couldn't talk to her without crying themselves and were at a loss at how to give her comfort. Those who had cycled back and those who were new to GEO had come to know me as a nice person who was very spiritual who sometimes had the right wise, words to say to make things better.

And so I knocked on the bars of Bernice's cell and asked if I could sit with her for a while. And I began to talk. I asked her if she was religious and she said she was Catholic but didn't go to church much, or pray very often. I could sense she was trying to answer that horrible, unanswerable question—"Why, God? Why?"—by finding some failing on her part that could explain why losing her baby made sense.

"Can I share something with you that might help?" I asked.

153

She agreed, and I began to tell her about the Brian Weiss books I was reading, and why I'd wanted to learn more about death because of my own experiences. I told her about losing my dad when I was a kid, and about how he came to visit me in a dream so vivid I knew—I just *knew*—it was actually him telling me that he was sorry to have left me, that he was still with me and loved me.

With her permission, I read her a section of his book *Many Lives, Many Masters*, about when babies die, it's because it's a part of their plan. They come for a reason, even if their visit with us is very short. Their lives, Weiss wrote, have a purpose.

Bernice's English wasn't the best because she'd spent much of her life in Mexico, but it was good enough that she felt she could read and understand the book, and asked if she could borrow it.

Bernice's attorney tried to make arrangements for her to go to her baby's funeral—in shackles and handcuffs, accompanied by a guard. For some reason, the judge refused. Word of the decision spread through the tank. Were we pissed off! When a mother is separated from her child through death, is there any excuse for not letting her say good-bye and kiss her baby one last time?

"We have to do something," the women agreed. We decided collectively to do our own memorial service for Bernice's baby at the same time the service on the outside was to be held. One by one, every inmate filed in silently and began to kneel on the hard grey concrete floor alongside Bernice. Some ladies brought in their plastic covered pillows to kneel on. We all held hands, heads bowed, and prayed together. I'm sure some of the women had long since given up on God, and had yet to open their hearts to Spirit again, but we were determined to pray in solidarity with Bernice. The tears flowed, and the women closest to Bernice hugged her and rubbed her back as she rocked on her knees. We remained there together, sharing her pain, touching hands, hugging Bernice, murmuring words of comfort.

And all because a judge who didn't know Bernice from any other "body" that came before his bench didn't think it was worth the flight risk to allow this young mother to say good-bye to her baby.

At the end of November, the doctors at one of the best hospitals in Sweden did a radical stem cell procedure on my sister. It was a procedure so extreme it sounded alarming to me. My cousin Rhonda had heard of this because of her mother's battle with cancer, and was very upset. The chances of survival were only about 25 percent, she said, which frightened me even more. But Sue was strong and her spirits were high. During her week in the hospital, she wrote letters to everyone in the family, including me. It was the longest letter I had ever received from her, and I felt reconnected to her. I wrote her back a very long letter as well, saying I was heartened by the fact that once she regained her health, we would surely be closer than we ever had been.

Sue beat the odds and was told the latest tests hadn't found any cancer in her system. She would have to take care of herself because her immunity was low, but it seemed the worst danger was over. When I spoke to her, she told me about the Christmas parties she was going to, and promised that she and my mother would also spend some time with the girls and Sergio on Christmas. "I know it's not the same as being with their mom," she said, "but we'll do our best to make it fun and keep them from being sad about you."

I said prayers of gratitude, and thanked the angels for bringing Sue through this difficult time—and for allowing my girls to have so much love in their home this Christmas.

At GEO, we were told that Christmas decorations were now forbidden because they were a fire hazard—as if they hadn't been the year before, or the year before that! It seemed to me just another way to take away what little joy we had. We would miss having snowflakes made from toilet paper wrappers taped to the walls, and cell bars wrapped in red streamers for a candy cane effect. The recreational director cooked up the idea of creating a dollhouse contest between all the tanks, and the next thing we knew, there was a camaraderie between the women to see who could make it the most beautiful and intricate. Each tank was given a large cardboard box and a few supplies, like colored paper and cotton, to get us started. The rest was up to us. Some of the women added "wallpaper" fashioned from photographs on the pages of interior design magazines that someone had donated to us. Others fashioned tables, chairs, couches, beds, and other miniature furniture by wrapping toilet paper around empty cardboard boxes that had held sanitary napkins and using toothpaste as glue. Each day, the little house became more and more elaborate. I was impressed by the women's handiwork, but couldn't help feeling blue. Another Christmas that I would spend in GEO instead of at home.

About a week before Christmas, Sue had fainted in her apartment and ended up in the hospital. And few days later, Sergio told me, "She's not doing well. Her immune system isn't up for this after that transfusion. Your mom says she's in ICU and she's gone into a coma."

"Oh my God."

"The doctors won't say what her chances are. They just said we should prepare for the worst. But let's imagine the best. Let's visualize that. There's always hope."

There was a long moment of silence as I took in what he'd just said. *This can NOT be possible. No. No. No. No! Sue would NOT die! I hadn't seen her in over two years and nine months. It was Christmas. She was going to beat this. She did before. No. No. No.*

"Your mother thinks we should tell the girls. Have them come to the hospital to see her. Just in case. I said I'd talk to you and see what you think."

"No. Not like that."

"I know. I feel the same way. They're so young and this is such a magical time, and with you not here . . . Let's not say anything except she's in the hospital and they shouldn't worry. They should just pray for her to get well soon."

When I called Sergio on the twenty-third, I could tell immediately that something was wrong, because he could barely talk. I felt that the room had just turned cold.

"What is it? What happened?"

He paused and then, his voice broke as he said, "She passed. Sue passed."

My body began to shake as silent sobs came over me. The ladies in the dayroom saw me, what was happening and brought me tissues. Someone sat next to me and put her arm around me.

I took a breath and spoke into the phone.

"What happened?"

I could hear Sergio's voice strain to get the words out without crying.

"The doctors told your mom that Sue wasn't gong to make it, that she wasn't going to recover consciousness. Stintan and Hans"—my aunt and uncle—"were there, so at least she didn't have to go through this alone. And then they turned off the life support. And it's strange but the moment they did, your cousin Rhonda called. Your mom picked up the phone and told her that Sue was dying in that moment and she'd have to call her back."

I couldn't talk, but Sergio could hear my sniffles and just kept on telling me what had happened. Someone put more toilet paper in my hand as I clutched the phone, my legs shaking uncontrollably and tears streaming down my face silently.

"Rhonda was calling every day for news," Sergio said, "but what are the odds that she calls at that very moment?"

"Not a coincidence."

"No, not a coincidence."

We didn't even have to say it aloud to each other, but we both recognized that Spirit had arranged a moment of serendipity as a reminder that we're all connected energetically and there's a larger plan that Spirit orchestrates.

Together, we decided not to tell the girls. We didn't want to ruin Christmas for them. It was hard enough for them to be without me, and to think that their favorite aunt was sick and couldn't be with them either, without getting the terrible news that she had actually passed. Alexa and Megan would open presents the next day as we always had. I would talk to them before they went to bed—but not today, when there was no way I could hold back my tears. No, let them have some peace. Then, on Christmas day, when the celebrations were over, Sergio would break the news.

After I hung up, my bunkie Irma, who had been very kind to me when she'd learned my sister was sick, helped me get back to my bunk. There, I sat down and waited, and then the grief came up. I let it flow through me and out of me as I cried and cried—for my sister, for this horrible situation, for my girls losing their only aunt, for me being so far away and not being able to do anything, for my mom having to lose her second child and having me be in this situation. It all sucked!

Soon, the chaplain came to talk to me, taking me to a quiet place where no one could hear us. I was told I could get a tranquilizer from medical, which I declined, but then a migraine came on. I couldn't sleep all night. All I could feel was pain—in my head, in my heart, in every cell of my body. The hours ticked away as I lay there silently, unable to think about anything, cry about anything, or do anything but be aware of how much it hurt. At one point, the voices of women down the hall laughing and talking started to bother me more, and more, and more—until I finally yelled out, "Shut the FUCK UP! SHUT UP SHUT UP SHUT UP!" and collapsed into sobs that drowned out their voices.

The next day I was numb and dazed. I did a little yoga, which helped a bit. I was able to hold in my grief as I talked to the girls and asked them about their presents, and wished them and Sergio a Merry Christmas. That night, Christmas Eve, I asked to go to medical for a sleeping pill. I hoped it might knock me out, and after I took it, I laid there hoping for the relief of a dreamless sleep. I feel asleep only to be roused a couple of hours later from the laughing and talking two cells down.

I couldn't take it. I got up and marched down the hallway to confront the women.

"It's Christmas Eve! People are trying to sleep. My sister just died. I can't be with my daughters on Christmas Eve, goddamn it. All I want is to sleep. Is that so much to ask? What part of shut the fuck up do you people not understand?"

I marched off, leaving them silenced, and returned to my bunk where I laid awake, the pill having lost its potency. It seemed like forever until I finally slept and could escape this hell for a few hours.

For days, everyone avoided me, even the women who had comforted me when Sergio broke the news over the phone—everyone except my bunkies. Some of the younger women who were new to GEO and didn't know me decided I was trying to rule the tank. The gossip spread. On New Year's Eve, I was fed up with the tension and the whispers. I went up to every single woman in the tank and said, "Do you have a problem with me? Because if you do, I want to know about it so we can talk it through and deal with it."

Only three people said yes, and we did talk it through. They could see where I was coming from, and even expressed their condolences about my sister. I understood that they had just been trying to distract themselves from spending a holiday in jail, too. I apologized for yelling, and said, "It was really just that I had to sleep. You get it, right?"

The air was cleared in time to greet 2009 and the hope of change. Change, hope—those were the themes that fall of 2008, at least on the outside. On the inside, where I sat in my jail cell, "hope and change" wasn't about a new president. My hope for change was that I would go home and never, ever see this place again.

That night, everyone was having a party in the dayroom. I hadn't officially been invited. After all, most people had been trying to avoid me.

My bunkies felt bad about what I was going through and figured I didn't want to laugh and talk with anyone. But I made peanut butter fudge for everyone with ingredients from the commissary and brought it into the dayroom, smiled, and made the best of things. I think I may have laughed at some point.

Then, at midnight, the entire building seemed to rock from all the shouts of "Happy New Year!" the cheers, and the banging on the metal tables. Everyone around hugged me as if we were old friends celebrating together as we always had. Just a few hours before, so many of them had been gossiping about me, or glaring at me, but now—whoosh. Out with the old, in with the new.

Hope. Change.

Please, God, I prayed in my bunk. *Bring me home.*

Chapter Eleven

· ·

Volo, Roll Out!

S
hortly after New Year's Eve, Sue came to me in a vivid dream, just as
my father had those many years ago. The details of how Sue and I
encountered each other that night as I slept are lost to time, but even
as we spoke in that mysterious land of dreams, I knew I really was talking
with her spirit. I do remember that Sue looked healthy, as she had been
when I'd last seen her years before. She told me she was very happy on the
other side, and said that now she would be able to help me in my situation
more than she could when she was alive. She promised to watch out for
Alexa and Megan and be present with them, too. She also told me I would
receive a gift that would comfort me and be exactly what I needed, and that
she had a hand in bringing that gift to me.

When I opened my eyes the next morning, I lay in my bunk as still as
can be, reconnecting with that fantastic feeling of being with her. My entire
spirit felt lighter. I held on to that feeling for as long as I could before it
faded and the sounds of the tank invaded my consciousness.

"I love you, Sue," I said to her silently.

Our souls have a perfect, intricate plan for all of us—I truly believe that.
And if we open our eyes, we see the evidence everywhere. The next day, as
I pulled a book out of its sliced-open mailing envelope and read its title, it
struck me that although it had been returned to the sender and delayed in
its arrival, the timing was perfect. In fact, the timing was so perfect; I knew
this gift had arrived in my hands because of Sue.

The 15-Minute Miracle by Jacquelyn Aldana was my book angel Margaret's Christmas gift to me. Back in November, when it arrived at GEO, it had been returned to the author's small publishing house because apparently, someone at GEO figured it had come from an individual, not a publisher, and therefore might contain contraband. It was returned to the author, who resent it (thank goodness). Just as Sue had promised me the night before, and in perfect timing, I had received a gift that would give me comfort and direction.

The 15-Minute Miracle shows a formula for retraining your mind and attracting the life of your dreams. I was up for anything at this point. I had been wondering whether there was an energy block holding me here in jail. I couldn't imagine why I was still in GEO after all the healing work I had done. In these last few years, I had helped many women open their hearts and spirits to the unseen world of God and the loving universal consciousness. It made sense that I had to stay here for their sake—and perhaps for mine. Our paths were meant to cross.

Yet now, Bernice was gone and the tank was full of young, childless women that I didn't feel any emotional connection to—and they didn't seek me out to ask about my spiritual practices or engage me in conversation. So what purpose did my being here serve? I was certain that being on the outside, I could live according to my purpose better than I could in GEO. Apparently, the universe didn't agree with me. How frustrating!

In meditation, I continued to open up to any messages from Spirit that would help me to understand what more I had to do for my circumstances to shift and reflect my vibration, which I felt was high and in alignment with freedom. Looking at the book, I knew my next step was to work with its program while remaining open to more messages and trusting in the timing of the universe.

For weeks, I had felt very lonely and isolated. After hearing about my sister's death, inmates and COs had approached me to say they were sorry for my loss, which was kind of them. But what more could they say? To most of the women, I was basically a stranger. To the COs, I was supposed to be just another "body" in a cell, so it was heartening when they did show some sympathy.

Despite all my forgiveness and healing work, I couldn't help being angry about losing Sue and remaining in jail. Why did she have to die of cancer while I was still here? It was so hard to accept that I wasn't able to say good-bye in person or see her one last time—it was so unfair! And my innocent daughters didn't deserve to be without their mother for so long. Damn it, I was pissed off! What more did I need to do to align with freedom and get out of this place at last?

One of the problems I had been struggling with was that it was easy to *think* positively, but hard to actually *feel* positive by this point. *The 15-Minute Miracle* offered tangible actions I could take to retrain my brain so I could create feelings of hope and joy. Frankly, I needed a new spiritual practice or technique to reignite my hope. I really didn't know how much longer I could take this situation.

In the back of the book, I found the author's phone number was listed and followed my intuitive urge to call her. The first two times I called, I heard a "hello," and then a recording that said, "This call is from an inmate at the Western Region Detention Facility." The person on the other end hung up immediately when she heard those words. Well, that was understandable! I thought for a moment about how to get around this problem. Then, I called my cousin Rhonda and asked her to place the call for me so I wouldn't have that intimidating message be my introduction to Jacqueline Aldana!

This time, she didn't hang up, and I told her that I was a huge fan of her book and how it was helping me. Then, I explained my situation and apologized for the scary recording on my earlier calls. Jacqueline agreed to work with me over the phone, coaching me in one-hour sessions. I knew that meant less phone time with Sergio and the girls for a little while, but it felt important.

I told her that Sergio would have to pay her by credit card, and she said she would send me some materials. We set up the first call for 7:00 a.m. California time a week later. I explained that early mornings would be the only chance to have privacy in the dayroom because few inmates were up and walking around the tank that early. She called me at our appointed time to begin our first session. She started by teaching me about the Emotional Freedom Technique, also known as EFT or tapping: To use the technique, you make statements about yourself while tapping on acupuncture points on your body to affect the flow of energy. That way, you can release any energy blocks that are causing your vibration to remain low and preventing you from healing and forgiving yourself and others. Jacqueline told me to use my fingertips to tap rapidly on my brow, the space under my nose, and so on, repeating the affirmation script that was suggested for me. *Even though I'm scared*—or whatever the difficult emotion is—*I deeply love and respect myself. Even though I'm really upset, I deeply love and respect myself.*

At first, I didn't have any emotional response to the words I was saying. The tapping didn't seem to be loosening up any fear, anger, or grief. I just noticed the sensation of tapping the acupuncture points on my head and chest, and under my arms. It felt very odd doing this process, but after the first few times, I noticed I was starting to feel lighter and a sense of ease, like some of the pressure being lifted off of my chest so I could breathe more deeply. If anyone had walked in on me, I'm sure they would've looked at me strangely and kept their distance! But I had already determined that even if someone saw me, I wouldn't let my ego get in the way and try to pull me back into my head and out of my body and emotions. I didn't care if anyone thought I was odd or gossiped about me. I had to do this.

Every phone session with Jacqueline was so powerful that I knew it had to be changing me energetically. And the work definitely helped me to focus on all that was good in my life instead. The one person in GEO I could talk to about this was the librarian. I told her it was an incredible book and technique, and she couldn't help noticing how quickly my mood and demeanor changed even though I had just spent the last couple of weeks mourning my sister. She even ordered ten copies of the book for the library, hoping it might have a powerful effect on other inmates who read it.

Then, I had a vivid dream about a powerful lion as well as a canary in a cage who finally became free. For me, the message was clear: I was where I was supposed to be. When I was released, I'd be able to "sing the song I was meant to sing," as it said in Jacquelyn Aldana's book. And I would have the courage to do this—that was the significance of the lion, I decided. I felt some comfort at last.

There was also another idea in *The 15-Minute Miracle* that strongly resonated for me. It explained that often, people want to help us, but they offer the help they think we need instead of the help we really need. I knew there was conflict between Sergio and my extended family, who was frustrated by my situation and wanted to help but were having a hard time accepting how Sergio and I were handling matters. In particular, they continued to believe the girls should be told the truth about what was happening to me. As I thought about how well meaning my relatives were, I realized that I had to stop being frustrated in return and have compassion for them. My girls were lucky they had so many people concerned about their welfare. Holding on to that thought was far more positive, and less stressful, than focusing on the conflict.

Weeks passed and then, at my hearing in March 2009, the marshals forgot to come and get me. I had been in GEO so long that I was off their radar. In fact, this was the third time they'd left me standing by the door, dressed and ready to be shackled and accompanied underground to the courtroom. I went back to sleep, did my yoga session, and called my attorney's office at 8am. After lunch, things were straightened out and I was taken to court in time for my hearing.

It was a hearing where Mike was finally allowed to argue my case, and he did very well. We were both cautiously optimistic. When I spoke to Sergio later that day, I said, "You know, I'm tired of saying, 'I'm waiting to hear news.'"

I told him that the emotional freedom technique was helping because at this point, I really needed to acknowledge how difficult it was to feel positive. Affirming what I was thinking and feeling and *then* shifting my thoughts and emotions felt right. After all, it had been three exhausting years and my situation continued to be uncertain. My spiritual techniques had helped immeasurably, but my hope had been flagging and EFT was reviving it.

By this time, Sergio and I realized we needed to sell our dream apartment in Sweden, even though the real estate market that was crashing and we were afraid that we would lose money. It was a hard decision for us, but according to our contract with the apartment board, I could only sublease the space for two years before the owner had to move back in. We didn't want to try to fight that. The sale of the apartment was yet another loss I couldn't do anything about.

I wrote to the new secretary of state, Hillary Clinton, to see if she could somehow help to get my case dismissed. All extradition cases go through her office, and I figured that as a mother, she might sympathize with my plight and decided that my human rights had been violated. My research into the UN's position on human rights—research I'd done while working in GEO's library—made its way into her letter as well as one I wrote to Michelle Obama, the new first lady. She had daughters around Alexa and

Megan's ages, so I thought she might feel moved by my story and take action to help me. I wasn't going to write off any possibility of any potential ally in my fight to achieve my freedom and go home to my family.

"Who's that? Your babies?" a woman asked me one day as I stood at the opening to my cell checking out some new photos my mother had sent me. Mail had arrived, and the mood in the tank was temporarily lifted, as it always was when we heard from our kids and the people we loved.

"My babies, indeed! I can't believe how tall they've gotten!"

I smiled just as another woman, a newcomer named Gaby, glanced over my shoulder to look at them. I knew Gaby only spoke a few words of English, but I invited her into the conversation.

"That's Alexa. She's ten. And Megan. She's nine."

"So close in age!" said the other woman. "That's nice. Hey, is that snow?" she said, leaning in. "I've never seen it for real!"

"Uh huh. We get a lot of it in Sweden, right up through the spring. The girls build snowmen in front of our house."

I glanced at Gaby and saw a strange look on her face. Abruptly and wordlessly, she walked away. I thought it was an odd reaction, but then thought nothing more about it.

A few weeks passed, and I noticed that when I was up extra early in the mornings, performing my spiritual techniques and rituals when everyone else was still asleep, Gaby was awake, too, and in the dayroom meditating, praying on rosary beads, or quietly chanting in Spanish. I walked by her one day and saw she was drawing an image of a pyramid, which seemed very unusual, so I struck up a conversation in broken English and Spanish (I'd picked up many words since arriving at GEO). She told me she was very intuitive and interested in spiritual topics. A few months earlier, she said, she had received a message from Spirit saying that she was going to go through a tough time and needed to be separated from her family. "And," she said, "I was suppose to meet someone from Sweden."

"Wow, really?"

"Yeah, so I'm thinking Sweden? Where would I meet someone from Sweden? And then you say 'I live in Sweden' and it was like—oh my God. Chills!"

We talked a little about premonitions and psychic predictions, and Sylvia Brown, whom we'd both seen on television recently giving her predictions for 2009. We also talked about how predictions don't always come true—and even if they do, they don't play out as you think they will. And sometimes, they're not specific, so you don't know what to watch out for. I said I had thought papers would get me out of GEO in November, but that November, and another, had passed.

Gaby told me her story: As a favor to a friend, she agreed to help a friend by driving a car to the U.S. from Mexico, where she lived. As she pulled it up to the border checkpoint, she suddenly realized that her life was going to change in a big way. Now, she had no idea how or why—unfortunately, she didn't know what I had learned about drug dealers stashing contraband in cars on the Mexican side. But, she explained, she knew that she was meant to experience whatever was about to happen. And when she saw my photographs and heard me say Sweden, she knew her premonition had come true.

Gaby and I spent hours together talking, and she taught me many rituals and ways of working with the spiritual world. She was able to do intuitive readings and brought in my family members. She explained that we have jobs on the other side after we pass, and Sue was working with cognitively disabled children, and my father was watching over people trying to get into the U.S. from Mexico on trains—a very dangerous thing to do, she said. I'd never heard of it, but I was intrigued by the idea that my father was involved in helping people come from Mexico to the U.S. given his connection to Mexico in my childhood.

Gaby said that our need to meet was probably part of the reason it was taking so long for my case to be dismissed. We were meant to influence each other. I felt she might be right, and asked if she had any sense of when I would be going home. She didn't think it would be very soon—she said it would take a little time and the papers were the key, and that I'd be completely exonerated when it was all over. She also told me that I wasn't going to have to go to Mexico.

What she said matched with the other intuitives Sergio and I had consulted with, so Gaby's reading felt reassuring. I learned a lot from her spiritually, and missed her greatly when she rolled out a few months later in July 2009.

I felt very alone without my spiritual buddy. The night before she was taken, she'd said she had a very important message for me: that I would be receiving a gift and a very strong female spirit had come to tell her to tell me that. She drew a picture as she was explaining things to me on a small piece of paper. I was so distracted by my sadness at losing her, and my happiness for her because she was getting out and going home to Mexico that I didn't think to keep her drawing of this woman or angel with a gift. She threw it in the trash as she was packing up her things to leave just a few hours later as another group was called to roll out at 3:00 in the morning.

About a month after Gaby left, a person from another cell came to me because she'd found a piece of paper in her bible that wasn't there before. When she showed it to me, I smiled. It was the drawing that Gaby had made the night before she left. How did it find its way into the bible this woman's bible two rooms away from where Gaby had been, without the woman knowing it? I knew it was a message for me, but what did it mean? At least it felt reassuring that something positive would be coming my way soon.

I was continuing to use the 15-Minute Miracle process and EFT in the hopes of removing any energetic blocks that were keeping me here. I was feeling more and more that just as I was meant to be in GEO to help Bernice after she lost her baby, I was here to connect with Gaby as well, and there was a larger plan involving both of us that had to play out. For some reason, I still had to be in GEO even though Gaby had left—that's the belief I held on to.

I had a new project to focus on and I was feeling more and more that it was a big part of why I still hadn't had my case dismissed. By this point, I'd written over two dozen Joy books and decided to self-publish them. I began to write up a business plan and Sergio started to check into how I could publish the books, and perhaps even make a doll based on Joy. Alexa and Megan sewed crude versions of what the Joy doll might look like and Sergio sent pictures of them to me with their usual letters. I spent hours perfecting the text for the website we would build, and sketching out the graphics. I put my heart and soul into getting the Joy Enterprises project ready to roll. I was having fun with it and had a renewed sense of faith that I would be released soon. There was no logical reason why I should have regained my optimism, but with the EFT and the other spiritual practices I was continuing to use, my positive attitude made a serious comeback.

Wrapped up in the excitement of planning the line of Joy books and adjunct products, I kept thinking, "This is what I'm supposed to do! This is why I'm here right now—to have no distractions and perfect this concept."

Sergio shared my excitement. He was already getting quotes on the packaging and other details. When we talked about the business plan's details, we temporarily forgot that I was in jail until the CO would come by and tell me why time was up. Sometimes, I even laughed at the contrast between me in my work mode and me sitting on my bunk in the cell, wearing prison greens. But Sergio and I were inspired—and the girls shared in our enthusiasm for Joy. This fictional little girl had the magical ability to keep my family feeling connected and sharing a positive experience when we were all struggling to hold on to hope. I also had received a clear message that I would be taking all I learned back to the business world—but I couldn't fathom how that would happen at that point.

In the summer of 2009, as I planned and analyzed and sketched and wrote, I realized that my deep, burning passion was to help people learn how to cope with life no matter what's going on and to live triumphantly. I had learned so much that I could teach others. I was prepared to walk out of GEO with an 80-page business plan and a product line ready to launch!

Gaby was back in Mexico, and Sergio was able to talk to her in October and again in mid-November. She said she'd been told by her guides on the other side that my case was cleared and we'd be receiving news anytime— actually, she said we'd hear by the end of November, but Sergio didn't tell me the details because he didn't want to disappoint me if Gaby was wrong.

Thanksgiving approached, and I very rarely left my cell because fears of the tank being devastated by the swine flu epidemic forced us into weeklong quarantine. We weren't allowed to get to the roof and enjoy the fresh air and sunshine, or go to the library or chapel. I did yoga in bed as best I could. Several of us pulled out our boxes from under our beds, and we pushed them out into the hallway to step on and off them for thirty or forty minutes to do step aerobics. It was boring but better than having no exercise at all.

I didn't ask for a flu vaccine, and Sergio and I decided that the girls they shouldn't get them either. They were the only ones in their classes that didn't, because the fear pandemonium spread all the way to Sweden, too. I don't believe in subscribing to mass fear about the flu. To me, the fear of getting sick is the real danger. Fear leads to inflammation and lower immunity. And I certainly wasn't going to start giving in to fear—about anything. I was doing all the things I could to boost my immunity: avoiding anyone who was sick, eating as healthfully as I could, exercising, and engaging in my spiritual practices to alleviate stress.

There was an infirmary that some of the women chose to go to when they became ill. It wasn't a very accommodating place, so I think some of them simply went for a change of scene. In all that time in GEO, the worst thing that happened to my health was that my migraines got worse starting in late 2007 and by 2009, a Tylenol and aspirin weren't helping much at all. I began getting at least one a week. One nurse in medical was a migraine sufferer and she took pity on me, letting me lie down in a totally dark room in the infirmary with blankets over me and an ice pack on my head. I would sleep there for a couple of hours until I felt better. Twice, she had to give me a shot to relieve the pain and nausea. I begged for my Excedrin Migraine, and she managed to talk the doctor into ordering it for me. She told me that my over-the-counter medicine was cheaper than the shots anyway. My guess is that cost savings, and not the doctor's concern for my comfort, is what led to my finally getting the medicine. I knew the headaches were stress related, but I was doing everything I could to relieve stress—or everything I was willing to do. I just wasn't going to have loud "shower sessions" like Sandy had done!

In all seriousness, I noticed that the inmates who had serious physical problems, such as heart disease or diabetes, seemed to get very good medical care. I have to credit the system where credit is due. At least two women who came through GEO had cancer, and they told me they would never have been able to afford treatment on the outside. In fact, they both got caught smuggling illegal aliens across the border, which they were doing to raise money to pay their doctors. Getting caught was actually a blessing for them in that sense.

When it came to the smaller stuff, however, the medical attention was minimal. I only had my teeth cleaned three times while I was there, once a year in keeping with their policy—at the second two times, it only took five minutes, tops! I knew once I got out, I'd have to get to a dentist as soon as possible. I saw many women with infections in their gums who were in severe pain but had to wait a long time to get any dental care. It seemed barbaric to me that GEO was okay with pulling teeth as treatment but not filling cavities. Was that really cheaper for them? How much were they saving, really?

Since they expected women to be in and out rather quickly, I suppose some bureaucrat thought it was unnecessary to offer anything other than emergency medical treatment. They certainly weren't thinking about someone like me, stuck in GEO for three years and eight months already with no clear end to my situation. Even so, I spent Thanksgiving trying to be grateful for all that I had instead of thinking about all that I had lost. It was hard, but I was determined to do it.

Around this time, Megan told me about a dream she had, where I was behind bars in black-and-white striped clothes. There was as pile of money behind me and a green, ugly sheet on the wall—and she heard loud, knocking noises. She didn't recall any more of the nightmare, but it scared her. I reassured her just as Sergio had when she'd awoken in the middle of the night. Afterward, I thought about how odd it was that she'd dreamed of me wearing a prison-like uniform.

There were other unusual dreams she and Alexa had, too. The dreams seemed to indicate they were in tune with what was happening to me— and that I might be coming home soon. In September 2009, Megan had dreamed that Sergio had written me a letter that said, 'my dear love, I'm so glad that we all can be together again. I can't wait for this next month to see you on October 19th. It will be a joy to my heart.' It was so detailed—she actually remembered seeing all those words written in his handwriting— that she truly believed it would come true. It didn't, but we couldn't shake the feeling that it was a message. Also that fall, Alexa dreamed I would come home on November 19th. Why, suddenly, were they both having dreams about me coming home—with dates popping up in the dreams?

Once Alexa heard about Megan's dream of me behind bars, she began having the same dream, and she ended up having it several times. She refused to believe I was actually in jail, however, and we told her it was just a dream. To this day, she swears she believed I was simply staying somewhere in the San Diego area, tied up with work, as we'd explained when I was first arrested and detained. But kids are naturally intuitive.

We all had such high hopes that something was going to happen in October or November, but I also felt I was running out of time. I really wondered if I had done the right thing in fighting the extradition. Had I overestimated the risk of agreeing to go to Mexico? Should I have taken the chance? My girls were growing up without me and another Christmas was just around the corner. I spent a lot of time meditating and I kept getting the same message—I would be going home. I refocused myself, dug deep inside my well of inner faith, and trusted that it was going to happen. I knew it would only happen if I believed in my miracle with all my heart.

On the morning of Tuesday December 1, 2009, the facility was having a lot of phone problems because they were installing a new system. Ms.

Jeffries, the counselor who helped inmates with personal issues, came by and said excitedly, "Karin, your husband called and said you have to call your attorney right away. You can do it when the phones are back online."

My stomach knotted. *Oh, God! Oh, God! Now what's going to happen?* I begged Ms. Jeffries to help me get to a phone. She knew that because of how long I'd been there, any news coming from attorneys was a big deal for me. She went out of her way to make arrangements for me to make a call from one of the visiting rooms where detainees can speak to their lawyers. I dialed Mike's number and held my breath in anticipation, but I only reached his secretary. I told her to please let him know about the phone problem at GEO and that I would do my best to keep calling until I got through to him otherwise, he could come to see me too.

I tried in vain to get a dial tone on the dayroom phone, and when I finally did, I dialed quickly, hoping Sergio would pick up and that the long-distance call wouldn't get cut off. Strangely, it seemed that the long distance service was working but not the local calls.

"What is it? I got your message. The phones are all screwed up, and I can't get a hold of Mike!"

"It's good! It's good! Listen to Mike's email—I'll pull it up. Here. 'It looks like Mexico is dropping the charges. Tell Karin to call right away.'"

"Oh my God! Dropping all the charges?"

"You heard it. He wouldn't send it if it weren't true."

"I don't want to get excited." Could I really stand another disappointment?

"I know. Let's just breathe. And stay positive. This could be it! We'll both keep trying him and each other."

After I hung up, I was a nervous wreck and couldn't talk to anyone. I was carrying a secret so big it felt as if the room might start spinning, but somehow, I managed to keep silent about what seemed to be the miracle I had been waiting for all these years.

Later, the counselor got me to a private room again and I got through to Mike.

"I've received an email from the prosecutor and Mexico *seems* to be dropping the charges. That's how I read it. I don't know any other details right now, but if this is true, I want to get you out on bond immediately. Can Sergio put up some money for the bond?"

"Absolutely. Whatever it is, he'll find the money."

"Call me on Friday and I'll give you an update. I really think this is it and I can get you out. But we have to be prepared after all that's gone on."

Those few days went slowly but inside in my gut and soul, I knew this was it. It was what we had been waiting for all along. I was sure I'd hear good news when I phoned Mike. Fortunately, the phone system was working again.

"The prosecutor has agreed you can get out on bond, and the hearing is Monday," he told me. "There aren't any official documents yet—just an email. But that's good enough for him, and there's no sense in your sitting incarcerated if the charges have been dropped, so he agreed you can get out."

I think I floated off my chair.

"You're going to court on Monday for a bond hearing. Now I've made arrangements with the Swedish consulate for you to stay there until we know more. You can call Sergio to let him know. Monday was the earliest court date I could get for you. But I'm going to try to get you out then."

Sergio had made arrangements for the $10,000 bond, which John Assaraf put up for me on the verbal promise that Sergio would wire him the money. The weekend went by slowly, but I was on cloud nine!

That Monday morning, the marshals forgot about me yet again. Although I initially felt a wave of panic—of all the days to not get picked up for court, did it have to be this one?! But then I thought, "You know, the angels must have planned this so I could do my morning rituals and center myself!" I was so elated, so sure I was mere hours away from freedom that I didn't even mind. How could I get upset over such a little thing when my miracle truly seemed to have arrived at last?

Sure enough, after lunch, I arrived in the courtroom in my usual garb—handcuffs and green uniform, the shackles and handcuffs removed before I stepped through the door and onto the plush carpet of the formal oak-paneled room, entering civilization for a brief few minutes. But this time, it was a very different experience from the usual three-minute-long ritual. The prosecutor handed Mike some legal documents Mike hadn't seen before, which the judge said were from Mexico. As Mike looked at the pages, the judge read aloud the words "all charges have been dropped."

My head was reeling. They talked about the bond having been posted and the plan for my staying at the consulate. The feeling of relief in my body was so great I could hardly focus on the conversation between Mike and the judge. Mike said that the government of Sweden had given their word that they would be responsible for me. The prosecutor was waiting to get the official documents through the right channels, and with the Christmas holidays approaching, he decided to let me out on bond and schedule a court date for January 15, 2010—five weeks away.

Five weeks?! My eyes were on Mike, but it was clear from the conversation that followed that as far as the judge was concerned, everyone else's need to be home with their families was more important than my need to be home with mine. After years of the justice system treating me as just another inmate whose feelings were irrelevant, why should I be surprised by that?

Hours later after returning from the court run that evening, I dashed to the phone. Sergio was waiting for my call in the wee hours of the morning in Sweden. We had mixed feelings. On one hand, we were ecstatic. On the other hand, it was sinking in that I was still shackled to the legal system for another Christmas season. Sergio said he'd talk to Mike about the possibility of him and the girls coming to San Diego, but by the early morning, I heard from Sergio that the two of them had decided that wasn't a good idea for various reasons. We would have to spend the holidays apart.

I felt myself getting upset, but what could I do? I thought bitterly, how long was my family going to be punished? Then, knowing that thought was not going to help me one bit, I brushed the resentment aside. After being away for so long, over so many holidays, I could take it and be patient.

When I finally told people in the tank that morning that I was going free on bail, and then home for good because we'd confirmed by email that Mexico had dropped the charges, everyone who knew me was in shock. The word spread like wildfire. I had been in GEO for so long that some COs were convinced I had set a record for incarceration there. The hours ticked away as I sat in my bunk reading, my two boxes of books packed up. That afternoon, I kept waiting to hear the words I'd been waiting 44 months to hear: "Volo! *Roll out!*"

Now, the way the story is supposed to go, I walked out of there just as I'd envisioned doing, but the judge had forgotten to sign the papers so I was told, "Sorry, but you'll have to stay here 'til he comes back in the morning and everything's in order."

AAARRRGGGHHH!!!!

I was on the phone first thing the next morning begging them to get the papers before the judge as soon as possible. I waited for hours, calling Sergio, the Swedish consulate, Mike, then Sergio again. Finally, when I got

Mike on the phone that afternoon, he told me that indeed, the missing signature was there.

"It's there?"

"It's there."

My stomach dropped like when you've just gone over the crest and start heading down the biggest decline on a roller coaster. My heart raced and I exhaled for the first time in nearly four years.

Usually, they announced over the loudspeakers to everyone that someone was going out, but around dinner time, a CO came up to me, handing me a large plastic trash bag, and said in her thick Russian accent, "I can't believe I'm going to tell you this, but here it is: Time to roll out!"

I put everything else I had besides the books into a big bag. Everyone hugged me and wished me luck. Several inmates said to me, "What are we going to do without you?" It was bittersweet for them, and I felt bad that they had to stay, but after saying good-bye to so many women who had rolled out, I let myself feel the joy of it being my turn at last.

Before I could leave, I had to follow some exit procedures, including a trip to the medical wing for a quick evaluation by the doctor. I was directed at last to a holding cell about three times the size of the cell I had been living in, and was told Mike was on his way. They brought me all the clothes I'd had on me when I entered the facility nearly four years before.

In front of the CO, I began to remove my GEO uniform so I could put on the clothes I had been arrested in 1352 days before. I almost put on my old panties but they had been stored so long, the CO said I could keep my ugly granny panties that the jail had issued me—at least until I could buy some new ones that weren't so institutional. As I slipped on my black velvet jeans, they felt delicious against my skin. My brown shirt and cashmere sweater were softer than I remembered. And my supple leather ankle boots—I'd forgotten how much I loved wearing them. Everything still fit! I was surprised because I had lost so much weight at the beginning, but apparently my healthy habits had brought me back to the weight I'd come in at.

I stood there for a moment, back in my old skin and in the clothes of the wife and mother I had been that March day in 2006 when I was swallowed into the belly of the beast, U.S. penal system. It felt wonderful to be dressed like a normal person again! Yet I couldn't help thinking about what a different person I was on the inside now. There was no mirror to look into, but I glanced down at my hands. My body was still the same, or mostly the same. And I was still Karin Volo, a person with two names—not just the "Volo" who was told to roll out.

So much had transpired since that long ago day, and I had grown so much, that I felt disoriented. Who was I now? How would I fuse my two lives together, the past and the present? Who would I be when I stepped out of that door? How would this experience live within me?

I was interrupted by a guard who came into the holding cell to hand me $100 in cash, which was the maximum allowed, and promised I'd receive the rest of the money left over in my jail account as a check in a couple of weeks. I opened my leather backpack purse and took out my wallet. When I opened it, I glanced at the photo on my driver's license. The Karin of the past was gone—no, not gone exactly. Just absorbed by a new me, the me who had survived my spiritual boot camp. I'd been here longer than I'd been in college! Had I really signed up for all these lessons?

There were all sorts of crazy little things I'd learned that simply made me realize that creativity can be a lifeline to joy. I thought about fashioning makeup from colored pencil tips, about making crafts from whatever you have on hand—and about opening yourself up to the creative flow that could lead you to write a book or even a series of books. I thought about hiding hard-boiled eggs under my bunk, and how I had learned the importance of gratitude and valuing the little luxuries in life. Learning to spit out my toothpaste into the toilet instead of the sink beside—which took forever to empty because of the pencil wide drain (yet another security measure I never understood)—maybe that was a lesson in taking control over your environment in small ways to make it more tolerable and functional.

I thought about the women I'd met, and what they'd told me about drug addiction and being set up when they were only doing a favor for a friend down in Mexico. They taught me that women can be incredibly resilient and strong, and even women who hadn't accomplished much according to how most people define success had amazing, inspiring stories about rising above their circumstances.

I thought about Bernice's wails when she learned her baby was gone, and the anger all of us shared when we heard she wouldn't be allowed to go to the memorial service. The power of women to support each other could be humbling and deeply inspiring. I had never truly realized that before. And even the power communication through the grapevine, hearing later that she'd had a healthy little girl while at another holding facility, feeling happy for her yet sad for her family knowing that her husband needed to take the newborn home without Bernice.

I thought about my angel work, and Gaby, Ellen, Julie—so many women who had shared a cell or a meditation session, who had laughed with me about the Bengay and Two Hole Jones's outrageous nickname. The grey prison walls were as cold and real as could be, but as I looked at them for the last time, I realized that they would fade in my memory as I embraced freedom again. The lessons I had learned were indelible, even if the moments, the conversations, and the faces of women I'd shared a tiny cell with for months would disappear along with the intensity of the anxiety and frustration that had plagued me again and again. I would remember what I needed to remember: that every moment is a moment we can spend in fear or in love, in waiting or in living.

I choose love and life.

"Your lawyer's here," said the guard at last. As she slid back the metal bars, I slipped my backpack over my shoulder. Then, I picked up a box of books, and walked toward her. A few steps later, I spotted Mike talking to some guards at the intake desk. His eye caught mine and we exchanged a look of amazement. He seemed tired, but he smiled and walked toward me to take my box as the CO handed me my second box of books.

A moment passed as we watched the intake CO hang up a phone and walk toward us with some papers.

"Okay, everything's in order. So follow me," said the guard as she came out into the hallway and began to walk us out the back door. Her keys jangled as she opened the back door and my eyes adjusted to the darkness of the evening.

"Good luck," she said.

The evening air felt fresh and danced with life as it skittered across my face, loosening tendrils that brushed against my skin. I closed my eyes momentarily and opened them again, as if this long awaited moment were a dream that would disappear in the blink of an eye, but it didn't.

Miracle.

We began to walk down the street to Mike's car, carrying the boxes. The sounds of the street seemed foreign to me after so many years on the inside. The metallic echoes were gone—no more buzzing of fluorescent lights. I looked up and saw the stars in the black sky—and realized I hadn't seen them in 44 months. I took a deep breath and filled my lungs with the gift of the cool evening breeze. There was a fluttering in my gut as I grinned ear to ear. Was I really here, outside, free?

I started to laugh. I couldn't help it! I had visualized this scene thousands of times and couldn't quite take in that I was actually experiencing it. I stopped for a moment at a corner and looked back at GEO, still chuckling. Silently, I thanked God for my freedom.

I glanced over at Mike, who was shaking his head in disbelief.

"I can't believe you're here!" he said. "I can't believe we're walking on the street!"

"I KNOW!!!" I screamed it in total jubilation. There was a man sitting at the bus stop across the street and I saw him flinch, startled by my shout. "Sorry!" I shouted merrily to him.

"I probably shouldn't tell you," Mike said, "but I almost didn't get you out. The judge only signed the order release for one of your cases, not both. But I reminded them of the bond and somehow, we made it happen. Honestly, Karin. I don't have a logical explanation for this. But you're here, outside GEO, and thank God for that!"

I looked at him and said, "Mike, I know *exactly* how this happened."

He looked at me quizzically.

"My prayers have finally been answered. This is the miracle I've been waiting for! This universe aligned with me in perfect timing. It doesn't matter exactly *how* it happened in this world. I mean, in the legal sense. The fact is it actually *did* happen. It was meant to, because I—all of us, everyone working together—" I meant the angels, too, but I didn't say that. "All of us manifested a miracle. And it *is* a miracle."

As we paused in front of his car, he looked at me curiously. "You know, you may make a believer out of me yet!"

Chapter Twelve

· ·

Feet on the Ground

M ike drove me to the Horton Plaza mall where we met Eric, the Swedish Consul, who would set me up to stay in their offices and help me out with practical support as I waited for my court date. After saying good-bye to Mike, I got into Eric's car, and he casually asked me to fill him in on my story. How do you condense nearly four years of madness into a casual story you tell to someone who knows little about the U.S. and Mexican criminal justice systems, little about you or how you came to be in trouble with the law—and who is navigating heavy city traffic while you're talking? But here I was, trying to weave a narrative that would make sense to a stranger. I could tell from his questions that I was skipping over important details I'd come to take for granted—for instance, the fact that facing a judge in Mexico was out of the question if I valued my personal safety. But my difficulty in explaining for the first time just what had happened didn't really matter to me. What did matter was I next to a stranger who was extending me trust, and who was treating me not as a body but as a person, a citizen. Knowing that I had the Swedish government looking out for me gave me some sense of security.

I was grateful for Eric's help, but it was disorienting to be out of jail at last. I felt like an alien trying to explain my world to someone on another planet. It was as if I was getting used to breathing in another atmosphere and unsure of the ground beneath my feet. Was I really here, safe, in the world outside of GEO?

As we came closer to the office building where I'd be staying that night, Eric apologized for the accommodations. "I'm sorry that there aren't any beds at the consulate," he said. "All we've got is an air mattress set up in one of the offices."

"I don't mind. That's better than what I had in GEO."

"And there's no shower. We'll have to figure what you can do about housing. I don't think they really understand this isn't a residence—it's an office. But we're happy to help in whatever ways we can. Mike says you could be here until January depending on how the hearings go?"

"Yes, that's what I understand."

He paused for a moment.

"You'll miss Christmas with your family?

"It's possible. But I don't want to think about that. What's most important is I'm really going home. That's what I focus on every day. The fact that I'm free. Well, I mean, almost."

Eric suggested we stop at a store so I could buy some toiletries. I had been so sensory deprived since March of 2006 that being outside and seeing the sights along the busy streets of San Diego was highly stimulating to my eyes and ears. But then we entered a nearby Walmart. Bright colors were everywhere, and people, and sounds—music, carts, cash registers, announcements. I stood there bewildered for a moment, taking it all in. It was as ordinary a scene as could be, but I might as well have been ET, it felt so odd to me. As soon as we walked in, I stopped. I shook my head and looked at Eric.

"I know I'm supposed to do something right now, but I have no idea what."

"Let's grab a cart so you can put your things in it," he replied kindly.

"Of course! That's normal, isn't it?" I felt totally clueless!

I stood in the oral hygiene section, mesmerized for a moment by the sheer number and variety of toothbrushes—and every one had a proper, long handle! There was toothpaste of every size and in every flavor, and dental floss, dental tape, dental thread, you name it. Had I always enjoyed this much freedom to make a decision? The array of choices was bewildering.

When I was arrested, the U.S. Marshals kept my carry-on bag, which bounced between the Swedish consulate and John Assaraf's office until about two years ago when it ended up at the consulate. Eric assured me he had seen it there, but he wasn't sure of the contents. I couldn't recall what I had in it either—and I was pretty sure whatever liquids inside it were pretty crusty by now. I placed in the shopping cart some moisturizer and other toiletries, a prepaid cellphone that my now former bunkie said I should get, and a pair of jeans and a couple of tops so I would have something to wear. After all, I had nothing but the clothes on my back that I had been wearing when I was arrested and they didn't feel so clean after four years in storage. And I purchased a box of my favorite tea: Earl Gray.

After our trip to Walmart, Eric drove past to the local shopping center and showed me where the grocery store was—close enough to walk to from the consulate. He asked if I wanted any food. I wasn't hungry, but then I saw an ice cream store. I asked if we could stop so I could get a scope of my favorite ice cream. The mint chocolate chip was deliciously cold and sweet and I savored every spoonful as we drove to the consulate.

When we reached our destination, he led me to an office with a desk and a queen-sized air mattress with sheets that took up the rest of the room.

"So Karin, if you need anything, just let me know," he said before leaving me alone in the space. I felt a little strange being in a building after hours, but I snapped out of the feeling very quickly. I called Sergio right away and gave him the phone number to call me back on.

As we caught up on details, it just didn't seem real to be talking to him from the "free world"! We decided Sergio wouldn't say anything to the girls; I would, when I called them at the usual time, which would be the next morning for me and shortly after school for them.

"Don't tell my mom I'm out," I said. "I don't want her to slip up and let them know because that would spoil the surprise. What should we say?"

"Well, we don't want to say you're on your way home soon. We have to keep it vague until we know you're on that plane."

We thought about it for a bit and realized our best bet was to tell the girls I now had access to new phone system, which meant they could call me and talk as long as they liked. We would tell them they wouldn't have to write letters to me anymore.

Sergio had to go wake up the girls for school but would call me back. I hung up, made myself a cup of hot tea—not lukewarm!—and went through my carry-on bag. There were some clothes in it, as I'd remembered, and presents I'd picked up for the girls: colorful hair bands, hair rollers, and birthday candles, which you can't find in Sweden. I had no idea if the girls would still be into this type of stuff after so much time had passed. But I had fun imagining how happy they would be when I could give them their presents in person. That would be the gift they most wanted. Could it be their Christmas present?

I also found my mp3 player. Now, there was something I'd missed: listening to music whenever I felt like it. Unfortunately, the batteries were long dead. I would have to pick some up in the morning.

I repacked the carry-on and sat for a moment. It was marvelous to be in this room where it was quiet, by myself, with true privacy for the first time in years—eerie, but marvelous.

Sergio called me back as promised and we talked for an hour, with no recording to interrupt us after twenty minutes. It was heavenly!

The next morning before the embassy workers arrived, I got up, folded up the sheets, and made a trip down the hall to the bathroom. It seemed strange, but fabulous, to put new contact lenses I had found in the suitcase in my eyes instead of wearing the regular glasses I had been stuck with in GEO. As I slipped into my new jeans and a burgundy t-shirt, I realized it would be a while before I was over the thrill of being able to wear normal clothes again.

When I got back to the office suite, the office manager had come in early. He was an elderly gentleman, full of energy as he gave me a warm welcome. I told him I'd be setting out on foot for the shopping center I had seen the night before, about a mile away. "Would you like a ride?" he asked.

"No, I'd rather walk. It's been a long time since I had a walk!" I told him.

When I got outside under the sunny skies, I was utterly amazed to smell freshly mown grass and drink in all the greenery around me. Even the small trees on a busy city sidewalk, and the flowers in the planters, seemed to spill over with color and vibrancy. I squinted in the bright sunlight and looked up at a sky that was bluer than blue, stretched like an unbroken canopy over my head, with no chain-link fence in sight. I could hear birds singing around me—I'd forgotten what that sounded like. It felt completely new to me and as electrifying as a symphony played in my honor to celebrate my freedom.

I paused by a school to watch children playing, listening to the sounds of them laughing and calling to each other. It made my heart ache for my girls. I felt as though I were discovering a whole new world, a new planet. But as good as it was to be back in the world, I longed to feel my daughters' arms around me. I wanted to kiss them and hug them like I'd never let them go.

I stopped by a Jamba Juice and ordered a shot of wheatgrass along with fresh squeezed orange juice and warm oatmeal with apples and cinnamon in it. The smell of fresh food was incredible, nothing like the smell of a meal at GEO. I felt myself detoxifying as I slowly savored my breakfast and inhaled the scents around me. My cells were doing a happy dance!

Then, I went back to the embassy to call home, and became further energized by my conversation with my daughters. When they heard that our phone calls wouldn't be limited anymore, my daughters became so excited that I couldn't help laughing out loud in shared joy.

I also called Sharon, Margaret and my cousin, Rhonda. They were all stunned to hear I was actually calling from the Swedish Consulate, but of course, they were incredibly happy for me. We talked for a long time about the journey they had been on with me. I could never have handled these past four years without their support. I also called my mom and told her I was out on bond and waiting to hear more news. I think she was very relieved to hear that she could just pick up the phone and call me for a change. (In fact, after that, she started calling me in the middle of my day, which was very late at night for her, just to say good-night.) To have regular contact with her only living child was so important to her, and it was something she'd be deprived of for too long. It felt so good to talk for as long as I wanted to my family and friends!

Just before I was supposed to have lunch with some women from the consulate, one of them took me to a nearby gym to get a membership so that I would have access to a shower. It was not ideal, but it would make do. I signed up for a one-month membership of my own and looked forward to a real workout and a decent shower. Then, we went to lunch at a Thai restaurant—they insisted on treating me.

The smell in the restaurant was downright divine, and I couldn't help contrasting the fresh soup to the ramen noodles I had in GEO, highly processed stuff you stirred into lukewarm water. It was so delightful that I felt as though I'd never eaten soup before! I savored every bite.

One of the women offered to give me a ride to downtown San Diego, which was about twenty minutes away by car. As I wandered around, it gave my brain some time to register that I was really there, wearing my own clothes, by myself—a free woman. I made my way to a waterfront park and sat on a bench to people watch and began reviewing everything that had happened. I was so grateful for all of our attorneys and the hard work they had done. I was so grateful for the judge in Mexico who had taken the time to review the case and closed it out. I was glad, and surprised, that the prosecutor had been nice to me in the end. I was deeply thankful that my miracle had come, even if I didn't know exactly how it came about. I didn't have to know. It was enough to simply have the miracle! And I was incredibly grateful for having Sergio in my life and for the blessing of having my daughters.

I sat there silently giving thanks to all of our friends and supporters, our mentors and spiritual advisors, my family here and on the other side, all of my angels, and all of the wonderful authors whose books had helped me on my spiritual journey and transformation. I was grateful to be alive and in this wonderful world. I relished every second of it.

I heard the far-off voice of someone calling for his dog. How long had it been since I'd seen a dog? And the colors! I couldn't get used to them. I had been living with drab dark green, grey, black, and dingy yellows and whites for so long I couldn't quite process the bright green of the grass, the bold red on the stop signs, the patterns of purple and turquoise on the blouse of a woman walking by, or the bold yellows and oranges on advertisements splashed on buildings and signs. I still couldn't quite take in the magic of freedom that filled my senses.

That night, after picking up some supplies including some batteries, I took myself out to dinner alone. I chose a nice restaurant, The Fish Market, on the waterfront and splurged by ordering lobster. It had been a long time since anything had tasted so wonderful. Absolute freedom makes everything exquisitely delicious!

I managed to take a bus back to the consulate and had a nice long phone call again with Sergio. He was amused by all that I had to report about my experiences that day. Later, I put the batteries in my MP3 player and danced around in the room because I was so happy to hear my favorite music again. It filled my head and my soul. I listened to Andrea Bocelli sing *Il Diavolo e L'Angelo* from *Cieli di Toscana* over and over again, even as I laid down on the air mattress, and gradually, I drifted off to sleep. It's a dramatic and joyful song that put me into the perfect state to relax into my body. Excitement and unadulterated relief are better than a sleeping pill for a good night's rest!

Over the next couple of days, I did my best to adjust to living in an office building. It felt strange just to be truly alone, to be able to close a door or open it and know that no one could come along and barge into my space. I was thrilled to be by myself and not have other people in authority over me dictating what to wear, what to eat, what to do, when to talk and when to keep quiet. Such freedom was almost mind-boggling for me, and I ecstatically embraced it with arms and soul and spirit wide open.

So much seemed unfamiliar, though. I felt like an idiot, trying to remember how to turn on a cell phone the next day. A nice woman at the consulate started to show me and I suddenly began to cry. It was such an ordinary skill I had taken for granted, but I'd been deprived of ordinary experiences for so long that I had forgotten that you have to press something to get the power on. My shoulders shook as I began to sob. I'd lost so much. I felt violated—as if my soul had been raped. The woman put her arm around me, and her compassion brought up another wave of emotion. Finally, it subsided. "Thank you," I said to her softly.

On the second night I was out of GEO, I had sushi with John and Maria Assaraf, who invited me to come to their house the following Sunday. I took them up on the offer, and that bright weekend morning, we drove along the coast to get to their place. I was able to see the ocean for the first time in years, and it took my breath away! It made me realize just how much I had missed being outdoors. Later, I sat by the Assaraf's pool in the sunshine and read a book all afternoon. It was pure bliss! Afterward, I took a long bath and saw my naked body in a full-length mirror for the first time since I'd been back in Sweden. All the mirrors I'd looked into had shown only my face, neck, and chest. I stood for a moment, taking in my reflection, being thinner than I had thought. I realized that there were many everyday experiences that wouldn't seem everyday to me again for some time. Seeing my full body for the first time in years reminded me of who I was, a whole person, not a number or a "body" moved from cell to hallway to elevator and courtyard and back.

It was very relaxing to be in a real house, and the Assarafs' was beautiful with its surrounding orange grove and marvelous view. It made me wish even more for home. I could handle my temporary situation, but if I had to be here, it would be nice to be someplace with a kitchen and a private bathroom. In the middle of the night back at the consulate, I had gotten my period and had to dash to the bathroom on the other side of the building. On the way, I unexpectedly ran into some male janitors. It was very awkward and simply smiled nervously as I walked past them with a bag of toiletries in my hand. I hadn't been allowed to look at or encounter men other than guards and lawyers for nearly four years, so I was unnerved and even scared. For a moment there, I thought, "Oh no! What are they going to do to me?" Then I realized they had been just as uncomfortable as I had been. My feeling of being in an alien world intensified, and I put out to the universe that I'd like to have someplace else to stay if I had to stay here much longer.

I brought up this incident with the pre-trial service counselor I met with, hoping she could help. She was very nice woman, and I told her that this whole experience had left me feeling emotionally violated. I was incredibly grateful to be out, but my situation was still very far from ideal. I desperately wanted to be home. She promised to recommend to the judge that the court provide me with more appropriate space, and explained that I couldn't leave town without the court's permission. I also couldn't move anywhere without their official okay.

Then, she asked me to tell her about my case. Once again, I had to tell an abbreviated version of my story, but she asked a lot of good questions about my life, my family, and even asked about what had happened before I met Sergio and came to the U.S. for a visit. Afterward, she put her pen down and said, "Have you ever gone to counseling?"

I shook my head.

"I think you could use it," she said, and she recommended someone she thought would be very good. "I'll recommend this to the judge. And your lawyer will have to file a request for it as well."

I thanked her, and as we ended the meeting I realized that although I wasn't truly free yet, I could live with that. The amount of freedom I'd experienced in the last few days was exhilarating, and the feeling hadn't warn off yet.

There was an older gentleman, Jon, working part-time at the consulate who had just moved into a new apartment. Shortly after meeting me and hearing about how I came to be living in the offices, he offered to let me stay at his place and sleep on his sofa. He reminded me of my grandfather and I had a really good feeling about taking him up on his offer. His apartment was small, he explained, but he had a fold-out sofa—and of course, a private bathroom! I was eager to move in, but I had to get court approval. As it turned out, they let me move to Jon's but refused to pay for counseling services. Apparently, I would only be able to return to normalcy in baby steps.

The night I finally got the news that I could stay at Jon's after all, John Assaraf invited me to a Hanukkah party at his house. "You should get out. Be around people," he said encouragingly. I went, and it was enjoyable, but in all honesty, it was challenging. After all, it was my first social event in years, and I had no idea how to explain who I was and why I was here. I had to relearn how to interact with people. There was a man there named Ken Druck who said he had followed my story and wanted to help me. "I'm a professional grief counselor," he explained, "And I won't charge you. It's the least I can do considering what happened to you. So, whenever you need it, I'll be here for you."

The universe was taking care of *everything* for me!

Slowly, I realized it was okay to do some things I wanted to do. Having been deprived of the dignity of privacy and freedom for so long, I found it hard to nurture myself. It's as if I'd forgotten how to be good to Karin. Sergio and I talked about this, and he encouraged me to get some pampering. I located a nearby salon and got a massage, manicure, pedicure and facial for around $150. Afterward, I took myself out to a nice dinner that night at an Italian restaurant, went to see a movie, and strolled through a bookstore, visiting my favorite authors and books. But I was tired of reading and wanted other types of experiences now, like watching movies in a theater, listening to music of my choice, and even being online on a computer.

As I said, Jon had a sofa bed, but I decided that sleeping on the sofa would be good enough. All night long, I felt like a rotisserie chicken, carefully turning so as not to fall off. By morning, my back was hurting, so the next day I decided to put the cushions on the floor and sleep on them. A few days after that, I mindlessly laid them out on the floor and suddenly stopped. What was I doing? There was no reason I couldn't pull out the bed. True, I didn't want to inconvenience Jon any more than was necessary, but really, he had told me it was fine to sleep there! Looking over at the makeshift bed I'd fashioned from cushions, I realized that they formed a sleeping space the size of my bunk. I had become so used to that little space to sleep in that I had unconsciously recreated it out of habit!

Well, enough of that, I decided. I pulled out the mattress, made the bed, and settled in, allowing my body to stretch across the queen-sized mattress. There was a lot to get used to again, and a lot to leave behind.

I saw the counselor, Ken, several times during this waiting time. He made me realize that even though I was out and probably was going home I would still need a lot of time to adjust. I needed to be prepared for the reactions. I needed to have patience with myself, as I would most likely experience PTSD (post-traumatic stress disorder). Talking to Sergio, I realized he had it, too. We were both scarred emotionally and mentally from the ordeal. Sergio was looking into our family getting counseling upon my return to Sweden so that we could get our lives back to normal as soon as possible. It helped to look forward to that, especially as Christmas approached.

During those weeks at Jon's, my three friends from the Los Angeles area came to see me and we went out to dinner. Like a kid in a candy store with a five-dollar bill in her pocket, I couldn't decide what to get so I ordered six appetizers because I wanted to try them all! My friends laughed and indulged me. Then, Christmas eve morning, I visited the Assarafs at their home and distracted myself by talking to their family and friends before heading back to Jon's to pretend that this was just another day—and tomorrow was just another day on the calendar, too. For the fourth time in my life—Christmas 2009, I couldn't allow myself to think about the holiday.

But the holidays passed, and in Jon's apartment in La Jolla, I felt my entire energy change. I had a bathroom and kitchen and was living a five-minute walk from the beach. Every morning, I got up early and took a long walk to the ocean, sometimes in the evenings, too. I hopped on his daughter's bike, which she'd been so kind to loan to me, and experienced the freedom of the wind in my hair as I steered myself wherever I wanted to go. Those bike rides and walks were very healing for me.

In retrospect, those weeks in limbo were actually a gift from the universe. They were my halfway house, and I needed an interim adjustment period. As the weeks went by, I relearned how to grocery shop and cook a meal. I was buying so many fresh fruits and vegetables—something I'd yearned to eat for so long!

I had to reconnect to myself and replenish myself so when I went home I would be able to give back to my family. We were talking three hours a day and I was getting to know my daughters again. I liked who they had become since I had seen them last. Sergio and I were able to reconnect on a much deeper level with no censorship. Finally, we could say what we wanted to say to each other! All the things we held back on the jail phones could now freely and spontaneously flow. It was a truly wonderful release for us both.

We set up Skype on John Assaraf's laptop that he'd loaned me during the holidays so I could finally see the girls. Megan and Alexa had helped Sergio set up an external video camera on his old computer, so when they heard him talking to me, they came into the room and looked over his shoulder so I was able to see them all. It was like water to a woman dying of thirst and it brought in another whole dimension. My daughters were so beautiful and they had grown so much! Tears of joy streamed down our faces. I wanted to unwrap their blankets and count their toes and fingers… just as when they were born. They did cheerleader splits and stunts for me in front of the Skype camera. What a balm for a mother's heart! I'm sure the shock showed on my face, but they were too busy smiling and waving and crowding into the camera frame to notice. Sergio looked different, too—a little more haggard but as handsome as ever. I hadn't seen him since March of 2007, except in snapshots.

We were getting closer to being together again.

One morning on my walk to the beach, I saw a cat. I stopped and called it over, and it lay down and I patted its tummy. It was purring, and its fur was so soft! I stood up and started walking but suddenly, my foot slipped. I had stepped in dog poop. I laughed out loud. It was amazing to me that I actually *could* step in dog poop! *Welcome to planet earth. It's a beautiful place, except for the dog poop!* It was such a normal, everyday thing, and it delighted me. Who would have believed I could enjoy stepping in dog poop?

As I reconnected to my body and my soul, my days fell into a routine: Get up, walk on beach, come home, talk to the girls, take a long bike ride, explore La Jolla, go grocery shopping, come home, and fix a wonderful meal. (Jon loved having a roommate who wanted to cook, and I felt this was how I could contribute to living there.) After dinner, I would walk, and then I would talk to Sergio before going to bed.

I still planned to tell the girls where I had been for four years just as soon as I got home, where I could be with them physically, holding and hugging them. However, my plans went awry. One day, Sergio told me his daughter from his first marriage was very angry with him for having been distracted for so long, and who could blame her? She didn't ask for the situation and neither did Sergio, and his daughter was old enough to suspect that we were hiding something important from her. She did some Internet research on me and confronted her father.

"You'll have to tell Alexa and Megan now," he said. "And I'll tell my son."

I sighed. Of course, I couldn't blame his daughter for wanting to know the truth. And we couldn't ask her to remain silent—that would only make the situation harder for her.

The next day while visiting with the girls on Skype, I told them everything that had happened. They were very distressed. They had no idea I had been in jail. I reassured them that I had been okay, and that the charges had been dropped but I had to continue with the legal process for a while. I simplified the story so they could understand it, and asked them how they felt. Were they angry that I had kept the truth from them?

They insisted they weren't, and when I talked to each of them separately, they both said the same thing: "Mommy, I would have been so scared if we'd known. I'm really glad you didn't tell me everything." Megan was only ten, and her first reaction was, "Are they going to come and take me too?" I said, "Absolutely not, sweetie." Children tend to think somehow things happen because of something *they* did.

I told both of my girls they could ask me anything they wanted, and as the days passed, they might have more questions, too. I explained I was out on bail and I didn't know when I was coming home. We needed to be grateful that we had the chance to talk this way where we could see each other. The girls felt very bad for me, and we all cried through the conversation. At least they could see I was okay. I showed them the whole apartment through the laptop camera. Jon walked by in the background a couple of times, and I explained who he was.

It was a huge relief to have no more secrets between us. They had been six and eight when I was arrested and now, at ten and eleven, they were old

189

enough to understand why I had been away so long. I just wished I could have held back on having the conversation until I was home because my situation was still somewhat uncertain.

On January 12, I called Mike to see if he had heard anything about the hearing three days away. He explained that one of three things could happen: The best-case scenario would be that the papers would have arrived and I'd be free to go home immediately. The second scenario would be that the papers had not arrived and I would have to wait longer. The third would be they would take me back into custody, which he felt was unlikely, but he wanted me to know that was a possibility. Mike was a little nervous and didn't trust anything about the situation given all that had transpired over four years. He didn't actually say that, but I knew that was what he was thinking. We had endured so many bad twists and turns!

I, on the other hand, wasn't nervous at all. I knew in my heart of hearts that it was over. There was no way I was *not* going home. My faith was strong. I called the travel agent to reserve my ticket home, trusting that it would happen.

Two days later, the morning of the fourteenth, I got a call from Mike on my cell phone as I was talking to Sergio on the landline. My stomach dropped.

"Call me back," Sergio said softly. I knew he felt it, too—fear that this was bad news. It had happened so often.

I hung up on Sergio and managed to croak out a hello to Mike.

"I have two things to say," he said. "The first is that your court time has been changed from tomorrow afternoon to tomorrow morning."

"Okay. I'll let everyone know. And the second thing?"

"The second is: Pack your bags. *You're going home!*"

I burst into tears. "Oh, my God! Is it really over? Tell me everything!"

"The prosecutor has not received the paperwork yet, but he's dismissing *both* your cases."

Without even thinking I said, "What? He's doing something nice for me?"

I could feel Mike grin on the other end of the phone. "Yeah. I can't believe it either. I think he's just so tired of this case."

Everyone was tired of it!

Tears were running down my face.

"Karin, I just can't tell you how happy I am for you! So hang up, call Sergio and give him the good news, and then, book your flight!"

With shaking hands, I called Sergio and said through the tears of joy, "Sergio, it's over. I'm coming home!"

We were both totally overwhelmed and still not quite able to believe it. *Has this actually happened? Have we crossed the finish line? Are we there? Can we breathe now?*

Sergio finally told me through his tears, "Stop crying and get your ticket!"

Earlier, I had reserved a ticket for the following Monday and they said they would hold it for me until late Friday afternoon. My hearing was to be in the early afternoon, so I'd have news by the time I had to make a decision. I called about flights and realized that it was much too expensive to fly home earlier than Monday, but that was okay by me.

The following morning, January 15, 2009, Jon drove me to court and in a matter of minutes, the judge looked down at me from his bench and said, "Well, that's it, Ms. Volo. Your cases are dismissed."

When we walked out of the courtroom, the pre-trial services woman gave me my passport. I was free to be a free human being once again, to travel and to go home. There were big hugs all around. I decided I'd take a road trip to visit my friends in Los Angeles before leaving, which I was free to do. We ended up staying up late talking like teenagers! Then, I went back to San Diego, packed up and said good-bye to everyone, and left for the airport with Jon, who was kind enough to drive me.

As I went through the boarding procedures, I couldn't help but remember the last time I had tried to board a plane to go home 45 months before. Then, I consciously put those thoughts out of my mind and focused on going home and hugging my family for the rest of my life. As the plane took off, I could feel a layer of my stress being left behind. I had visualized this so many times, and now it was happening! On my walks in La Jolla, I had seen planes taking off, flying low over the ocean, and I kept thinking, *soon I'm going to be on that plane!*

I landed in Stockholm, and when I left baggage claim, I made my way through the gate, peering through the crowd. And in a magical moment, my eyes met Sergio's.

He held a bouquet of flowers for me, and I could see him tearing up. I picked up my pace, trying not to run, until I last I walked into his open arms.

Home. I was truly home.

He kissed me softly and said, "Mission accomplished."

With tears streaming down my cheeks, I responded, "I'm finally here!"

He smiled. "It took you long enough!"

Just to feel his arms around me was overwhelming. The tears threatened to turn into a cascade, and I was trying not to make a scene, so I said, "Let's get out of here." We walked to the car and drove home holding hands.

That morning when the girls had left for school, he had told them he had to go over to their friend's house after school let out. In planning our reunion, I had insisted that both girls had to arrive home at the same time. The first thing he did was call Alexa on her cell phone and tell her, "You have to come home now. Go pick up Megan and bring her home with you right away."

I was so nervous. It was starting to get dark outside and my palms were sweating.

"We're home," I heard Alexa say as I sat hidden in the living room.

My heart began to pound. My throat tightened.

Sergio was standing where he could see both them and me as well. He spoke calmly to them, covering up his own excitement. What an actor!

"Hi, girls. Are you ready to talk to your mom?"

They were busy taking off their coats and their winter boots and they both automatically said *yes.*

He asked them a second time to get their attention. "Are you ready to talk to your mom?"

Wondering what was going on they both gave him a long, drawn-out "*Yes....?*"

I did my best not to giggle.

"Okay," Sergio told them. "Then come into the living room."

My stomach was doing flip-flops as excitement coursed through my veins. As the girls entered the room, I stood up and said, "Because here I am!" and opened my arms wide.

"*Mommy!!!*"

Their screams danced through the air as we ran into each other's arms. We hugged so tightly we could barely breathe.

They cried and cried, unable to get any words out amid the tears of utter joy and relief.

I glanced over at Sergio, and laughed. He was crying and smiling as much as we were, and he came over to join us in a group hug.

We couldn't talk. It was simply too emotional and precious to hold each other. It had been exactly 1400 days since we had last been able to do this, and it was like holding them as babies just after they came out of my belly—overwhelming! We instinctively didn't want to spoil the moment with words, but to savor it deeply.

I kissed them and kissed them, over and over again. I didn't want to let them go!

They started talking at once.

"How are you here?" they wanted to know.

"You wanted to be surprised, so here I am," I replied.

As they pulled away to look at me, I looked at them. They were so tall! And so thin, their baby fat melted away with the years. And they were so incredibly beautiful.

To be able to look into their eyes, touch their hair, kiss their cheeks, and hold them so tightly that our hearts melted together…it was truly heaven on earth.

The nightmare was truly over.

Today was the day I came home.

Afterword

J ohan Ernst Nilsson, a Swedish adventurer and a friend of Sergio and mine, told us recently that everyone always thinks reaching the summit of Mount Everest is the goal. What most people don't realize is that the descent is just as dangerous, if not more so because you are physically spent coming down and it's easy to make mistakes because when you're tired.

When I returned home, I naively thought that I would be able to return to my everyday life and live like a normal person again. I was told by our crisis and trauma expert that when people experience a major trauma as our family had, the time to recover is generally as long as the trauma had been. Boy, I did not want to believe that it was going to take me another four years to feel normal again! But it *did* take time. I certainly hadn't expected symptoms from PTSD, but there were undeniably there for all of us.

For the first year, I couldn't talk to anyone other than my closest friends and family. I couldn't meet people who had known me before all this happened. I didn't want to tell anyone what I had been through. When I did start to share my story, I found it easier to talk to strangers or to do interviews online where I didn't see people in person. I also had some short-term memory loss, which I was told was normal and temporary. And I had some primitive, instant fear reactions to things that reminded me of GEO. I was in an appliance store with Sergio shortly after returning to Sweden and suddenly I froze. My heart raced and my breathing became shallow as two security guards walked toward us briskly, probably on their way to the break room. It was just like at the Swedish consulate when I ran into the janitors.

195

those sorts of reactions faded, in part because of the years in therapy.

worked with several techniques. I talked about what had course, but I also did art therapy to express what I'd experienced about it. And I did EMDR (eye movement desensitization and ng), which helped me to retell my story in a way that removed the c getic imprints of fear and anger that can shape thoughts and influence us at a cellular level, creating stress-related illness and disease. I also continued doing tapping, meditation, and using affirmations and other techniques I had worked with in jail. I studied the brain and heart and how energy works from scientific and metaphysical levels. After eating so much processed food for four years, I wanted to eat only organic foods and remove toxic chemicals we're exposed to every day, so I switched to fluoride-free toothpaste, nontoxic and all-natural personal care and household products, and I began studying nutrition and natural healing.

My experience had been life changing, and after my return home, I told Sergio that I just couldn't go back to the executive search business. I knew I was supposed to teach others what I had learned to manage such dire circumstances. I also knew I was supposed to take this into the business world. I just had no idea how to do that.

Sergio and I ended up writing a book called *Engage!*—which was not what we had originally intended—and pleasantly surprised us by becoming an international best seller. For almost two years, we researched fifteen amazing companies that are leading the way to a new business mindset that uses business as a force for good for the people, planet, and profits, and we were able to define the formula to inspire other companies on that path. When we discovered positive psychology, we found a decade of research that proved that all the things we had done as a family during those tough years are things that can help employees and companies thrive. This is what inspired us to write *Engage!* And to start working with companies to discover their purpose and to flourish. So eventually, I found that I could combine my professional experience with my personal experience in a way that could make a positive impact and have a far reach.

You never know what life has in store for you. Sometimes you just have to roll with the punches and pick yourself right back up. I have learned that life does not happen *to* us, it happens *for* us—so that we can learn, grow, and have the opportunity to be the best that we can be. I don't consciously remember signing up for a spiritual boot camp in jail, but I believe I did so before I was born into this life.

I will be forever grateful to Sergio for standing by my side, believing in me, and giving my girls a stable home and pretty decent childhood despite everything. He has had serious ramifications from the PTSD. After all, I had a lot of time in jail to master techniques for overcoming fear and stress, while he was spending enormous amounts of time in the practical work of raising his children as well as Alexa and Megan, running our business, and trying to get me home. It's easy to underestimate the amount of stress a caretaker goes through, and Sergio's journey back has been long and arduous. I have been so blessed to have him in my life.

My daughters have gained so much knowledge and insights through this journey that have empowered them. The *Bringing Joy* series helped keep our family together and taught them great tools to manage whatever life might throw at them at a very young age. They have become master manifesters, and I so admire the intelligent, beautiful young ladies they are becoming. Megan has embarked on a modeling career, and she has a clear sense of who she is on the inside. I feel confident that she will avoid the pitfalls of the fashion industry because of her inner strength and her self-awareness. She has a clear vision of what she wants for herself and manifests the jobs she wants that are right for her. Alexa doesn't have a clear vision of what she wants to do in the future at the time of writing this, but that's natural for a teenager. In this time of uncertainty and possibility, she's applied what she learned from me and Sergio in those years when I was away. In a speech to her class, she said that my strength taught her "everything is possible as long as you fight for it and always see the goal in front of you." When she knows what she wants, she pursues it with determination. I'm confident she is well equipped to handle whatever life might throw her way.

This whole ordeal has opened doors I never expected. The *Bringing Joy* stories blossomed into an entire book series with twenty-seven books! This has lead me to collaborating with Neale Donald Walsch and helping parents through his School for the New Spirituality as well as co-writing *Bringing Joy to God*, which is based on the twenty five core principles in the *Conversations With God* series. It's been wonderful to see this imaginary little girl's adventures, which kept me connected with my own daughters and with Sergio while I was in jail, touch other people's hearts and help them to teach their children about important universal truths.

The telling of our story has become a part of the healing process for me. When I can be vulnerable and share this horrific experience without feeling afraid, and I can encourage people and lift them up when they're feeling scared or powerless, I feel that I'm living out my purpose. Plus, sharing my story often puts people automatically in a place of gratitude. They see that their problems aren't nearly so bad after all and they are thankful that they haven't had to go through something like this! No matter where you are in life, you can always find someone who has it harder than you've had it. Choosing to write this book, which I began shortly after coming home, is a part of my life's purpose. Sharing my story through my writing, blogging, inspirational speaking, and now this book, is a way that I hope to leave a legacy of inspiring others to be their very best versions of themselves.

Thank you so much for reading my story—I really appreciate that! Please recommend it to your friends and loved ones so that together we can spread this empowering message far and wide.

If you want to read more in depth about the specific lessons we learned that helped us to not only survive but to thrive going something so difficult, or if you just want to stay in touch, I have a short PDF document as a gift that you can download at www.KarinVolo.com/lessons.

It is my hope that in reading this story, you've been inspired to start your own journey to be fully empowered and to bring joy into your life!

With love and joy always,

Karin
June 2014

Acknowledgements

∙∙

There are so many incredible people that have helped us on this journey that without their support, we probably wouldn't be where we are today. There are far too many names to include everyone but I have to give a shout out to several significant individuals.

To our inner circle who gave us love, a new perspective, and hope when there was very little: Sharon (my soul sister for life), Margaret (my other mother and book angel), Rhonda (my dearest cousin who has always been more like a sister), Beth (your support and letters during those years was important—I miss you!), John (mentor, friend, and inspiration), Mimi (your pictures keep me connected to the girls as they grew up!), Harriet (gracias por todo mi amor!), and Carmen (your visions of hope kept us going). To my dear friends for life, Steffani, Jenny, Vesna, Kina…thank you for all the love. Wanda, you have been invaluable to me and our family—thank you for all your wisdom!

For all my book mentors who without your books, I would not have learned to thrive and grow: Neale Donald Walsch, Louise Hay, David Hawkins, Doreen Virtue, Gregg Braden, Dr. Brian Weiss, Diana Cooper, Laura Day, Colette Baron Reid, Jacquelyn Aldana, Deepak Chopra, Sonia Choquette, Don Miguel Ruiz, Jean Slatter, Eckert Tolle, Marci Shimoff, Jack Canfield, Rodney Yee, Ester & Jerry Hicks, and so many others.

To all the interesting women I met from all walks of life who openly shared their stories and their hearts—I've learned so much from you!

This book would not be in this form without the loving support from Alice Anderson (you really helped me put form to it—thank you for listening to me for so many hours!) and Nancy Peske, my developmental editor who is a master at weaving with words.

To all the amazing people who made up our legal team—your hard work and dedication was much appreciated.

And to everyone who has believed in us, had faith in us, and came into our lives at exactly the right time when we needed you—thank you from the bottom of my heart!

Recommended Reading List

A Course In Miracles, New Christian Church of Full Endeavor, Ltd., Wilconsin Dells, WI 2005

Andrews, Andy, **The Traveler's Gift,** Thomas Nelson, Inc, Nashville, TN, 2002

Aldana, Jacquelyn, **The 15 Minute Miracle Revealed,** Inner Wisdom Publications, Los Gatos, CA, 2003

Assaraf, John and Murray Smith, **The Answer,** Atria Books, New York, NY, 2008

" **The Complete Vision Board Kit,** Beyond Words Publishing Inc, Hillsboro, OR, 2008

Baron-Reid, Colette, **Remembering the Future: The Path to Recovering Intuition,** Hay House Inc, Carlsbad, CA, 2006

Braden, Gregg, **The God Code,** Hay House Inc, Carlsbad, CA 2005

" **The Isaiah Effect,** Three Rivers Press, New York, NY, 2000

" **The Divine Matrix,** Hay House Inc, Carlsbad, CA, 2007

Browne, Sylvia, **The Other Side and Back,** New American Library, New York, NY, 1999

" **Life On the Other Side,** New American Library, New York, NY, 2000

" **Book of Angels,** Hay House Inc, Carlsbad, CA, 2003

" **Book of Dreams,** The Penguin Group, New York, NY, 2002

Bryant, Alice, **The Message of the Crystal Skull,** Llewellyn Publications, St. Paul, MN 1989

Byrne, Rhonda, **The Secret**, Beyond Words Publishing Inc, Hillsboro, OR, 2006

Chopra, Deepak, **Life After Death**, Three Rivers Press, New York, NY 2006
" **Quantum Healing,** Bantam Books, New York, NY, 1989

Choquette, Sonia, **The Phychic Pathway**, Three Rivers Press, New York, NY, 1995
" **Trust Your Vibes,** Hay House Inc, Carlsbad, CA, 2004
" **Ask Your Guides,** Hay House Inc, Carlsbad, CA, 2006

Coelho, Paulo, **The Alchemist**, HarperCollins Publishers, Inc, NY, NY 1994
By the River Piedra I Sat Down and Wept, HarperCollins Publishers, Inc, New York, NY 1998
" **The Pilgrimage**, HarperCollins Publishers, Inc, NY, NY 1998
" **The Zahir**, HarperCollins Publishers, Inc, NY, NY 2005

Cooper, Diana, **Discover Atlantis**, Findhorn Press, Scotland, UK, 2007
" **A Little Light on Angels,** Findhorn Press, Scotland, UK, 1996

Day, Laura, **The Circle**, Tarcher/Putnam, New York, NY, 2001
" **Practical Intuition**, Villard Books, New York, NY, 1996

Desikachar, T.K.V., **The Heart Of Yoga**, Inner Traditions International, Rochester, VT, 1999

Drosnin, Michael, **The Bible Code**, Touchstone, New York, NY 1997

Dwoskin, Hale, **The Sedona Method**, Sedona Press, Sedona, AZ, 2007

Dyer, Dr. Wayne, **The Power of Intention**, Hay House Inc, Carlsbad, CA 2004

Eadie, Betty, **Embraced By The Light**, Gold Leaf Press, New York, NY, 1992
" **The Awakening Heart**, Pocket Books, New York, NY 1996

Emoto, Masaru, **The Hidden Messages in Water,** Beyond Words Publishing, Inc. Hillsboro, OR 2001

Frankl, Viktor, **Man's Search for Meaning**, Beacon Press, Boston MA, 2006

Gilbran, Kahlil, **The Prophet**, Alfred A. Knopf, Inc, New York, NY, 1923

Gladwell, Malcolm, **The Tipping Point**, Little, Brown and Company, New York, NY, 2000

Greene, Brian, **The Elegant Universe**, Vintage Books, New York, NY, 2000

Harra, Carmen, **Everyday Karma**, Ballentine Books, New York, NY, 2002

Hawkins, David R. MD, PhD, **Power VS. Force**, Hay House Inc, Carlsbad CA, 1995

Hay, Louise, **You Can Heal Your Life**, Hay House Inc, Carlsbad, CA, 1999 (1984)

Hicks, Ester and Jerry, **The Amazing Power of Deliberate Intent**, Hay House Inc, Carlsbad CA, 2006

" **Ask and It Is Given**, Hay House Inc, Carlsbad CA, 2004

Ilibagiza, Immaculee, **Left To Tell,** Hay House Inc, Carlsbad, CA 2006

Kersten, Holger, **Jesus Lived In India**, Penquin Books, New Delhi, India, 2001

Lazlo, Ervin, **Science and The Akashic Field**, Inner Traditions, Rochester, VT, 2004

Marx Hubbard, Barbara, **Conscious Evolution**, New World Library, Novato, CA, 1998

McTaggart, Lynne, **The Field**, HarpersCollins, New York, NY, 2002

Meeder, Kim, **Bridge of Hope,** Multnomah Publishers, Sisters, OR 2006

" **Hope Rising,** Multnomah Publishers, Sisters, OR 2003

Meyer, Marvin (Translator), **The Secret Teaching of Jesus**, First Vintage Books, New York, NY, 1986

Pagels, Elaine, **Gnostic Gospels,** Vintage Books, New York, NY, 1979

Puryear, Anne, **Steven Lives!**, Pocket Books, New York, NY 1992

Renard, Gary R., **The Disappearance of the Universe**, Hay House Inc, Carlsbad CA, 2002

Ross, Allen, **Mitakuye Oyasin We are All Related,** Wicâoni Wastâe, Denver, CO, 1997

Ruiz, Don Miguel, **The Four Agreements,** Amber-Allen Publishing, Inc, San Rafael, CA 1997

" **The Mastery of Love,** Amber-Allen Publishing, Inc, San Rafael, CA 1999

Schiffmann, Erich, **Yoga The Spirit and Practice of Moving Into Stillness,** Pocket Books, NY, NY, 1996

Shimoff, Marci, **Happy For No Reason**, Free Press, New York, NY, 2008

Slatter, Jean, **Hiring the Heavens,** New World Library, Novato, CA, 2005

Smith, Gordon, **Spirit Messenger,** Hay House Inc, Carlsbad, CA 2004

Tolle, Eckert, **The New Earth**, Dutton, New York, NY, 2005

Van Praagh, James, **Talking to Heaven,** New American Library, New York, NY, 1999

Virtue, Doreen, **The Lightworker's Way**, Hay House Inc, Carlsbad, CA 1997

" **Divine Guidance**, St. Martin's Press, New York, NY, 1998

" **Healing with The Angels**, Hay House Inc, Carlsbad, CA 1999

" **The Chrystal Children**, Hay House Inc, Carlsbad, CA 2003

" **Angel Medicine**, Hay House Inc, Carlsbad, CA 2004

" **How To Hear Your Angels,** Hay House Inc, Carlsbad, CA 2007

Vitale, Joe, **The Attractor Factor**, John Wiley & Sons, Inc, Hoboken, NJ, 2005

Walsch, Neale Donald, **Conversations with God, Book One,** Hampton Roads Publishing Co, Charlottesville, NC, 1995

" **Conversations with God, Book Two,** Hampton Roads Publishing Co, Charlottesville, NC, 1997

" **Conversations with God, Book Three,** Hampton Roads Publishing Co, Charlottesville, NC, 1998

Weiss, Brian, **Many Lives, Many Masters**, Fireside, New York, NY, 1988

" **Only Love Is Real,** Grand Central Publishing, Inc, New York, NY, 1997

" **Messages from the Masters,** Grand Central Publishing, Inc, New York, NY, 2000

" **Same Soul, Many Bodies,** Free Press, New York, NY, 2004

Yee, Rodney, **Moving Toward Balance,** Rodale Inc, Emmaus, PA, 2004

Get Connected!

If you want to connect with me, here's how…

www.KarinVolo.com

- ✓ Be empowered and get your Joyometer with free training!
- ✓ For Inspiration speaking or media, please use the contact form on this website

For Companies:

www.Evoloshen.com

- ✓ Find out how to get engaged and become a purpose driven company
- ✓ Get certified in engagement – check out www.EvoloshenAcademy.com

For Parents:

www.BringingJoyToTheWorld.com

- ✓ Read these transformational books to your children and open up a world of deep conversations

Social Media:

@KarinVolo
@Evoloshen
@BringingJoy

www.Facebook.com/InspiringYourVeryBest
www.EvoloshenFan.com
www.Facebook.com/BringingJoy

One last note for you…since you have purchased this book, you're making a bigger impact!

Sharing my story has always been about the bigger message and wanting to make a positive difference. Because I believe in giving back, the royalties of this book are going to support a wonderful not for profit called:

NOT FOR SALE

NOT FOR SALE PROTECTS PEOPLE AND COMMUNITIES AROUND THE WORLD FROM HUMAN TRAFFICKING.

There are more than **30 million people around the world affected by slavery** – more than at any point in history.

Not For Sale has supported thousands of people around the world back to lives of freedom and meaning.

By working together, we can create a world where no one is for sale. Join us in giving dignity and empowering people affected by human trafficking!

Find out more at **www.notforsalecampaign.org**

About the Author

Karin Volo, an expert in engagement, career, personal and organizational development, is known as the Chief Joy Bringer. She is a co-author of the international best selling book, *Engage!* With 15+ years experience working with international Fortune 500 companies on two continents, she has insights on business building, cultural transformation, and high performance.

Karin works with cultural development, employee engagement, leadership mentoring, professional inspirational speaking and writing. She uses her professional skills and draws from her personal experiences to help individuals and companies thrive.

She is also the author of the *Bringing Joy* children's series, a regular blogger on *Huffington Post*, a faculty member at the Institute for Inspired Organizational Cultures, and an expert judge on employee engagement in both the UK and the US.

Karin's passion is helping people better their lives through sharing all she has learned on her own journey. She uses her years of overcoming challenges as her platform to teach and inspire others. She is a dedicated wife and mother. Her personal purpose is bringing joy to the world.

Made in the USA
San Bernardino, CA
03 March 2016